The Year 1800, Or the Sayings and Doings of Our Fathers and Mothers 60 Years Ago, As Recorded in the Newspapers and Other Periodicals, Prepared by F. Perigal

Frederick Perigal

Nabu Public Domain Reprints:

You are holding a reproduction of an original work published before 1923 that is in the public domain in the United States of America, and possibly other countries. You may freely copy and distribute this work as no entity (individual or corporate) has a copyright on the body of the work. This book may contain prior copyright references, and library stamps (as most of these works were scanned from library copies). These have been scanned and retained as part of the historical artifact.

This book may have occasional imperfections such as missing or blurred pages, poor pictures, errant marks, etc. that were either part of the original artifact, or were introduced by the scanning process. We believe this work is culturally important, and despite the imperfections, have elected to bring it back into print as part of our continuing commitment to the preservation of printed works worldwide. We appreciate your understanding of the imperfections in the preservation process, and hope you enjoy this valuable book.

THE YEAR 1800,

OR

THE SAYINGS AND DOINGS OF OUR FATHERS AND MOTHERS

60 YEARS AGO.

As Recorded in the Newspapers and other Periodicals.

Consisting of Extracts from—

THE TIMES, MORNING CHRONICLE, MORNING HERALD, ST. JAMES'S CHRONICLE, MORNING POST AND GAZETTEER, LONDON CHRONICLE, STAR, PORCUPINE, TRUE BRITON, LONDON GAZETTE, LLOYD'S EVENING POST, OBSERVER, BELL'S WEEKLY MESSENGER, READING MERCURY AND OXFORD GAZETTE, JOURNAL DES DÉBATS, ANNUAL REGISTER, GENTLEMAN'S MAGAZINE, EUROPEAN MAGAZINE, SCOTS' MAGAZINE, AND UNIVERSAL MAGAZINE.

PREPARED BY

F. PERIGAL,

AUTHOR OF "THE CHART OF THE NAVY OF GREAT BRITAIN FROM THE EARLIEST PERIOD OF HISTORY."

London:

THOMAS SANDERSON, 77, FLEET STREET, E.C.,

EDINBURGH: W. P. NIMMO.   DUBLIN: McGLASHEN & GILL.   GLASGOW: H. CAMPBELL.
LIVERPOOL: W. GILLING.   MANCHESTER: DINHAM & CO.

AND TO BE HAD AT ALL BOOKSELLERS AND RAILWAY STATIONS.

1860.

Just published by the same Author,

A SECOND EDITION OF THE

CHART OF THE NAVY OF GREAT BRITAIN FROM THE EARLIEST PERIOD OF HISTORY,

COMPILED FROM HISTORICAL PUBLICATIONS, OLD RECORDS, PARLIAMENTARY RETURNS, AND OTHER AUTHORITIES.

OPINIONS OF THE PRESS.

Among recent statistical publications is *A Chart of the Navy*. It has been condensed with much skill and clearness, and is calculated to prove highly useful. Details are embraced of all the changes and "reconstructions" of the Royal Navy from the reign of Henry VIII, together with a general view of the increase of the mercantile marine.—*Times, July 5, 1859.*

This *Chart* exhibits at a glance the rise and progress of the Royal Navy, showing its total force in each reign, and the numbers of ships in the several rates since the system of classification was adopted by Charles I. The relative strength of the Navy at the principal periods of our history may, therefore, be readily compared by means of it. Such a compilation as the present will be very useful.—*Mechanics' Magazine, July 8, 1859.*

This is a compilation of the various events connected with the Naval History of Great Britain, commencing in the last century B.C. down to the year 1857. It is the first attempt which we remember to have seen, of collecting and publishing, in the form of a Chart, a comprehensive record of events in our Naval history. Mr. Perigal deserves great credit for the manner in which he has produced this first edition, and we hope that the publication will receive the extent of support to which it is fairly entitled.—*The Artizan, August 1, 1859.*

Mr. F. Perigal, of the Admiralty, has prepared a new copy of his useful *Chart of Naval History*, which shows the naval strength of the country as it stood at the commencement of the present year.—*Times, July 28, 1860.*

PUBLISHED BY

J. D. POTTER, 31, POULTRY, AND 11, KING STREET, TOWER HILL,

(*Agent for the Admiralty Charts*).

AND TO BE HAD OF ALL BOOKSELLERS.

Price 1s. in *Sheets*; or *lined, bound and lettered*, 3s. 6d.

THE YEAR 1800,

OR

THE SAYINGS AND DOINGS OF OUR FATHERS AND MOTHERS 60 YEARS AGO.

PREFATORY REMARKS.

This publication exhibits a variety of occurrences of general interest, as they were recorded in the newspapers and other periodicals of the last year of the eighteenth century; it will serve to illustrate the state of social life in this country at that particular period, and enable the reader to judge of the important advances which have been made in our public and domestic condition, during the intervening time.

The year selected is interesting on various accounts :—a general war existed; Napoleon had become First Consul, and projected an invasion of England, Talleyrand being his Foreign Secretary; Pitt, who had long been Prime Minister to George III, was making grand efforts to carry on the War with vigour; Nelson was pursuing his glorious career; many other celebrities were living; and the course of events then being enacted, has had a powerful influence in securing for us the prosperity and happiness we now enjoy, both nationally and individually.

A comparison between the years 1800 and 1860, will remind us of the immense progress made in that brief interval, and enable us the better to appreciate the advantages which we possess in many respects over our immediate predecessors.

In 1800 the streets and houses were not lighted with gas; steam travelling, by land or sea, was unknown; the electric telegraph was undreamt of; the laws were harsh; commerce restricted; the slave trade flourished; the press-gang was in active operation; the pillory in frequent use; footpads and mounted highwaymen numerous; duelling and drunkenness fashionable; the old stage coaches slow and unsafe travelling; and the old watchmen an inefficient protection to life and property. Since then Parliament has been reformed; free-trade established; religious and political liberty greatly extended; and a thousand improvements and discoveries in the arts and sciences introduced.

The "news" communicated at that time was scanty and long after date, and the newspapers were of a very limited character; "The Times" (even then the leading paper) consisted of but 16 columns, of nearly 3 inches wide, and about 18 inches long, printed on very inferior paper; and it was by no means such a formidable business, as it now is, to wade through the quantity of matter it contained; its price was 6d. The staple subjects of all the papers were, Napoleon and the prevailing fashions, both of which were the daily themes of severe criticism; there were no well-written essays as "leaders," nor instructive dissertations on the money market and city affairs.

The articles here collected together have been selected from upwards of one thousand papers, issued during 1800, and it is hoped that the reader will derive both information and amusement from their perusal.

It was intended to have added to the collection a series of notes as a running commentary to its principal paragraphs, but the subjects comprised in them were found to be too multifarious to admit of this being done without too greatly extending the limits of the work.

Should this publication meet with an extensive amount of public support, it is contemplated to issue a similar collection of articles from the periodicals and pamphlets of other periods, so as to exhibit the manners and habits of the people of this kingdom at intervals sufficiently separated to secure a distinctive character to each epoch selected for such delineation.

F. PERIG.

CONTENTS.

		Page
1.	Prefatory Remarks	3
2.	Advertisements	5
3.	Home and Foreign Affairs	17
4.	Parliamentary Proceedings	23
5.	Naval and Military Intelligence	31
6.	Shipping News	36
7.	The Union with Ireland	36
8.	Police Reports	37
9.	Law Courts	38
10.	Provincial Trials	45
11.	Sentences and Punishments	46
12.	Highway Robberies	48
13.	Various Crimes and Offences	49
14.	Duelling	52
15.	Prize Fights	53
16.	Volunteers	53
17.	Rifles	55
18.	High Price of Corn and Dearness of Provisions	55
19.	Science	62
20.	Metropolitan Improvements and other Local Matters	64
21.	A Voyage in a Hoy	68
22.	Theatres and Exhibitions	69
23.	Sports and Feats	70
24.	Curious Incidents and Facetiæ	72
25.	The Court and Haut Ton	74
26.	Fashions	79
27.	The Fine Arts	85
28.	Lotteries	88
29.	Varieties	89

I. B.

THE Answer of a Letter to an Officer of Hereford is, "That he was."

THE Expenses attending the Ring are at present ten guineas.

W. P. S. will meet with the Friend he sought for if he will send a line of address, directed for R. C., to be left at the Penny Post-office, Wood-street, Cheapside, till called for.

ABSENTED himself from his friends, near a month ago, a sprightly youth, about 10 years of age. Whoever will give information of him to Mr. Badfield, No. 2, Blossom's Inn-gateway, Laurence-lane, Cheapside, so that he may be restored to his friends, will be handsomely rewarded. Had on when he went away a blue coat, pink striped waistcoat, and brown great coat. Provided he will return to his friends immediately, he will be received, and everything amicably adjusted.

INTERESTING intelligence.—To who it may concern.—If F. Cozani will give himself the trouble to call on Mr. Woodhouse, No. 10, Little Brook-street, he will hear of something that most likely will afford him much pleasure.

IF the person who left his home on Saturday, the 15th instant, between one and two o'clock in the afternoon, will return, he will be received with paternal kindness and affection, and all that has passed be forgotten. With a man of good sense and disposition this advertisement, doubtless, will prevail.

WANTED to purchase, a place in a public office, either under Government or otherwise, on a permanent establishment, where attendance is not required after 4 o'clock: the salary not less than 200l., or from that to 250l., and if with a prospect of future preferment would be liked the better. Apply personally or by letter, to I. D., at Mr. Houseman's, No. 31, Threadneedle-street.

THE young man, who left his employer's counting-house in the city, on Wednesday last, is most earnestly entreated to return immediately. If he does not appear by Saturday, the 26th inst., his name and all particulars will be advertised, and a reward offered for his apprehension.

IF the person does not return immediately, who got himself intoxicated at the Oakley Arms, Oakley-street, St. George's-fields, on Sunday evening last, and was brought home in a coach to his situation by two strangers, and the next day absconded from his employ, a prosecution will be issued against him, and certain means used for his discovery.

A CAUTION.—Whereas Elizabeth, the wife of me, the undersigned, W..D.., of Farley-hill, in the parish of Swallowfield, in the county of Berks, shopkeeper, has lately eloped from me without any just or reasonable cause, and I having great reason to suspect she has been seduced from me by some ill-designed person or persons, having wantonly threatened that she intends to contract debts in order to ruin me, I do hereby caution all persons from entrusting the said Elizabeth, my wife, as I shall not pay any debts she may contract.—Witness my hand this 3rd day of April, 1800. W..D..

MATRIMONY.—A Gentleman of a small fortune, and have been brought up very gentely, and of a good character, and of a respectable family, and about 30, and have been brought up in the country, and never been in any trade whatever, and very agreeable company, his fortune being but small, taken this mode of some lady that has got a good fortune in her own hands, to the amount of 4 or 5,000l. or more, that wish for domestick happiness, and to be united to a gentleman of strict honour. Sunday and Satterday excepted for an interview, but letters post paid taken in. Direct for C. D., No. 5, Barron Street, Panton Vile, Islinton.—(The foregoing is verbatim.—ED.)

FOR a Wife.—Any marriageable lady, with 300l., under the age of 21, or with 500l. above that age, and who will convince me of her esteem, with her own handwriting in answer to this, and glory in her public and sacred affection, I, Sir J.. D.., Baronet, will settle eleven thousand pounds a year upon her, and other estates she may bring with her; and will ever study to increase her happiness, and indulge her ladyship to the highest degree in my power, for her making the kindest and quickest steps to matrimony; and I will get her one thousand pounds a year more by my well known practice of physick, that appears in one of my Bills in the Court of Equity. I shall impatiently wait to see your signal with your second finger on your left hand; with it make a snug scratch between your eyes, before you pass by me, on the terrace, or elsewhere, to denote your, or, a lady's intention, to meet me in the alcove near my house in Windsor Castle, when the clock strikes one; where you may find me every dry day. If you are alone, I shall hope to see you instantly move towards the alcove. I shall introduce the subject by asking you if you can tell me how the ladies approve of the enterprizing and remarkable printed marriage offer that Sir J.. D.. has made them, with dictations so nice, for the use of their favourable pens, and limitations that they cannot be impeached.

N.B.—Pray let me tell your attorney (my sweetest comforter) about another noble estate in Hereford-shire that must be yours for ever, if I die first, and that the unintended joint act of me and my brother, has made me only a tenant for life in this estate we so intailed, as his joint act (after his death) could not be obtained. This joint act was inadvertently inserted by our attorney, when we mortgaged this estate to A * * S * *, Esq., in Brook Street, Grosvenor Square, for two thousand pounds.

FOR a Wife.—Qualified Ladies, justice obliges me to give you a fortnight's notice, that I have a letter lately from London, that tells me His Majesty's knights here are shortly to have £600 a year added to your income, and that I have candid accounts in prints, as large as a newspaper, to read to you for your perfect satisfaction! Come ye together, and see me at church in my new grand physical feather'd wig: I may modestly say, report declares I am captivating. See further in this paper of the 20th of October last.

Windsor Castle.   J..D..

TO the Fair Sex.—If the young lady, who a young gentleman in the city appointed to meet at the west end of the town on Sunday morning last, will send a line to him, mentioning where she may be seen or heard of, it will be very thankfully received. Address, by post, to J. W. H., to be left at the Bank. Honour may be depended on.

B

ST. JAMES's Church.—A gentleman, who stood in the north-west gallery on Friday last, near to a lady who was in a front seat of the back part of the gallery, dressed in black, with black ear-rings, and was seated between an elderly lady and a young lady: after the service was over, the gentleman saw them get into a carriage that was waiting for them near to Eagle-street, and they went on towards the Haymarket. If the lady alluded to is in that situation as to permit her for a moment to consider and think of the cause of this advertisement, no doubt but she will remember the person who would think himself greatly honoured by her inclination to know the true motive of this address.

A CARD.—If the gentleman who followed and paid so much attention to a lady last Sunday night, between the hours of 9 and 10, from Holborn, to Charles-street, Middlesex Hospital, and accidentally tore her glove, really felt the solicitude he expressed for her, and earnest desire of seeing her again, he may obtain an interview by addressing a line, mentioning any occurrent circumstance, to C. G. M., 175, Oxford-street.

A CARD.—If the lady who a gentleman handed into her carriage from Covent Garden Theatre, on Wednesday the third of this month, will oblige the advertiser with a line to Z. Z., Spring-garden coffee-house, saying if married or single, she will quiet the mind of a young nobleman, who has tried, but in vain, to find the lady. The carriage was ordered to Bond-street. The lady may depend on honour and secrecy — nothing but the most honourable interview is intended. The lady was in mourning and sufficiently cloathed to distinguish her for possessing every virtue and charm that man could desire in a female that he would make choice of for a wife. Deception will be detected, as the lady's person can never be forgot.

TO A. Z.—If the lady will give herself the trouble to send where her letter was directed, she will find one left for her, containing every wished-for information.

A SITUATION under Government, or elsewhere. A premium (adequate to a salary of 100l. per annum and upwards) will be given to any lady, or gentleman who will procure the advertiser any situation (except that of a clerk) in any public office. The most satisfactory references can be given, and the strictest secrecy may be relied on. Direct to A. B., No. 57, Chandos-street, Covent-garden.

ONE thousand five hundred pounds will be given to any person who has influence to procure for the advertiser an appointment of writer either to Bengal or Madras. Address to A. Z., at the British Coffee-house.

THIRTY guineas will be given for a Freeman's Presentation to Christ's Hospital. Apply to S. B., No. 13, Russell-court, Covent garden.

AN active man, of respectable character and connections, habituated to business, who writes a neat, expeditious hand, understands accounts and book-keeping, having 5 or 6 leisure hours every day, offers his service to any respectable person in the vicinity of Charing-cross, to manage his concerns, keep his accounts, collect debts, &c., or would engage as a deputy, and perform the duty of any infirm gentleman in a public office, who might wish for a temporary or permanent retirement. Address to F. F., at Messrs. Byfield and Co., Charing-cross.

FROM 100l. to 400l. will be given to any lady or gentleman who has interest to procure the advertiser a permanent situation under Government, or any of the public offices. The advertiser possessing a general knowledge of business, would not object to employ the above sum in trade, where his personal attendance would be required. Address, post paid, to A. B., Steven's Coffee-house, Bond-street.

ARMY.—A Major and Lieutenant-Colonel of Fencible Regiments of Infantry, with permanent rank, wish to exchange into old regiments of the line, giving a proper difference. Letters (post paid) addressed to Mr. George Williams, George's Coffee-house, Haymarket, will be attended to.
N.B.—The Major would exchange on half-pay without any difference.

TO Majors of Infantry.—Any major of a regiment of the line willing to sell out, may hear of a purchaser, by applying in person, or by letter, to Mr. Hughes, at No. 149, Strand, where a reference may be had to the party desirous of purchasing. No army broker need apply.

WANTED to purchase a cornetcy in an old regiment of dragoons.—Apply at the office of this paper, where a reference, nigh at hand, will be given.

EXCHANGE of Preferment.—A gentleman holding a desirable living, an easy day's journey west of London, in a very genteel neighbourhood, worth 500l. per annum would exchange it for any kind of ecclesiastical emolument worth 400l. per annum. Apply by letter (post paid) to A. B., No. 77, Cornhill.

CHAPEL.—Any gentleman having a chapel to dispose of, either in the metropolis, its environs, or the country, is requested to address a line to C. L., at Peele's Coffee-house, Fleet-street.

A YOUNG Gentleman, of good connections, who holds a situation in a public office, which occupies but a small part of the day, wishes to engage his intermediate hours, viz., from 10 or 11 in the morning to 4 in the afternoon, in the service of a merchant or in extra writing, which may produce some little addition to his income. Address to G. B., at Lloyd's Coffee-house.

A YOUNG man, in a public office, who is disengaged generally after 2 o'clock, wishes to employ his leisure hours in a counting-house. Any gentleman wanting such an assistant, may be waited upon by the advertiser, by addressing to M. G., Will's Coffee-house, Cornhill.

CLERKS in public offices, who have a few hours for about four days in the week, may hear of employment, by sending a specimen of their writing, and address, directed to M. C., at Brown's Coffee-house, Mitre-court, Temple.

Fire at Vauxhall.
THE proprietor of Vauxhall Gardens, returns thanks to the public, and to the neighbourhood in general, for their timely assistance in stopping the progress of the flames, and particularly to the gentlemen of the Lambeth and other Volunteer Associations, for their spirited and indefatigable exertions during the whole time of the fire.—Vauxhall Gardens, July 1, 1800.

FRIENDLY Advice.—If a Young Gentleman, who left his house and business on Tuesday evening last, will return, or appoint an interview with any of his friends, everything which has passed will be forgot.

WANTED, a youth of genius, for a copper-plate engraver. Apply at Messrs. Whiltows, copper-plate makers, Shoe-lane, Fleet-street. A premium is expected. He will have the advantage of the Goldsmith's Company.

A LADY going to Nottingham in a week or two, wishes to make a third in a chaise. A gentleman and lady, or two elderly gentlemen would be preferred. Address X. Y., No. 2, Clement's-court, Milk-street.

AMERICA.—An advantageous offer. Any gentleman, who can command a thousand pounds, and would wish to take a voyage to America, will have an opportunity of realizing some thousands in a short period; by a speculation perfectly free from risk. Letters, post paid, from principals only, will be attended to. Address to A. B., at Mr. Glover's, grocer, No. 49, corner of Compton and Dean-street, Soho.

THE Cutter "Enterprize," of Guernsey, Amice Lecocq, Commander, a prime sailer, armed with 4 guns, small arms, &c., and having excellent accommodations for passengers, will sail from the Port of Weymouth, for the Island of Guernsey on every Thursday, winds and weather permitting. All gentlemen or ladies, who will take their passage on board the said vessel, may rely on every care and attention being paid them. Price for cabin passengers 1*l*. 3*s*. 6*d*.

General Post Office, Dec. 31, 1799.

THE post boy carrying the mail on horseback from Wigan to Chorley, in the county of Lancaster, was stopped about five o'clock in the morning of Sunday the 29th inst., in a lane between Worthing Mill, and Worthing Hall, by a man on foot, who struck the boy with a sword, and pulled him off his horse, which the robber then mounted, rode away a short distance, tied the horse to a stake in an hedge, and took away the mail and bags.—The following bags of letters were in the mail:—

Liverpool to Chorley.	Warrington to Chorley.
ditto to Blackburn.	ditto to Blackburn.
ditto to Preston.	ditto to Preston.
ditto to Lancaster.	ditto to Lancaster.
ditto to Kendal.	ditto to Kendal.
ditto to Penrith.	ditto to Penrith.
ditto to Carlisle.	ditto to Carlisle.

Wigan to Chorley, with letters for Blackburn, &c. ditto to Preston, with Letters for Preston, and all places to the north thereof.

Whoever shall apprehend and convict, or cause to be apprehended and convicted, the person who committed this robbery, will be entitled to a reward of two hundred pounds, over and above the reward of forty pounds given by Act of Parliament for apprehending highwaymen; or if any person, whether an accomplice in the robbery, or knowing thereof, shall surrender himself, and make discovery, whereby the person who committed the same may be apprehended and brought to justice, such discoverer will be entitled to the same reward of 200*l*., and will also receive His Majesty's most gracious pardon.

By Command of His Majesty's Postmaster-General,
FRANCIS FREELING, Secretary.

POST Chaise party for Exeter or Truro.—Any gentleman or party going down this week, may be accommodated with the advertiser's post-chaise gratis. To be left in preference at Truro. Or the advertiser himself will take a seat with one or two persons; to leave town on Saturday morning. Address to A. B. Batson's Coffee-house.

LONDON TO READING COACH OFFICE.
The London Coach Office, King-street, Reading.
ORIGINAL
Post Coaches to London.

A POST Coach every morning at seven o'clock, to the Black Lion, Water-lane, Fleet-street, London, through Twyford, Maidenhead, and Slough; returns from the Black Lion, every afternoon at one o'clock the same road (Sundays excepted), and arrives in Reading early the same evening.

A POST COACH
Every Tuesday, Wednesday, and Friday mornings at nine o'clock, through Wokingham, Bracknall, and Sunning-hill, to the Black Lion, Water-lane, Fleet-street, London, and returns from the Black Lion, every Tuesday, Thursday, and Saturday mornings at eight o'clock, the same road.—Passengers and parcels book'd at the Rose Inn, Wokingham.

A POST COACH
Every Tuesday, Thursday and Saturday mornings at nine o'clock, through Wokingham, Binfield, Winkfield, Warfield, and, *by permission* through the park, to the Black Lion, Water-lane, Fleet-street, London, and returns from the Black Lion, every Monday, Wednesday, and Friday mornings at eight o'clock, the same road.

SUNDAY'S COACH
From London at eight o'clock in the morning: from Reading at nine o'clock in the morning, through Twyford, Maidenhead, and Hounslow.

The above coaches call at Hatchett's New White Horse Cellar, Piccadilly, going in and coming out of London, where passengers and parcels are carefully book'd.

John Williams, Edward Elms, Samuel Williams and Co., proprietors, who return thanks to their friends for past favours, and humbly solicit a continuance of the same.

N.B. No parcel above five pounds value accounted for if lost, unless specified when book'd and paid for accordingly.

Market for the Camp.

NOTICE is hereby given, that a market-place will be established between the 23 and 24 milestone on the road from London to Bagshot, for such persons as may wish to bring provisions and vegetables for sale to the troops to be encamped on Windsor Forest, on the 9th of June, 1800, where they will receive every encouragement.

LAMPS Stolen.—Rewards.—Whereas many lamps have lately been stolen from the lamp irons in the streets of this city, notice is hereby given, that a reward of three guineas will be paid to any person who shall apprehend or convict any offender or offenders of the said offence.—Also, a further reward of five guineas will be given on the conviction of any person or persons for buying or receiving any of the said lamps.—The rewards will be paid at the Pavement Office, Guildhall, where any information touching the said offences will be received.

PURSE Found.—Left by a Lady at Messrs. Bicknells, the corner of Old Bond-street, a purse containing guineas, &c. If the owner will call, it shall be immediately restored.

THE amusement of Turnery is of late become one of the favorite employments of the nobility and gentry of easy fortune, contributing in a great degree, not only to their pleasures, but also to their health, by the exercise it gives, especially to people who love retirement. It also is of real utility, as being key to all the mechanical arts, for those who love, and study it is science; and also proves a great benefit towards learning practical geometry.

From a firm conviction of these facts, there is now offered to the nobility, and all the amateurs of this art, every sort of tool and instrument, turning machines, of every construction, for wood, ivory, tortoiseshell, gold, silver, steel, iron, and every sort of metal.—Turning machines for ovals, excentrics, &c.—Also portable forges, and a lathe for what is termed to wave or guillochee; also proper grindstones, and, generally speaking, all that has any affinity to this useful and pleasing art. The waving machines have hitherto been known to, and practised only by foreigners, who are mostly inhabitants of the metropolis; but gentlemen may now learn this most amusing and useful art.—The turning of metals is certainly the most difficult part, and as gentlemen are often deterred from pursuing this employment, from the impossibility of receiving proper instructions, they can now obviate this difficulty, at least for ten miles round Henley, as lessons will be given on this head; also on practical geometry.

Gentlemen may also be furnished with, or have made to their models, every thing that appertains to agriculture. Some models, now finished, being of real national utility, are offered for inspection, particularly a new invented machine for pump boring, and for conductors; a very curious and useful crane; a small churn in glass, with which a lady may make 2lb. of butter in seven minutes, without either fatigue or at least inconvenience; churns on a larger scale, which will be of great use to dairymen; various useful inventions for twisting or winding thread or wool.—All sorts of machines, for manufactures, mended, or new-constructed; screws of every size.—In short, turnery of every sort will be done, in either gold, silver, wood, ivory, tortoiseshell, steel, and all sorts of metals.—Models of all that is here offered are ready to be seen, by referring, by letters, post paid, or personally, to Mr. Narton, Henley-upon-Thames.

Burns, the Airshire Bard.

THE friends of the Widow and Children of poor Burns are hereby informed that the London subscription for their benefit is now closed, and has produced the sum of five hundred pounds 3 per cent. Reduced Consols, of which the following are the particulars: this Stock has been transferred this day into the names of the provost and magistrates for the time being of the town of Air, who have kindly undertaken to patronise this distressed family, and to husband with the utmost care this little sum for their relief.

Naval Architecture.

No. 6, Crescent, New-bridge-street, Sept. 30, 1800.

A GENERAL Meeting of the Society for the Improvement of Naval Architecture will be held at this place, on Thursday, the 9th day of October, to enable the treasurers to sell Stock, according to a resolution of the committee, for the purpose of paying the expense of printing the experiments made by the society on the resistance of water to bodies of different forms (and which are now ready for delivery) and for other purposes.

JOS. BROCKBANK, Sec.

Subscription for the Capture of French Privateers, Armed Vessels, &c.

Merchant Seamen's Office, Feb. 20, 1800.

AT a General Meeting of the Subscribers, held here this day, Sir Richard Neave, Bart., in the chair, the following statement of the accounts was laid before the meeting:—

Sums subscribed .. .. Total £4,026 18 0

Expended in acknowledgments of plate to several officers of His Majesty's Navy, for their very meritorious services in the protection of the trade of this country £2,432 14 11
Gratuities in money to wounded and other seamen, who have exerted themselves in defending and protecting their vessels against the enemy.. .. £1,007 7 10
Advertisements £333 16 3
Stationery and other incidental charges £235 0 0
The corporation, for the relief of Seamen in the Merchant's Service .. £17 19 0

Total .. £4,026 18 0

It is with the greatest satisfaction the Committee can acquaint the subscribers, that in the numerous instances wherein they have been able to pay a tribute of distinction to those meritorious officers in His Majesty's Navy, who have more particularly signalized themselves in protecting the commerce of the country, the notice of the committee had been universally received with expressions of the utmost sensibility; and that the sums of money presented to the officers and crews of other vessels, had been acknowledged with the sincerest gratitude, perfectly according with the original intention of the institution, and confirming its objects. That they have only to regret that the meritorious services of many brave men must already unavoidably have escaped their notice; and that the abilities of the fund did not afford the means of testifying their sense of the distinguished actions which were daily claiming their regards.

RICHARD NEAVE.	THOMAS BEDDINGTON.
BEESTON LONG.	ALEX. CHAMPION.
WM. MANNIN.	ROBERT CURLING.

St. George's Volunteer Regiment.

WHEREAS I, J*** H*** the younger, now living with Mr. Guest, a Pastry-cook, No. 205, in the Strand, having on the 14th day of August last, riotously and tumultuously assembled with other persons, to the amount of several hundreds, and excited and encouraged them to riot, and violently assaulted with dirt and otherwise, divers of privates of the St. George's Volunteer Regiment, then attending a funeral at the parish church of St. Clement Danes, in the county of Middlesex, and for which offence I have been indicted at the last general sessions of the peace in and for the said county; but in consideration of my youth, and promising never to offend again in like manner and paying the costs of the prosecution, Colonel, the Earl of Chesterfield, and the officers of the same regiment, have stopped the prosecution, upon my making this public declaration, acknowledging my offence, begging pardon of the regiment, and particularly those men who I so undeservedly assaulted, and which I hereby do, and hope that all His Majesty's subjects will take warning by this, and avoid offending in like manner.—As witness my hand this 25th day of October, 1800.

J*** H*** the younger.

Witness, GEO. WILLINGHAM, Ensign St. George's Volunteer Regiment.

ORIGINAL Manuscript Sermons may be purchased, written with accuracy, elegance and energy.—Apply either personally, or by letter, to Publius Tacitus, No. 1, White Rose-court, Coleman-street.

THE Society of Friends, commonly called Quakers, having been for some time calumniated as oppressors of the laborious and indigent classes of the community, by combining to monopolize those necessary articles of life, corn, and flour think themselves called upon to vindicate their own innocence and integrity, and to assert that no such combination or monopoly hath existed, or doth exist; either with respect to corn, and flour, or any other article whatever; and that they abhor such wicked and baneful practices.

Aggrieved by the unjust reproach, they not only assert their innocence, but put in their claim for possessing an equal degree of sympathy for the wants of the poor, with their fellow citizens of any description.

If any man will come forward, and prove that the charge of forestalling, monopolizing, or regrating, which they solemnly deny to attach to the Society, or any other improper conduct, whereby the necessaries of life are inhanced in price, can be fixed on any one, or more individuals, they are far from desiring to skreen such from justice; but at all events, they claim for the Society in general a pl.... opinion of their countrymen, and freedom from the insults which they have so long patiently borne.

Signed on behalf of the said Society, at a meeting held in London the 6th of the 10th month, 1800, and by order thereof, by

JOSEPH FOSTER, Clerk.

Volunteer Corps.

AT a General Meeting (convened by advertisement) of several gentlemen, members and well-wishers to the Volunteer Corps, held the 19th of February, 1800, at the City Coffee-house in Cheapside, it is considered that the Volunteer Corps have been beneficial to their country, and have received the approbation of their sovereign and the country at large.

That the Corps ought to meet with every encouragement, and that all attempts to injure them or diminish their numbers, ought to be zealously guarded against.

That it has been generally understood all Volunteers serving under Officers bearing the King's commission, were exempted from the duty of wearing hair powder, which if not, many Corps (particularly those which are not composed of opulent men) would be considerably reduced by resignations.

Resolved therefore, that it be recommended that no Volunteer send in his resignation until after a General Meeting is called, and that the commanding officers of the several Corps in and near London be requested to attend the said meeting.

Resolved that such General Meeting of Officers and Gentlemen Volunteers be held at the London Tavern, in Bishopsgate-street, on Wednesday the 26th day of February instant at 12 o'clock.

Resolved, that the thanks of the gentlemen present be given to the Rt. Hon. The Lord Mayor, for his polite letter and information.

Resolved, that the thanks of the gentlemen present be also given to the gentleman who sent to this meeting his able opinion in favour of the exemption claimed by the Volunteers.

T. A. PICKERING, Chairman.

To the Public.

WHEREAS the scarcity of Rags has greatly increased the price of every kind of Paper, which has occasioned a Company to establish a manufactory, by His Majesty's letters patent, for extracting printing and writing ink out of printed and written paper and converting the same into perfect white paper, fit for printing, writing, and other purposes, which is the first establishment of that nature.

They flatter themselves, that such an useful undertaking, so beneficial to the country, and which, of course, will reduce the price of paper, will meet with the approbation and support of the nobility, gentry, and public at large. It is requested they will save all waste paper, for which they will be paid the full value.

Public offices, gentlemen of the law, merchants, and others, who have always quantities of waste paper and old books unsold, and which are often burnt, not wishing to have them exposed to the public, find now an opportunity to convert them into money, being certain that they will be torn to pieces, and remanufactured. If every family would save their letters and old writing-paper, which are generally burnt and not regarded of any consequence, it would annually produce such a quantity that very few rags would be required to be imported and thereby save considerable sums of money which now go to foreign countries.

Stationers, if they consider this establishment in its true light, will be guided by self-interest to support it with their waste paper, at a just price, because the exportation trade must be lost to this country if the high price of paper continues.

Printers have already experienced, that many presses have stopped working, on account of the high price and want of paper, which, most certainly, has operated on the commerce of booksellers and the business of bookbinders; it is therefore hoped that the trade in general will prefer selling their waste paper to this manufactory; many of them having, with patriotism, rendered their assistance to this concern.

Places of receiving, at No. 9, Sheffield-street, Clare-market; and the Neckinger Paper Mill, Bermondsey. Mr. Fox, No. 52, Orchard-street, Portman-square, is likewise empowered to contract for waste-paper.

Persons, residing in the country, who have or will collect their waste paper, are requested to address as above.

London, January 1, 1800.

Whig Club.

THE next meeting of the Whig Club will be on Tuesday the 14th instant, at the Crown and Anchor Tavern, Strand, Lord Holland, in the chair.

STEWARDS.
LORD WM. RUSSELL, M.P.
LORD ROBERT SPENCER,
H. ST. ANDREW ST. JOHN, M.P.
JAMES BROGDEN, ESQ., M.P.
JOS. RICHARDSON, ESQ., M.P.
JAMES MACKINTOSH, ESQ.,

Dinner on the table at four o'clock,

R. W. CLARKSON, Sec.

Coachmakers'-hall, Foster-lane, Cheapside.

Parents and Guardians

ENTRUSTED with the education of youth may in a short time have them completely formed to appear in the first circles with that elegance and distinguished ease which is ever attendant on true politeness and good breeding.

☞ Boarding Schools attended.

N.B.—The morning academy for ladies only, is open, and will be continued till His Majesty's Birth Day, from eleven o'clock till three.

THE amusement of Turnery is of late become one of the favourite employments of the nobility and gentry of easy fortune, contributing in a great degree, not only to their pleasures, but also to their health, by the exercise it gives, especially to people who love retirement. It also is of real utility, as being key to all the mechanical arts, for those who love, and study this science; and also proves a great benefit towards learning practical geometry.

From a firm conviction of these facts, there is now offered to the nobility, and all the amateurs of this art, every sort of tool and instrument, turning machines, of every construction, for wood, ivory, tortoiseshell, gold, silver, steel, iron, and every sort of metal.—Turning machines for ovals, excentrics, &c.—Also portable forges, and a lathe for what is termed to wave or *guilloshee*; also proper grindstones, and, generally speaking, all that has any affinity to this useful and pleasing art. The waving machines have hitherto been known to, and practised only by foreigners, who are mostly inhabitants of the metropolis; but gentlemen may now learn this most amusing and useful art.—The turning of metals is certainly the most difficult part, and as gentlemen are often deterred from pursuing this employment, from the impossibility of receiving proper instructions, they can now obviate this difficulty, at least for ten miles round Henley, as lessons will be given on this head; also on practical geometry.

Gentlemen may also be furnished with, or have made to their models, every thing that appertains to agriculture. Some models, now finished, being of real national utility, are offered for inspection, particularly a new invented machine for pump boring, and for conductors; a very curious and useful crane; a small churn in glass, with which a lady may make 2lb. of butter in seven minutes, without either fatigue or at least inconvenience; churns on a larger scale, which will be of great use to dairymen; various useful inventions for twisting or winding thread or wool.—All sorts of machines, for manufactures, mended, or new-constructed; screws of every size.—In short, turnery of every sort will be done, in either gold, silver, wood, ivory, tortoiseshell, steel, and all sorts of metals.—Models of all that is here offered are ready to be seen, by referring, by letters, post paid, or personally, to Mr. Narton, Henley-upon-Thames.

Burns, the Airshire Bard.

THE friends of the Widow and Children of poor Burns are hereby informed that the London subscription for their benefit is now closed, and has produced the sum of five hundred pounds 3 per cent. Reduced Consols, of which the following are the particulars: this Stock has been transferred this day into the names of the provost and magistrates for the time being of the town of Air, who have kindly undertaken to patronise this distressed family, and to husband with the utmost care this little sum for their relief.

Naval Architecture.

No. 6, Crescent, New-bridge-street, Sept. 30, 1800.

A GENERAL Meeting of the Society for the Improvement of Naval Architecture will be held at this place, on Thursday, the 9th day of October, to enable the treasurers to sell Stock, according to a resolution of the committee, for the purpose of paying the expense of printing the experiments made by the society on the resistance of water to bodies of different forms (and which are now ready for delivery) and for other purposes.

JOS. BROCKBANK, Sec.

Subscription for the Capture of French Privateers, Armed Vessels, &c.

Merchant Seamen's Office, Feb. 20, 1800.

AT a General Meeting of the Subscribers, held here this day, Sir Richard Neave, Bart., in the chair, the following statement of the accounts was laid before the meeting:—

Sums subscribed .. .. Total £4,026 18 0

Expended in acknowledgments of plate to several officers of His Majesty's Navy, for their very meritorious services in the protection of the trade of this country £2,432 14 11
Gratuities in money to wounded and other seamen, who have exerted themselves in defending and protecting their vessels against the enemy.. .. £1,007 7 10
Advertisements £383 16 8
Stationery and other incidental charges £235 0 0
The corporation, for the relief of Seamen in the Merchant's Service .. £17 19 0

Total .. £4,026 18 0

It is with the greatest satisfaction the Committee can acquaint the subscribers, that in the numerous instances wherein they have been able to pay a tribute of distinction to those meritorious officers in His Majesty's Navy, who have more particularly signalized themselves in protecting the commerce of the country, the notice of the committee had been universally received with expressions of the utmost sensibility; and that the sums of money presented to the officers and crews of other vessels, had been acknowledged with the sincerest gratitude, perfectly according with the original intention of the institution, and confirming its objects. That they have only to regret that the meritorious services of many brave men must already unavoidably have escaped their notice; and that the abilities of the fund did not afford the means of testifying their sense of the distinguished actions which were daily claiming their regards.

RICHARD NEAVE.	THOMAS BEDDINGTON.
BEESTON LONG.	ALEX. CHAMPION.
WM. MANNIN.	ROBERT CURLING.

St. George's Volunteer Regiment.

WHEREAS I, J*** H*** the younger, now living with Mr. Guest, a Pastry-cook, No. 205, in the Strand, having on the 14th day of August last, riotously and tumultuously assembled with other persons, to the amount of several hundreds, and excited and encouraged them to riot, and violently assaulted with dirt and otherwise, divers of privates of the St. George's Volunteer Regiment, then attending a funeral at the parish church of St. Clement Danes, in the county of Middlesex, and for which offence I have been indicted at the last general sessions of the peace in and for the said county; but in consideration of my youth, and promising never to offend again in like manner and paying the costs of the prosecution, Colonel, the Earl of Chesterfield, and the officers of the same regiment, have stopped the prosecution, upon my making this public declaration, acknowledging my offence, begging pardon of the regiment, and particularly those men who I so undeservedly assaulted, and which I hereby do, and hope that all His Majesty's subjects will take warning by this, and avoid offending in like manner.—As witness my hand this 25th day of October, 1800.

J*** H*** the younger.

Witness, GEO. WILLINGHAM, Ensign St. George's Volunteer Regiment.

ORIGINAL Manuscript Sermons may be purchased, written with accuracy, elegance and energy.—Apply either personally, or by letter, to Publius Tacitus, No. 1, White Rose-court, Coleman-street.

THE Society of Friends, commonly called Quakers, having been for some time calumniated as oppressors of the laborious and indigent classes of the community, by combining to monopolize those necessary articles of life, corn, and flour think themselves called upon to vindicate their own innocence and integrity, and to assert that no such combination or monopoly hath existed, or doth exist; either with respect to corn, and flour, or any other article whatever; and that they abhor such wicked and baneful practices.

Aggrieved by the unjust reproach, they not only assert their innocence, but put in their claim for possessing an equal degree of sympathy for the wants of the poor, with their fellow citizens of any description.

If any man will come forward, and prove that the charge of forestalling, monopolizing, or regrating, which they solemnly deny to attach to the Society, or any other improper conduct, whereby the necessaries of life are inhanced in price, can be fixed on any one, or more individuals, they are far from desiring to skreen such from justice; but at all events, they claim for the Society in general a place in the good opinion of their countrymen, and freedom from the insults which they have so long patiently borne.

Signed on behalf of the said Society, at a meeting held in London the 6th of the 10th month, 1800, and by order thereof, by
JOSEPH FOSTER, Clerk.

Volunteer Corps.

AT a General Meeting (convened by advertisement) of several gentlemen, members and well-wishers to the Volunteer Corps, held the 19th of February, 1800, at the City Coffee-house in Cheapside, it is considered that the Volunteer Corps have been beneficial to their country, and have received the approbation of their sovereign and the country at large.

That the Corps ought to meet with every encouragement, and that all attempts to injure them or diminish their numbers, ought to be zealously guarded against.

That it has been generally understood all Volunteers serving under Officers bearing the King's commission, were exempted from the duty of wearing hair powder, which if not, many Corps (particularly those which are not composed of opulent men) would be considerably reduced by resignations.

Resolved therefore, that it be recommended that no Volunteer send in his resignation until after a General Meeting is called, and that the commanding officers of the several Corps in and near London be requested to attend the said meeting.

Resolved that such General Meeting of Officers and Gentlemen Volunteers be held at the London Tavern, in Bishopsgate-street, on Wednesday the 26th day of February instant at 12 o'clock.

Resolved, that the thanks of the gentlemen present be given to the Rt. Hon. The Lord Mayor, for his polite letter and information.

Resolved, that the thanks of the gentlemen present be also given to the gentleman who sent to this meeting his able opinion in favour of the exemption claimed by the Volunteers.
T. A. PICKERING, Chairman.

To the Public.

WHEREAS the scarcity of Rags has greatly increased the price of every kind of Paper, which has occasioned a Company to establish a manufactory, by His Majesty's letters patent, for extracting printing and writing ink out of printed and written paper and converting the same into perfect white paper, fit for printing, writing, and other purposes, which is the first establishment of that nature.

They flatter themselves, that such an useful undertaking, so beneficial to the country, and which, of course, will reduce the price of paper, will meet with the approbation and support of the nobility, gentry, and public at large. It is requested they will save all waste paper, for which they will be paid the full value.

Public offices, gentlemen of the law, merchants, and others, who have always quantities of waste paper and old books unsold, and which are often burnt, not wishing to have them exposed to the public, find now an opportunity to convert them into money, being certain that they will be torn to pieces, and remanufactured. If every family would save their letters and old writing-paper, which are generally burnt and not regarded of any consequence, it would annually produce such a quantity that very few rags would be required to be imported and thereby save considerable sums of money which now go to foreign countries.

Stationers, if they consider this establishment in its true light, will be guided by self-interest to support it with their waste paper, at a just price, because the exportation trade must be lost to this country if the high price of paper continues.

Printers have already experienced, that many presses have stopped working, on account of the high price and want of paper, which, most certainly, has operated on the commerce of booksellers and the business of bookbinders; it is therefore hoped that the trade in general will prefer selling their waste paper to this manufactory; many of them having, with patriotism, rendered their assistance to this concern.

Places of receiving, at No. 9, Sheffield-street, Clare-market; and the Neckinger Paper Mill, Bermondsey. Mr. Fox, No. 52, Orchard-street, Portman-square, is likewise empowered to contract for waste-paper.

Persons, residing in the country, who have or will collect their waste paper, are requested to address as above.

London, January 1, 1800.
Whig Club.

THE next meeting of the Whig Club will be on Tuesday the 14th instant, at the Crown and Anchor Tavern, Strand, Lord Holland, in the chair.
STEWARDS.
LORD WM. RUSSELL, M.P.
LORD ROBERT SPENCER,
H. ST. ANDREW ST. JOHN, M.P.
JAMES BROGDEN, ESQ., M.P.
JOS. RICHARDSON, ESQ., M.P.
JAMES MACKINTOSH, ESQ.,
Dinner on the table at four o'clock,
R. W. CLARKSON, Sec.

Coachmakers'-hall, Foster-lane, Cheapside.
Parents and Guardians

ENTRUSTED with the education of youth may in a short time have them completely formed to appear in the first circles with that elegance and distinguished ease which is ever attendant on true politeness and good breeding.
☞ Boarding Schools attended.
N.B.—The morning academy for ladies only, is open. and will be continued till His Majesty's Birth Day, from eleven o'clock till three.

To Wearers of Hair Powder.

AS several paragraphs have appeared in the newspapers, tending evidently to mislead the public mind respecting the wearing of hair powder, under an apprehension that its use is the principal cause of keeping up the price of bread, the perfumers have called upon their committee to contradict such groundless assertions, by assuring the public that it is not the fact. The following statement may be relied on:—The British starch makers have left off making some time on account of the high price of corn; and the perfumers have received the sanction of government to import foreign starch, in consequence of which they have obtained an ample supply of an excellent quality, and a sufficient quantity to last until our own granaries can again afford to furnish their usual abundance; they have every reason to hope that the large quantity already arrived, and on its way, will soon enable them to make a considerable reduction in the price of hair powder.

We are, with the highest respect, the public's most obedient humble servants,

WILLIAM GATTIE,
JOHN DAVISON,
THOMAS GOLDIN,
RICHARD ROSSER,
ANDREW JOHNSTONE,
SAMUEL BERRY, Chairman
to the Committee.

N.B.—Not entitled to drawback on exportation.

DRESSED this day, at the Spring-gardens Coffee-house, Cockspur-street, a live turtle, and sent to any part of the town as per order.

Perfect Likeness.
(By His Majesty's Special Appointment).

JONES'S Reflecting Mirrors, at one guinea each, for taking likeness in profile or full face: also, landscapes, and views from sea, &c. They are made on so easy a plan, that a child of ten years of age cannot fail to take a perfect likeness with them. Perfect likeness taken in miniature profile at 2s. 6d., and painted on glass or crystals, in a style of superior elegance, from 5s. to 18s. each. Profile likeness in colour, from 15s. to 1l. 15s. each, gilt frames included. His impression profile plates, for ladies and gentlemen to take any number from 10s. 6d. and 15s. each. They will be found of the greatest utility to such ladies and gentlemen who travel, as they can be put into a small pocket-book, and to present a friend with a polite remembrance in one minute. Time of sitting, one minute, and one sitting sufficient. Miniature neatly painted from three to five guineas each. Specimens of the above paintings may be seen every day from eleven o'clock in the forenoon, till seven in the evening, at No. 4, Wells-street, third door from Oxford-street.

N.B.—Such who wish to see the effect of the above instrument, pay one shilling each, which will be returned on purchasing of either the above instrument, or sitting for an impression plate likeness.

⁎ Likewise his velvet writing paper and metallic pencils, made up in books at 2s. and 2s. 6d. each. Manufacturer in Ordinary to His Majesty. To be had as above.

Genteel apartments for a single gentleman.

MINIATURE Painting.—Likenesses in miniatures are taken by Miss Clark, great granddaughter of Theodore, King of Corsica, at her apartment, No. 4, Cockspur-street, Charing-cross. Attendance from 11 till 4.

Dancing.—Private Tuition.
Scotch and Irish Steps.

MR. HOPKINS has the honour to inform the nobility, gentry, officers in the army and navy, and his friends in general, that he continues to instruct gentlemen and ladies in the most elegant variety of the Scotch and Irish steps, with all the modern requisites of Dancing the Minuet, Louvre, Cotillons, Hornpipes, Reels, and English Country Dances, after the most approved and fashionable style; and the course of their attendance made convenient to themselves. He also attends at home such ladies and gentlemen as honour him with their address, by an application at his residence.

Naval Monument to perpetuate the Glorious Victories of the British Navy.

THE advantages which the British Empire have acquired by the unparallelled exertions of its victorious fleets, demand, in a peculiar degree the gratitude of the nation to those distinguished characters by whose skill, courage, and exertions, under the blessing of Divine Providence, those important victories have been obtained; victories which have so essentially contributed to check the progress, and to humble the pride of the tyrannical and destructive power, which threatened to overthrow the independance of every European state, and, indeed, to overthrow the whole system of social and moral government. To commemorate those important victories, and to do just honour to those brave men, it is proposed that a Grand Naval Monument shall be erected on some place which may hereafter appear most eligible.

That this national monument may be the sole effusion of British gratitude, it is proposed that it should be erected by general and voluntary contributions; and it is not doubted but a sufficient fund for this purpose will very speedily be raised. The monument is intended to display trophies descriptive of the victories obtained.

The plan to be conducted under the auspices of His Royal Highness the Duke of Clarence, Admiral of the Blue, &c., &c.: and the following Committee, who are to decide upon, the merits of the several designs offered for this national undertaking, and to superintend its execution:—

Earl Spencer, First Lord of the Admiralty; The Right Hon. William Pitt, Master of the Corporation of the Trinity House; Sir Andrew Snape Hamond, Bart., Comptroller of His Majesty's Navy; Sir Peter Parker, Bart., Admiral of the Fleet; The Hon. Samuel Barrington, General of Marines; Evan Nepean, Esq., Secretary of the Admiralty; George Rose, Esq., Secretary of the Treasury; The Governor of the Bank of England; The Chairman of the East India Company; and Alexander Davison, Esq., Treasurer.

Subscriptions to any extent, and of the smallest denomination, from all persons whatsoever, who may wish to hand down to posterity their names, as promoters of this Grand National Undertaking, will be respectfully received at all the banking houses; at Lloyd's Coffee-house; at the bar of the Crown and Anchor Tavern, Strand; and by the Treasurer, St. James's-square, London, as also by the mayors and chief magistrates of all the corporate bodies throughout the kingdom.

THE patent Tea-Kettle, which precludes the necessity of keeping a fire, to be had only at Lloyd's Manufactory, No. 178 Strand.

ANN JENNINGS. — Widow of the late John Jennings, upholder, &c., No. 15 Newgate-street, returns her sincere thanks to the numerous friends of her late husband, and begs leave to recommend Mr. Wm. Chivers, as his Successor, assuring them any orders they favour him with will be considered as an obligation conferred on herself and family.

THE Hudson's Bay Co., will expose to sale by the Candle. at their house, Fenchurch-street, on Wednesday the 9th inst., at 11 o'clock in the forenoon precisely, coat parchment, and cub beaver skins. Particulars of which are inserted in their printed catalogues. To be seen at their warehouse to the time of sale. Hudson's Bay-house, April 2, 1800.

THIS day is published, price 2s. a new edition of Proposal for Paying off the Whole of the present National Debt, and for reducing Taxes immediately, by H. M. Bird. Esq., one of the Commercial Commissioners for the city of London and its vicinity. Sold by T. & C. Rivington; and other Booksellers.

THIS day is published, price 1s. 6d., ornamented with a curious caricature print, contrasting the fashions, ancient and modern, The Last Dying Words of the Eighteenth Century—a Pindaric Ode, giving a humorous and chronological detail of all the remarkable events, fashions, characters, &c. &c., in the reign of William III, Queen Ann, George I, II, III, particularly a proof of the century's dissolution, ancient manner and fashions, full bottomed wigs, hoops, &c., ancient actors, playhouses, and authors, Mohawks, storms, prophets, murderers, conflagrations, ghosts, riots, balloons, modern fashions, pads, spencers, short waists, wigs, &c., crimps, boxers, cuffers, private theatres, Shakespeare's MSS., German and English dramatists, novelists, patent coffins and stoves, &c., processions, volunteers, taxes. revolutions, victories, intended union, Lord Mayor's election, &c., &c., by Andrew Merry, Esq.; Printed for J. Lee, No. 77, Fleet-street; and others.

BELL'S Bulletin News and General Reading Room has been opened six weeks; the literary and intelligent gratification which it has afforded to the subscribers, have given them perfect satisfaction. The plan — A commodious room adjoining the library is fitted up for the purpose, in which are provided all the morning and evening papers, the foreign papers by the Hambro' mails, as soon as they arrive, and all the new publications of the day; also, a terrestial globe of the best construction, and a collection of the best maps. At two o'clock every day, a bulletin of the news of the day, subsequent to the publication of the morning papers. up to that time; and also the price of the public funds up to one o'clock.

Subscribers to this plan are also entitled to the full use of the British Library, which contains one of the best collections of books in the kingdom. Subscribers on this plan pay one guinea per quarter, just half the price of any one of the daily prints. None but subscribers to this plan are admitted into the reading room.

Subscriptions to the library, as usual, one guinea per year, for all the new books and pamphlets; and quarterly subscribers, for books in ordinary, at five shillings per quarter. A most ample supply of new books is provided, and the most respectful attention paid to the punctual accommodation of the subscribers, at Bell's British Library, No. 90, Strand, opposite Southampton-street.

ASTLEY'S THEATRE.

MR. MENDOZA'S Benefit, and positively the last night but two of the Company's performing this season. Astley's, Westminster Bridge.—This present Monday, Oct. 13, will be presented, by particular desire (for this night only), and for the 7th time at this theatre, a spectacle romance, called "The Bridal Spectre, or Alonzo and Imogene." Alonzo, Mr. Crossman, and Imogene, Miss Smith. Mr. Mendoza will for this night only (being his first appearance these 7 years), and in the like manner as he exhibited his science of self-defence at the Theatre Royal, Covent Garden. spar with a gentleman, and several celebrated pugilists. After which, Mr. Johannot will sing an entire new song, written by Mr. Upton, called "The Forestaller, Monopoly, and the Cowkeeper." Also, in the course of the evening, the following comic songs, to be sung by Mr Johannot, written by Mr. Upton: "Mrs. Betty and Humphry Jenkins," with the celebrated Irish song, sung by Mr. Johannot, written by C. Dibdin, jun., and composed by Mr. Sanderson. called "Dermot O'Dogherty's Description of a Storm; Paddy M'Gree's definition of English bulls and their joint ideas of Matrimony." And an entire new song, written by C. Dibdin, jun., and composed by C. Broad, called "The Match Boy," containing a display of fashionable and unfashionable matches, matches for everything that can be matched, and a description of things impossible to be matched; in which he will introduce the old chaunt, as sung by an original character, well known as a match boy in every part of London, Westminster, and the Borough of Southwark. By particular desire, the comic ballet of "The Gretna Blacksmith." After which, a new song by Miss Gray, called "All the World for my Laddie." The whole to conclude with the serio-comic pantomime of "Quixotte and Sancho."

Doors to be opened at half-past 5, to begin at half-past 6 o'clock. Boxes, 4s. Pit, 2s. Gallery, 1s. Second Price at half-past 8 o'clock precisely. Places for the boxes to be taken at the amphitheatre, of Mrs. Connell, boxkeeper, from 11 till 3.

THEATRE ROYAL, DRURY LANE.

THIS evening will be presented "Pizarro." Ataliba Mr. Powell; Rolla, Mr. Kemble; Alonzo. Mr. C. Kemble; Pizarro, Mr. Barrymore; Cora, Miss Biggs; Elvira, Mrs Siddons. To which will be added "The Humourist."

To-morrow, "A Trip to Scarborough," with "Lodoiska."

KING'S THEATRE.

TO-MORROW Evening (11 Feb.) will, by particular desire, be performed the favorite serious opera, called "Semiramide," with chorusses. The music by Bianchi. The principal characters by Madame Banti, Senor Rovadino, and Senor Roselli, being his re-appearance after an absence of 4 years. After the first act, the last new divertisement. At the end of the Opera will be performed a Ballet, composed by M. D'Egville, called "Les Jeux d'Eglé." With new Dances. The music by Bossi. Principal characters by Mr. Deshayes, Mr. Laborie, and Mr. Didelot; Made. Hilligsberg, Made. Laborie, Madlle. J. Hilligsberg, and Madlle. Parisot.

Pit, 10s. 6d. Gallery, 5s.

N.B. The doors to be opened at 6¼, and the performance commence at 7¼ on Tuesday; but on Saturday evening the performance will positively begin at 7¼, in order to be finished in proper time.

Vivant Rex et Regina.

square, an Entertainment, entirely new, called "The Cake House."

Arrangement of the Recitations and Songs:—

PART I.

Re. Dregs and his Villa.
Song. Perpetual Youth.
Re. Conjugal *tête-à-tête.*
Song. The Lottery of Wedlock.
Re. Agreeable Company.
Song. Love and Reason.
Re. A Receipt to kill Wives.
Song. The Poet and the Paper.
Re. A Trial of Patience.
Song. Anna, Ann, Nan, Nance.
Re. Le Maître de Danse.
Song. The Grand Ballet.

PART II.

Re. The Captain and the Poet.
Song. Brother Jack.
Re. Sailors.
Song. Filial Love.
Re. A Return of Reason.
Song. The Sweets of Love.
Re. The Club.
Song. The Thing, the Kick, and the Go.
Re. The Mess.
Song. Jack at Greenwich.
Re. More Plotting.
Song. Great News.

PART III.

Re. Honest Caleb.
Song. Highgate Probation.
Re. The Saracen's Head.
Song. Another Cup, and then.
Re. Which is the way to Windsor?
Song. A little!
Re. The Two Doctors.
Song. The Canary Bird.
Re. Bits and Scraps.
Song. Echo.
Re. The Coup-de-grâce.
Song. The Union.

The whole is written, and composed, and will be spoken, sung, and accompanied by Mr. Dibden

Boxes, 5s.; Area, 3s.; Gallery, 2s. Doors to be open at Seven o'clock, the Performance to begin at Eight. Places for the Boxes to be taken at Mr. Dibden's Music Warehouse, Leicester-place, Leicester-square; where may be had the Songs in the Entertainments of Sans Souci; the novel of "Hannah Hewit;" "The Younger Brother;" "The History of the Stage," complete in five volumes, and every other article specified in his Catalogue. The "Union," "The Lottery of Wedlock," "The Poet and the Paper," "Love and Reason," and "Brother Jack," are already published. On Monday next will be published "Perpetual Youth."

Sans-Souci will continue open Mondays, Thursdays, and Saturdays, during the season.

YATTENDEN REVEL will be on Thursday, July 10, 1800; and for the encouragement of gentlemen gamesters will be given a good plain Hat, value 16s., to be played for at Cudgels; likewise a good plain Hat to be Wrestled for; and a Cheese, of 16s. value, to be Bowled for.

On the second Revel Day, July 11, will be given a good plain Hat, of 14s. value, to be played for at Cudgels; also a good Hat to be Wrestled for; likewise a Cheese, of 16s. value, to be bowled for; and a Cheese to be Run for by Men in Sacks; and other Sports.

READING ASSEMBLY.

THE First Assembly this Season will be at the Town Hall, on Tuesday, the 4th of November. To begin precisely at Eight o'clock. It will be moonlight.

MAILLARDET'S EXHIBITION, Spring-gardens, is now open, from 11 till 4 in the Morning, and from 7 to 10 at Night, brilliantly Illuminated in the Evenings. Anxious to preserve public patronage, which Maillardet acknowledges to have already so kindly received, he has added to his Museum as follows: 1. A figure of a Child, which with all the movements of real life, will execute (during the stay of the visitor) specimens of Writing and Drawing, equal to the most perfect productions of the first masters in those professions. 2. An exact representation of that rare and beautiful Insect, called Aronea, which, by being placed on a table, will traverse its surface, self-moved, in a variety of directions. 3. The Natural Imperial Scarabæus, which, seen through a glass, appears as if composed of Precious Stones, in all their variety of colours. Admission 2s. 6d.

Androides, or Animated Mechanism, No. 38, Norfolk-street, Strand.

THE Day Exhibition at One o'clock is resumed, for the convenience of Young Ladies and Gentlemen returned from School; and the additions lately made of the Volunteer, who goes through the Manual Exercise and Fires; and Harlequin Magician, who displays a scenic representation of the taking of Seringapatam, the Battle of the Nile, Britannia lamenting the Death of Lord Howe, and Rolla restoring Cora's Child (from Pizarro), make the Evening's Exhibition, at Eight o'clock, one of the most singularly curious and interesting that this Metropolis can boast.

Boxes, 2s. Gallery, 1s.

Cartwright's Musical and Philosophical Exhibition.

THE Theatre, at the Lyceum, in the Strand, which has been recently fitted up in an elegant and commodious manner, is now Open, and will continue *this* and every Evening, with a series of Performances by Mr. Cartwright on his improved Musical Glasses, and a grand display of new-invented Fireworks, by Inflammable Air. Mr. Cartwright will perform a very difficult, much admired selection of Handel, Fisher, and Shield; and particularly several celebrated Irish and Scotch Airs, for which the Musical Glasses are so peculiarly adapted. To conclude with the Philosophical Fireworks from Inflammable Air.

Boxes, 4s.; Pit, 3s.; Gallery, 2s. Doors opened at 7, to begin precisely at 8 o'clock, and conclude before 10. Tickets and places for the Boxes to be taken at the Lyceum, from 12 to 3 o'clock. Entrance to Boxes and Pit in the Strand; Gallery door in Exeter-street.

ERUPTION of Mount Vesuvius, vomiting forth Torrents of Fire, environed with spital streams of Burning Lava, and in her utmost state of Convulsion, as seen from across the Bay of Naples, with Storm and Shipwreck, is represented every evening at the Naumachia, Bouverie-street, Fleet-street; previous to which will be represented, for a few evenings, the Glorious Battle of the Nile, with every prominent manœuvre which occurred, from the evening of attack until the defeat of the enemy on the following morning. Doors open at Seven o'clock, and the Engagement to commence at half-past. Places for the Boxes to be taken at the Naumachia, from Eleven to Four.

By means of a Buzaglo the Naumachia is continually of an agreeable degree of warmth.

IT is with the utmost reluctance that Mr. Cartwright is compelled to decline the many solicitations he has received to continue his Performances longer than this Week, his Engagements rendering it impossible. That he may not be wanting in any mark of respect, he takes the liberty of acquainting the public that his Exhibitions will be repeated, with many Additions and Alterations every evening this Week, when they will close for this season.

NOTICE.—THE Public are respectfully informed that the beautiful View of Margate, at the Panorama, Leicester square, is shortly finally to close, to be succeeded by a View of Ramagate, which is in great forwardness. The View of Lord Nelson's Victory, which has given such general satisfaction, continues as usual.

The Panorama is open from 10 till dusk. Admittance to each Painting, 1s.

SINCE the arrival of the two noble Male Lions at Exeter Change, in the Strand, the concourse of spectators has been considerably more than at any former time since that truly grand Menagerie was first opened. One of the Lions arrived the 16th of November last, and the other on the 21st day of December last. They are both exhibited in the Great Room, with near two hundred other Animals; amongst which are four of the largest Bengal Royal Tigers ever seen in this country. Admittance 1s. each. In a separate apartment are a stupendous Elephant and six Kangaroos from Botany Bay. Admittance 1s. each. Also in another apartment is an Optical Exhibition, far excelling any thing of the kind hitherto invented. Admittance 1s. each, or the three Exhibitions for 2s. 6d. A Skeleton of a Whale, 66 feet long, and perfect in every respect, to be sold cheap.

N.B.—Foreign Birds and Beasts bought, sold, or exchanged, by C. Pidcock, as above.

Last Week of the Battle of the Nile.
At the Naumachia, Bouverie-street, Fleet-street.

THIS and every Evening during the present Week will be exhibited a truly grand and awful representation of a Storm and Shipwreck, accompanied with Thunder, Lightning, Rain, &c., in a style of correctness never before witnessed in this or any other country.

Previous to which will be displayed a representation of the Battle of the Nile.

By means of a Regulating Buzaglo the Naumachia is kept in an agreeable degree of warmth.

Places for the Boxes to be taken from 10 to 4.
Boxes, 3s. Pit, 2s.
Doors open at 7, and begins at half-past 7.

200 Guineas.

TWO Hundred Guineas was offered last week at Exeter Change, for one of the Royal Tygers for the purpose of baiting it with Bull-dogs, but the Proprietor, well-knowing the dreadful consequences that would follow, would not accept even ten times the sum for such a purpose, for of all animals the Tyger is the most terrible, having limbs superior to an ox, and talons that would tear a horse in pieces in a few moments. There is no less than four of those animals at the above place, together with a beautiful Lion, and a variety of Leopards, Panthers, Hyenas, near two hundred in number; other Foreign Animals, among which is a large Male Elephant, with ivory tusks standing out of his mouth, near a yard long. They are divided into three Exhibitions at One Shilling each, or the whole of the Collection for Half-a-Crown each person.

PANORAMA.—Leicester Square.

NOW Open, a correct View of Lord Nelson's Victory at the Nile, which though seen by daylight, appears as in the Action, at ten o'clock at night, the whole seeming only lighted by the fire from the ships, and those blown up and burnt, producing an effect seldom seen by the oldest seaman. Seven ships of the line are close to the observer, and appear as large as reality. This Painting, from the management of the light and colouring, has an effect equally good on a dark day as it has in the sunshine. The beautiful View of Margate continues open, as usual.

Hours from Ten till Dusk. Admittance to each, 1s.

MR. O'BRIEN, the celebrated Irish Giant, who measures near Nine Feet high, most respectfully informs the Nobility and Gentry, and Public in general, that he is just returned from the country, and has taken a lodging at Mr. Jameson's, Clock and Watch Maker, No. 8, Charing Cross, opposite the Admiralty, where he will exhibit himself for a short time only. Admittance One Shilling each.

Never before Exhibited,

AN Albino and Albiness, at Brooke's Original Menagerie, top of the Hay-market, No. 242, Piccadilly. These astonishing and beautiful productions of nature, the Girl nineteen years old, and the Boy seventeen, are elegant in form, their eyes of a sparkling red, and in perpetual motion; they are in fact Nyctalopes! Their hair is of the most snowy white and silken texture. The charming female is truly unique, and in transparency of skin much surpasses the lovely Circassians. As to words they are totally inadequate to express the singular curiosity of these wonderful phenomena, the uncommon and continued attention they have already experienced from personages of the first fashion and consideration, having had the honour of being exhibited before His Royal Highness the Prince of Wales, their Royal Highnesses the Duke and Duchess of York, the Duke of Cumberland, and Prince of Orange, Sir Joseph Banks, and many of the first Nobility and Gentry, who were all pleased to express themselves in the strongest terms of satisfaction in respect to them, is the most manifest proof of the high estimation in which they are held, and leaves not a doubt that ocular demonstration is only necessary to fill the mind with the most sublime ideas of the marvellous works of the Omnipotent. Their parents, who are of dark complexions have had several children, but alternately an Albino and a Brunette. Admittance 1s. each.

N.B.—All kind of Exotic Animals; and Birds bought, sold, or exchanged.

The Bous Potamous, or Amphibious Beef, to be seen alive.

NOW in Bloom, at Barr's Nursery, Ball's Pond, near Islington, a large American Aloo, having upwards of 23,000 blooming buds, supposed to be more than was ever before produced from any one plant in England, which, with the regularity of the chandelier branches (30 in number), gives it the appearance of one of the most wonderful productions of nature. Admittance 1s.

MILTON GALLERY, PALL MALL.

FUSELI'S EXHIBITION, with additional Pictures, is now Open, from Nine in the morning till Seven in the evening (Sundays excepted).

Admittance, 1s. Catalogue, 6d.

UNPARALLELED Benefits in the English State Lottery.—To be gained for only 15l. 19s., viz.: Sixty thousand pounds—Fifty thousand pounds—Forty thousand pounds—Thirty-five thousand pounds—Thirty thousand pounds—Twenty-five thousand pounds—Twenty thousand pounds—Ten thousand pounds—Five thousand pounds; besides prizes of 2,000l., 1,000l., 500l., and 16,730 prizes from 100l. to 18l.,—8l. 4s. will gain half the above sums,—4l. 3s. one quarter ditto,—2l. 2s. one eighth ditto,—1l. 1s. one sixteenth of the above benefits.

Mr. Nicholson, No. 16, Cornhill, opposite the Bank of England, is selling the tickets and shares in the greatest variety of numbers, and recommends to his friends and the public an early purchase, as the price will certainly advance before the drawing commences, and as a proof thereof, engages to return the difference of price in case tickets and shares should fall before the drawing begins. Schemes at large, gratis.

Orders from the country (post paid), accompanied with bank notes, good bills, post-office orders, or shares of prizes, will be executed on the same terms as if personally present; and from the very great and unexampled success that has attended the purchasers of tickets and shares at the above office in the last English and Irish Lotteries, it is requested that those who intend honouring Mr. Nicholson with their commands, will be particular in directing to No. 16, Cornhill. Very great encouragement will be given to clubs, societies, &c.

DIAMOND Lottery. By Act of Parliament, the valuable Diamond brought to England by the late Lord Pigot (estimated at nearly Thirty thousand pounds), is to be disposed of by Lottery of 11,428 tickets, at two guineas each, the first drawn of which in the ensuing English State Lottery will be the prize. The tickets are on sale, by appointment, at the Old State Lottery Office of Swift and Co. No. 115, Poultry, (where the model of the diamond may be seen); and also at their offices in Dublin and Glasgow.—Tickets and Shares in the Irish Lottery for November, and the English State Lottery, are on sale in great variety. Letters immediately answered, orders correctly and punctually executed, and the earliest account sent of the success of registered numbers. Schemes gratis.

ENGLISH STATE LOTTERY.—SIXTH DAY.
No. 2,075, a Prize of 100l. Nos. 42,192, 33,683, Prizes of 50l.

THE Inhabitants of the borough of Southwark have always been remarkably fortunate in the Lottery. On Saturday Messrs. Pidgeon and Whiteing received of Mr. Nicholson, No. 16, Cornhill, by his draft on his banker, Sir Richard Carr Glynn and Co., 1950l. for the Ticket No. 31,423, drawn on Friday, a Prize of 2000l. Mr. Hackelton a few years back got a prize of 10,000l., by buying his Tickets and Shares at Mr. Nicholson's office.

At a crisis of such importance, when the considerable sum of Ten Thousand Pounds is receivable by the First Drawn Ticket, on a morning so near at hand as Monday next—and the princely fortune of Twenty Thousand Pounds, to be determined by the First Drawn Ticket on the Monday immediately following, who, in justice to himself and family, ought to resist the powerful impulse, to purchase Tickets or Shares at the present very moderate prices?

IRISH STATE LOTTERY.
Eighth Day.—No. 24,350, a Prize of 15,000l.
Ninth Day.—Nos. 11,004, 18,468, Prizes of 50l.

BIRTHS.

ON the 26th May, Mrs. Ryland, wife of Mr. Ryland, Cornfactor, of a son, being the 8th in succession without a daughter.

Oct. 7, at Madrid, the Princess of Peace of a daughter.

14 Dec., the Lady of the Bishop of Carlisle of her 10th son.

MARRIAGE.

JULY 8, Right Hon. George Canning, M.P., to Miss Scott, youngest daughter of the late General Scott.

DEATHS.

DIED, on the 14th Feb., in Darlington, in the 90th year of his age, Gideon Philips, Esq., one of the people called Quakers. He has bequeathed to Mr. Combe, the present Lord Mayor of London, the sum of 500l., and to Mr. Sheridan 100 guineas!

Died on the 17th ult., in the 69th year of his age, of a long and painful illness, which he bore with Christian fortitude, at his house in Bloomsbury-square, Nathaniel Godbold, Esq., Proprietor and Inventor of the much celebrated Vegetable Balsam for the cure of Consumptions and Asthmas. He was a truly hospitable and liberal benefactor to the poor, and in his last moments directed that the balsam should be administered to the necessitous at reduced prices. He was a man of perfectly inoffensive manners, artless, and his temper gentle. In him the world has lost a valuable member of society, and his family a kind and indulgent parent. His remains were deposited on Saturday last at Godalming, in Surrey.

Died on Monday last, at Newington, in the 81st year of her age, Mrs. Favell, relict of the late Samuel Favell, Esq., of Tooley-street, Southwark. She was a lady of remarkable activity and energy of mind, and by a life of singular exertion, became the founder of the fortune of her house.

Died at East Dereham, Norfolk, William Cowper, Esq., of the Inner Temple, author of a poem entitled "The Task," and many other beautiful productions. He was born at Great Berkhampstead, Herts, Nov. 15, 1731. In 1791 he undertook the arduous task of translating the Iliad and Odyssey into blank verse.

Died at her house in Portman-square, in an advanced age, Mrs. Montagu, relict of the late Edward Montagu, Esq., of Denton Castle, Northumberland; distinguished for her benevolence to the poor chimney sweepers, whom she annually entertained with roast-beef and plum-pudding every May-day on the lawn before her house, and who will have great reason to lament her death. Mrs. Montagu was an excellent scholar, and possessed a sound judgment, and an exquisite taste. She peculiarly excelled in epistolary composition, and her letters, in point of learning, judgment, and elegance, far exceed those of her namesake, Lady Mary Wortley Montagu.

10 Feb., in his 57th year, Cardinal Altieri. He renounced his dignity while Rome was in the hands of the French; which step he repented publicly previous to his death, in a printed pamphlet, in which he entreats the pardon of God and the Church for his fear of men.

6 April, at Nice, of absolute want, the artist Corbion, master of the celebrated Viotti.

6 April, at Paris, Guillomain, the famous comic writer, author of 368 theatrical pieces.

HOME AND FOREIGN AFFAIRS.

New Year's Day—Holiday at all the Public Offices.

(1.) It is always with satisfaction that we avail ourselves of the return of the present season to acknowledge our sense of the obligation we lay under to the Public, for the very liberal patronage with which they have honoured the TIMES during many years; a constancy of favour which, we believe, has never before distinguished any newspaper, and for which the proprietors cannot sufficiently express their most grateful thanks.

This favour is too valuable and too honourable to excite no envy in cotemporary prints, whose frequent habit it is to express it by the grossest calumnies and abuse. The Public, we believe, has done them ample justice, and applauded the contempt with which it is our practice to receive them.

The conduct of the political part of this paper has met with an approbation too general and unqualified to admit even the possibility of variation. In giving our best support to His Majesty's Ministers, we are persuaded we advance the real interest of these kingdoms; and we trust that the services we are enabled to render both the Public and the Government are enhanced by the independence with which they are acquitted. We do not feel it to be our duty to disguise a public calamity, nor to pretend to rejoice as often as it is our duty to relate a disappointment; but we think that, in spite of any partial misfortune, it is incumbent upon us to recommend perseverance in the general system, and to claim the confidence of the people for an Administration which has defended them under so many dangers, both foreign and domestic, and conducted them happily to the present glorious period of the War, when we may look confidently to just and permanent conditions of peace, from the defeats and calamities of our unhappy enemy, or to a victorious campaign, the last of the War, in which the almost certain success of our arms and our Allies promise a still more splendid termination of hostilities, with a surer guarantee for the observation of peace.

We believe it will be thought, after so long experience, to be superfluous for us to assert the priority of this Paper in every authentic article of political intelligence; but it is a pleasant task to ascertain the justice of the public opinion in a matter so flattering to our own exertions, and so justly due to the favour which has crowned them.

During the long period of last winter, when all regular communication with the Continent was stopped, we were alone enabled to communicate foreign intelligence through the Paris journals, which we received exclusively for three months. We were the first to announce the notice of hostilities on the Continent, if the Russians did not quit Germany. By the mail which brought the news of the arrival of Mr. Grenville at Berlin, our Hamburgh correspondent announced that this mission would fail. We were also the first to announce the declaration of War by France against the Emperor and the Grand Duke of Tuscany; of the defeat of Jourdan by the Archduke; of the intended declaration of War by the King of Sardinia against the French, several weeks before hostilities actually commenced; of the re-capture of Leghorn and Florence; and of the subsidiary treaty with Russia two months before it was announced in Parliament. Latterly, we were the first to announce the unfortunate reverses in Switzerland, and the still more unfortunate misunderstanding between the Courts of Vienna and Petersburgh, which were generally disbelieved for some time, though we knew our information to be certain. With far greater pleasure we have within these few days announced the reconciliation of those great Powers.

The other departments of this Paper have been found, we trust, to be filled by gentlemen of integrity and talents; and the Parliamentary and Law Reports continue to be relied upon for their precision and truth. In every part of our publication we have uniformly endeavoured to avoid causing pain or the giving of offence to any individual, while we have attempted to sustain the public morals and the happiness which can only be derived from that source, and to inculcate not only obedience but love to the laws of our country.

It is by persevering in the same paths, that we alone lay claim to the continuation of that indulgence, which it is not with less pride than gratitude that we acknowledge.—"*The Times*," *London, January* 1.

(2.) We enter this day into the last year of the eighteenth century. It is likely to be as pregnant with calamities to mankind as any of those which went before it. The rage of contending Cabinets continues, though the violence of their people is extinguished, and the world is at length likely to see the true character of the War ascertained, by observing the mercenary character of the Government still active, when the panic which they excited, and the delirium which they made their pretext, have been corrected by the severe hand of adversity. The people of every country sigh for peace, and would, if they dared, demand it. All controversy about principles is over; and we have the fatal certainty that we are now only to suffer the continuance of bloodshed and expense, because, on one side, the Allies cannot compromise their ambition, and, on the other, the usurpers cannot consolidate their power. In this state of the world, it will be our pride to preserve the same vigilant, firm, and independent course which we have maintained through the whole period of the revolutionary convulsion—holding ourselves equally apart from the excesses of anarchy and from the debasement of corruption. —"*The Morning Chronicle*," *January* 1, 1800.

(3.) The total of the principal Debt of this country, as it stood on the 5th of January, 1800, is 451,699,919*l*. 11*s*. 5¼*d*., the annual interest of which is 19,813,569*l*. 1*s*. 8¾*d*.

(4). WHIG CLUB OF ENGLAND.—THERE was last night a most numerous meeting of this independent Society, when the Right Hon. H. C. Combe, Lord Mayor of London, was in the Chair. He was supported by the Duke of Norfolk, Duke of Bedford, the Earl of Derby, Lord John Russell, Lord William Russell, Lord Robert Spencer, Mr. Fox, Mr. Sheridan, Mr. Erskine, Mr. Whitbread, Sir John Aubrey, Bart., Sir Thomas Millar, Bart., Mr. Byng, Mr. Smith, Mr. Alderman Skinner, Mr. Brogden, Mr. Mingay, and a number of other eminent persons.

After the usual sentiments of the day, the Right Hon. Chairman gave "Mr. Fox," which was drunk with the warm and unbounded testimonies of regard that ever accompany his name.

Mr. Fox, after thanking the company for their unceasing kindness, said that he had taken occasion to state to them last year the determination he had made not to give an habitual attendance in Parliament, from the conviction that no efforts of his could be useful in a moment of such public indifference to everything truly valuable in our system. He had, however, broken in upon his plan of retirement, and had the night before assisted in a debate of a most important question in the House of Commons, no less than whether, after an experience of seven years of War, and calamity, and expense, we should, or we should not, listen to a proposal to negotiate for peace. He had no hesitation in saying, that the experience of last night convinced him more than ever of the propriety of his former determination, for he found the House determined to support the Minister, notwithstanding the opinion of the public, which he believed to be now, what it was confessed to have been years since, universally against the tenor of the answer which Lord Grenville has sent to Talleyrand Perigord. A majority of 265 votes against 64 on such a question convinced him that nothing was to be obtained. Not more than three votes were gained to the few who spoke the sense of the country, and yet a doubt was not entertained but that if the Chancellor of the Exchequer had observed an opposite conduct, and had agreed to negotiate, the same persons would, with heartfelt conviction, have voted with him in an Address of thanks to His Majesty for opening the road to peace. What, under such an appearance, could he say, but that the active power of the Constitution was gone, as it must be gone when the representative body does not respond to the public opinion. He felt more and more convinced of the propriety of his going back to his retirement, but this did not make him feel less happy in the kind confidence of such a Society as the present, which he considered as an asylum for the friends of liberty, whose use might be infinite. There was no saying how soon and how rapidly public opinion might change; and the revolution of opinion was the only revolution that he wanted. He said, however, that though he had resolved to withdraw himself from habitual attendance, he by no means wished to recommend it to others, who might be more sanguine.

The Duke of Norfolk, in a short and apposite address, said, that the spark of public spirit, when stifled everywhere else, had still maintained itself alive in the metropolis, and had manifested its force in resisting the mandate of corruption, and exercising its genuine rights in electing the Chief Magistrate, whose public conduct and whose principles they approved. He gave, therefore, "The Right Hon. the Lord Mayor and the independent Livery of London."

The Lord Mayor thanked the Club for coupling his name with the independent Livery of London. It was the proudest distinction he wished to enjoy. The principles of Whiggism had twined themselves round his heart, and the elevation to which he had been raised by the voice of the Livery, should not make him forget in life the principles which had recommended him to their favour; and after his death he wished for no prouder distinction on his tombstone than that he had lived the friend of Freedom and of Fox. He then gave " The Head of the ancient Nobility of England—the Duke of Norfolk."

His Grace said, that in describing him in his hereditary capacity, he could only say that he never found so much honour as when united with the illustrious descendants of the men who brought about the glorious revolution, and by whose noble efforts its principles were maintained.

"The Duke of Bedford."

His Grace thanked the Society for their partial favour, and assured them that as it was the pride of his life to adopt the sentiments and principles of Mr. Fox, he would through life act upon them.

"The Earl of Derby."

The noble Earl said, he was not so little known to the Club as to need professions. No effort of his should be wanting, but he felt that at such a time no effort of his could avail much. He should never be wanting at his post.

"The Hon. Thomas Erskine and the Trial by Jury."

He thanked the Club for the honour, and for joining his name with that grand institution of the realm—the Trial by Jury. It was not yet possible to *pack* a jury as another assembly could be packed. He had last night co-operated with his friend (Mr. Fox) in Parliament. He most cordially acquiesced in the retirement which he proposed to himself.

"Mr. Sheridan."

In an animated speech Mr. Sheridan expressed his gratitude. He lamented the condition of his country, when this was the only place in England where fifty gentlemen could meet and freely express their sentiments. It was no small compliment to that Club, that Mr. Fox, when he retired from attendance in Parliament, thought this Society still so earnest in the cause of genuine freedom and the true principles of the British Constitution, as to honour it with his presence. He felt that the new era of the War had aroused the attention and the interest of the people, and he was sure that if their opinions were to be obtained, it would be found that they were not ready to spend the last shilling of their property, and to spill the last drop of their blood, for the House of Bourbon. This was the true question at issue; for this was the single avowed purpose of the most savage, the most implacable, and the most bloody war that ever was waged. It would be well for the people of England to say whether they were ready to

sacrifice everything to the divine, sacred, hereditary, and indefeasible rights of the House of Bourbon. The national debt of England was between four and five hundred millions. *It might be placed under two heads—one half of it had been incurred in resisting the ambition of the perfidy of the House of Bourbon, and the other half of it in attempting to restore that House to the Throne.*
"Mr. Whitbread."

The Hon. Gentleman returned thanks for the honour; as did Lord William Russell, Mr. Byng, Mr. Alderman Skinner, Mr. Smith, &c.

Mr. Fox said, before he quitted the room, which he did early on account of a severe cold, he would propose a toast, which he had often given with more or less hopes of seeing the sentiment realised. He never saw it with less hope than at this time,—he meant "The cause of Liberty all over the World,"—which was drank with enthusiasm.

The Lord Mayor kept up the high conviviality of the day to a late hour.

(5.) MR. PITT, who was Chancellor of the Exchequer, on 24th February introduced the following Budget. The Supplies required for the year were:—

	£
Navy	13,610,000
Army	11,350,000
Ordnance	1,695,000
Miscellaneous Services	750,000
Interest due to the Bank	816,000
Deficiency of the Ways and Means of 1799	447,000
Duties on Land and Malt	850,000
Exchequer Bills issued on Income Tax	2,500,000
Bills issued on other Taxes	1,075,000
——— on the Vote of Credit of the last year (say)	1,907,000
Subsidies to German Princes	2,500,000
Expense of Russian Troops	500,000
Towards the reduction of the Public Debt	200,000
Probable Contingencies	1,800,000
	39,500,000

And the estimated means for raising the Supplies were:—

	£
Malt, Sugar, and Tobacco	2,750,000
Exports and Imports	1,250,000
Lottery	200,000
Tax on Income	5,300,000
Renewal of the Charter of the Bank	3,000,000
Vote of Credit	3,000,000
Surplus of the Consolidated Fund	5,500,000
Loan	18,500,000
	39,500,000

(6.) YESTERDAY afternoon, Captain Maitland, of the navy, and Lieutenant-Colonel Douglas, of the Marines, acting on board Sir Sidney Smith's ship "Le Tigre," arrived at the Admiralty with dispatches from that gallant officer, containing official advices of the capitulation and surrender of the whole of the French Army of Egypt, amounting to 8000 men, under General Kleber, to the allied Turkish and British Forces.

Advices were at the same time received from Lord Nelson, announcing the capture of the "Généreux" man-of-war, of 74 guns, commanded by Admiral Perez, together with a fleet of store-ships and victuallers, from Toulon, destined for the relief of Malta.

(7.) WHEN His Majesty came down to the House of Lords the other day, it was singular that it should have been thought proper to give the royal assent to two paltry private Bills along with the Union Bill. It would have been more solemn and dignified to have passed that Bill alone, as a measure of superlative importance, and not fit to be classed with inferior matters.

(8.) THE idea of an Union with Ireland was conceived before the last session of Parliament. In the session of 1798-9, an Act passed our Parliament prohibiting "the importation of *French lawns not made in Ireland!*"

(9.) THE 1st of February next is said to be the day appointed for the introduction of the Union Colours on board our ships of war, and also on the standards of different regiments.

(10.) THE inhabitants of the county of Waterford are required to keep within their dwellings, from one hour after sunset to sunrise, under penalty of being sent to serve in the navy or army.

(11.) IT is the intention of Government to render the circulation of specie in Ireland of the same value as it is in England. This regulation will be followed by a new coinage of gold and silver. We think this a favourable opportunity to introduce an entire new piece of gold coin, in commemoration of the happy connection between the two countries. One of the value of 14s. would be a convenient size, something larger than the half-guinea; His Majesty's head on one side, and on the other two sceptres with the imperial crown. The coin might very deservedly be named the Union; and although it may be considered a trifling matter in the opinion of some persons, experience proves that small circumstances often produce good political effects.

(12.) ON 5th Sept., the Island of Malta surrendered to His Majesty's forces under the command of General Pigot.

(13.) THE capture of Malta is felt to be of great importance to this country.

(14.) MR. FOX has nearly completed his great and desirable work. He commences the history of this country—which includes that of all Europe—where Hume left it off, at the Revolution of 1688. We know not with certainty to what period he intends to continue it. We have been informed only to the conclusion of the last reign, but other persons have assured us it will embrace a very great portion of the present, and events in which the Right Honourable author has been most immediately concerned.

(15.) By an Order of the King in Council, all ships arriving in any of the harbours of Great Britain from any of the ports of Virginia or Maryland, in the United States of America, are to perform quarantine in the same manner as ships coming from the Mediterranean.

(16.) SATURDAY's "London Gazette" contains a prohibition against the emigration of artificers, and an offer of 100*l.* reward, and a fine of 200*l.*, for the detection of persons enticing them away.

(17.) IF the system which the Duke of York is now carrying into effect, of abolishing the practice of making rank in the Army a matter of traffic, is followed up, we may expect to see the British army obtain that reputation for skill which it enjoys for courage. At present it is admitted that the former is by no means equal to the latter.

(18.) THE late Bill respecting the baking of Bread will have one effect not perhaps foreseen. It will abolish the good old orthodox and most *lamentable cry* of *hot cross buns.*

(19.) POLICIES have been underwritten at Lloyd's at a premium of twelve guineas, to return one hundred in case Preliminaries of Peace are signed between France and Austria within two months; and at a premium of twenty guineas in case preliminaries are signed between France and England.

(20.) POLICIES have been opened at Lloyd's within these few days, offering for a premium of twenty-five guineas to return one hundred in case there should not be a Peace between Great Britain and France on or before the 1st of January, 1802.

(21.) THE following is the construction which ought to be given to the introduction of Buonaparte's Letter to the King, beginning with the words *Liberty, Equality.* I take the *unpardonable Liberty* of addressing *your Majesty* on terms of *Equality.*

(22.) A CONJECTURE having arose in Governor Hunter's mind that the Land called Van Diemen's Land was not a part of the coast of New Holland but that it was probably a group of islands separated from its southern extremity by a strait, and being desirous of ascertaining the fact, he fitted out a two-decked boat, of 15 tons burthen, built at Norfolk Island, and sent her to the southward, under the direction of the second lieutenant and surgeon of the "Reliance" man-of-war. They passed through a wide and extensive strait, and completely circumnavigated Van Diemen's Land, entered two rivers in it, and went many miles up with their little sloop. The south extremity of this country lies in latitude 39° 00' exactly, and the strait is in some places more than a degree and a half wide, but studded with a few scattered steep islands. A chart of this discovery is preparing to be sent home.

(23.) LETTERS from Botany Bay mention that the colony promises in a very short time to be able to subsist itself without further assistance from the mother country. The bull and four cows which had strayed into the interior some years ago have been found, and have multiplied, in the course of eight years, to one hundred and seventy-four head.

(24.) A REGULATION has taken place at Calcutta, by which all newspapers are not permitted to be published till they have first been inspected by the Secretary of Government, and every article expunged that he may disapprove.

(25.) THE rockets used by the late Chief of Mysore in his wars proved very destructive to an army: on account of their weight they are thrown by engines, 600 of which were found in the arsenal at Seringapatam.

(26.) THE project of converting to Christianity the Otaheitans has failed. The last of the missionaries returned by the ship "Reliance."

(27.) AMONG the passengers who arrived on Saturday night at Dover from France, was a French gentleman, of the name of Pattes, who was committed to prison by the Mayor, for having returned to this kingdom after being compelled to quit it in October last.

The following is extracted from the French papers.

LIBERTY.—EQUALITY.

(28.) IN the name of the French People. 4 Nivose, year 8th of the French Republic, one and indivisible, December 25, 1799.

Buonaparte, Chief Consul of the Republic, to the French People.

To render the Republic beloved by our fellow-citizens, respectable to strangers, formidable to its enemies; such are the obligations we have contracted in accepting the Chief Magistracy. It will be dear to the citizens, if the laws, if the acts of administration, be always distinguished by the spirit of order, of justice, and of moderation. Without order, the administration is nothing but a chaos,—no finance, no public credit. With the fortune of the State that of individuals is destroyed. Without justice there is nothing but parties, oppressors, and victims. Moderation impresses an august character upon Governments as upon nations. It is always the companion of force, and the pledge of the permanence of social institutions. The Republic will be imposing in the eyes of foreigners if it respects in their independence the title by which hangs its own; if its engagements, founded on wisdom, formed with candour, are maintained with fidelity, it will be formidable to its enemies; if its armies by sea and land are vigorously constituted; if each of its defenders considers the corps to which he belongs as a family of which he is a member, and in that family an inheritance of virtue and glory; if an officer, formed by long study, obtains by regular promotion the reward due to his talents and exertions. Upon these principles depend the stability of the government, the success of commerce and agriculture, the greatness and prosperity of nations. In explaining them we have pointed out the rules by which our conduct is to be judged. Frenchmen we have told you our duties. It will belong to you to inform us whether we have fulfilled them.

BUONAPARTE, *Chief Consul.*
H. B. MARET, *Sec. Gen.*

(29.) THE French still call part of their forces the army of England; and, as that part has to contend with the Chouans, in case of another expedition the name may have some meaning.

(30.) A PARIS journal asks, "What, pray, have we gained by a ten years' revolution? Virtue? No! Riches? No! Liberty? No! Trade and navigation? No! we have even lost that portion which we once possessed! Conquests? Yes, alas, with woeful experience! Nothing else? Yes, universal detestation and contempt!"

(31.) IT appears by the report of Rhœderer to the Conservative Senate of France, that the number of French citizens who had refused and who had accepted the new Constitution were—

    1,562 persons had refused it,
    3,012,569   „   had accepted it.

The number of those who accepted the present exceed by more than 1,200,000 the number who accepted the Constitution of 1793, and about 2,000,000 more than those who accepted the Constitution of the year 3. Three millions of voters form a very great majority of Frenchmen of age to exercise political rights, and are almost the whole of the citizens, heads of families, who unite intelligence with prosperity.

(32.) IN a late debate in the Tribunate on the law concerning privateering, it was stated by Rayneaul, that 3,461 vessels had been captured by French cruizers in the course of the present War!

(33.) THE business of marriage in France has been the occasion of a great deal of trouble. The first edict was that there should be no more marriages on the Decadi. The ladies were not pleased with this, it was a restriction which they deemed, small as it was, too great. Shortly afterwards the government determined that marriages should be solemnized on no day but the Decadi. This was absolutely horrible; to wait ten days! They therefore wisely decided at length that every day was a marriageable day; and this has pacified the spinsters of Paris.

(34.) THE French are making a military road from Switzerland to Italy, by the Simplon Country. The Cisalpine Republic is to be charged with one-half of the expense of it. General Jareau is to have the superintendence of its execution.

(35.) AN attempt of a very serious kind was made in the evening of last Wednesday on the person of the First Consul, as he was on his way to the opera. The design appears to have been formed with much ingenuity, and he narrowly escaped destruction from the explosion of a machine filled with combustibles of the most powerful nature, and laid in the street through which he was obliged to pass. The explosion was so violent as to be distinctly heard in every quarter of Paris; and the effects of it were so fatal and instantaneous, as to kill five, and dangerously wound sixteen persons who were passing at the time. The circumstances and results of this attempt are certainly too strong to suppose that the conspiracy was not real. The enemies of *Buonaparte*, particularly in the metropolis, have been long known to be both numerous and determined; and it is not improbable that their present disappointment may stimulate them to measures of revenge more open and more desperate.

(36.) THE following account respecting the attempt, and the machine, which was to take away the life of the Chief Consul, appears in the "Journal des Défenseurs." The cask of powder which was blown up was hooped with iron, and contained a quantity of balls in such a manner, that the discharge must be a real discharge of canister shot. The carriage on which it was placed blocked up the street at the time when the first Guards of Buonaparte passed. They made it draw off, but after they had passed on, it returned. The guards which followed made it draw off a second time, and thus there were two very remarkable movements. At that moment it was conjectured that the explosion was to be made, by pulling the trigger of the gun with a string; these different movements altering the position of the carriage, prevented the cord from being sufficiently stretched in order to pull the trigger; and it was at that moment the coach of the First Consul, which drove rapidly, avoided the fatal blow.

Buonaparte was accompanied in his coach by Generals Lannes and Berthier, and his Aide-de-camp Lauriston, in going to the Oratorio the night of the explosion.

Madame Buonaparte, accompanied by her daughter, and Madame Murat, followed her husband. She was in the carriage when the explosion was made: the glasses of her coach were broke; her horses, much frightened, stopped; but she ordered them to be drove on.

(37.) ON a review of the last campaign in Italy, there were fought 16 battles, and 120 engagements; there were taken by the Allies 19 strong places, 4,301 pieces of cannon, 14 howitzers, 38 mortars, 129 waggons of ammunition, 80,759 muskets, 500,000 cartridges, and upwards of 13,000 quintals of powder. The enemy had 73,274 killed and wounded, and lost 78,401 prisoners. They had one General-in-Chief killed, and another wounded; and amongst the prisoners, we reckon 18 Generals of Divisions, and several others of inferior rank.

(38.) FROM 1792 to December, 1799, one hundred and eighty-eight pitched battles are stated to have been fought by the different armies engaged in the present war. Might not a statesman calmly ask—what has been gained to the common cause by this profuse expenditure of human life? Are the French nearer being extirpated than in 1792? Is France, republican or not, nearer being conquered, or beat into the restoration of the Bourbon race? How wild the imagination that can place any future probability against such experience!

(39.) THE new Pope, who has taken the name of Pius VII., is of a mild and humane deportment, of a middling size, rather stout, his hair black, and commands respect. On the morning of the 14th ult. (March), at eight o'clock, the first Dean of the Conclave appeared on the balcony of the Benedictine Convent of St. Giorgio Maggiore, at Venice, and announced to the people assembled there, that the election was at length happily terminated. The great news was immediately communicated to the neighbourhood by twelve pieces of cannon, which had been planted on the Piazzetta, opposite to the island, for several weeks past, and were answered by all the ships-of-war and merchantmen; the roaring of cannon was accompanied by the majestic sound of all the bells at Venice, and by the rejoicing of the inhabitants, exclaiming, "Evviva il nuovo papa!" In the evening the steeple of St. Mark, and many of the palaces and convents were beautifully illuminated, and the whole Island of St. Giorgio Maggiore seemed to be on fire, every window being illuminated by five rows of large wax candles, which, with some thousands of beautifully illuminated gondolas, and other small vessels, sailing up and down the canal, afforded a very grand sight. On the following evening, all Venice was illuminated; the same day, the Cardinals had the honour of kissing his Holiness's hand and foot, and of being admitted to the double embrace. The Prelates, Nobility, and other persons of rank, also had free admittance. The coronation was to take place on the 23rd ult.

(40.) THE lazaroni at Naples, regarding themselves as the best friends of the king, and the saviours of the monarchy, give themselves up to every kind of excess.

(41.) A.E.I.O.U.—These five vowels are written in this manner over the portal of the emperor's palace at Vienna, to signify, *Austriacorum est imperare orbi universe.* The inscription is as modest as it is true! Austria's empire is omnipotent universally.—[Editor's translation.]

(42.) IN consequence of the late disturbances at Vienna all foreigners have been ordered to quit that capital. No person is allowed to enter Austria unless provided with a passport from the Cabinet of Vienna.

(43.) THE fine gallery of paintings at Florence has been packed up and put on board the "Anne" frigate. This has been done by way of precaution, in case hostilities should recommence in Italy.

(44.) THE boundaries between the United States and the Spanish territories have been finally settled.

GENERAL WASHINGTON.
Philadelphia, Dec. 15.
(45.) IN the House of Representatives this morning, General Marshall presented four resolutions, to the following effect, viz.:—

Resolved,—That this House will wait on the President of the United States in condolence of this mournful event.

Resolved,—That the Speaker's chair be shrouded with black, and that the members and officers of the House wear black during the session.

Resolved,—that a Committee, in conjunction with one from the Senate, be appointed to consider the most suitable manner of paying honour to the memory of the man, first in war, first in peace, and first in the hearts of his country.

Resolved,—That this House, when it adjourn, do adjourn to Monday.

These resolutions were unanimously agreed to.

A Message from the President was received, communicating a letter from Tobias Lear, Esq., Private Secretary to General Washington.

The President's Message :—

" Gentlemen of the Senate, and Gentlemen of the House of Representatives,

" The letter herewith transmitted will inform you that it has pleased Divine Providence to remove from this life our excellent fellow-citizen, George Washington, by the purity of his character and a long series of services to his country, rendered illustrious through the world. It remains for an affectionate and grateful people, in whose hearts he can never die, to pay suitable honour to his memory.

"JOHN ADAMS."

"Sir, *Mount Vernon, Dec. 15.*

" It is with inexpressible grief that I have to announce to you the death of the great and good General Washington. He died last evening, between 10 and 11 o'clock, after a short illness of about 24 hours. His disorder was an inflammatory sore throat, which proceeded from a cold, of which he made but little complaint on Friday. On Saturday morning, about 3 o'clock, he became ill. Dr. Craik attended him in the morning, and Dr. Dick, of Alexandria, and Dr. Brown, of Port Tobacco, were soon after called in. Every medical assistance was offered, but without the desired effect. His last scene corresponded with the whole tenor of his life. Not a groan nor a complaint escaped him in extreme distress. With perfect resignation, and a full possession of his reason, he closed his well-spent life.

"I have the honour to be, &c.,
"TOBIAS LEAR."

George Town, Dec. 20.

On Wednesday last the mortal part of Washington the Great,—the father of his country and the friend of man,—was consigned to the tomb with solemn honours and funeral pomp.

A multitude of persons assembled from many miles round at Mount Vernon, the choice abode and last residence of the illustrious chief. There were the groves, the spacious avenues, the beautiful and sublime scenes, the noble mansion, —but alas! the august inhabitant *was now no more.* In the long and lofty portico, where oft the hero walked in all his glory, now lay the shrouded corpse. The countenance still composed and serene, seemed to express the dignity of the spirit which lately dwelt in that lifeless form. There those who paid the last sad honours to the benefactor of his country took an impressive—a farewell view.

On the ornament at the head of the coffin was inscribed "Surge ad judicium." About the middle of the coffin, "Gloria Deo." And on the silver plate—

"GENERAL
GEORGE WASHINGTON,
Departed this life on the 14th of December, 99, Æt. 68."

Between 3 and 4 o'clock the sound of artillery from a vessel in the river, firing minute guns, awoke afresh our solemn sorrow; the corpse was moved; a band of music, with mournful melody, melted the soul into all the tenderness of woe. The procession was formed, consisting of cavalry, infantry, guards (with arms reversed), music, clergy, the General's horse (with his saddle, holsters, and pistols), Colonels Little, Payne, Marstelle, Ramsay, Gilpin, and Simms, as pall-bearers, mourners, masonic brethren.

When the procession had arrived at the bottom of the elevated lawn, on the banks of the Potomak, where the family vault is placed, the cavalry halted, the infantry marched towards the mount and formed their lines; the clergy, the masonic brethren, and the citizens, descended to the vault, and the funeral service of the church was performed. The firing was repeated from the vessel in the river, and the sounds echoed from the woods and hills around. Three general discharges by the infantry, the cavalry, and 11 pieces of artillery, which lined the banks of the Polomak, back of the vault, paid the last tribute to the entombed Commander-in-Chief of the armies of the United States, and to the venerable departed hero.

PARLIAMENTARY PROCEEDINGS.

(46.) INTELLIGENCE was received yesterday afternoon (9th February), by his Grace the Duke of Portland, from Ireland, containing the result of the debate in the House of Commons of that kingdom on Wednesday last (the 5th). The despatch was forwarded from Holyhead on the same plan as the lottery expresses are.

On Wednesday last a Message was sent to the two Houses of Parliament from the Lord Lieutenant communicating the resolutions of the British Parliament on the subject of a Legislative Union between the two countries, which his Excellency recommended to the consideration of the Irish Legislature. On the Address to his Excellency, promising to take the matter into consideration, a long and very animated debate ensued, which lasted till late on the following morning. The Anti-Unionists again spoke with great violence, and appeared to have gained strength since the first day of the session, as the majority has only increased a single vote, notwithstanding all the recent elections. On the division the numbers were in favour of the Union :—

Ayes . . . 158
Noes . . . 115
Majority . . 43

The city of Dublin was considerably agitated during the whole time of the debate, and there is every reason to believe that tumult would have ensued had the military force not been so great. We are concerned to see so much opposition given to a measure, which we sincerely believe to be so much to the advantage of both countries.

(47.) WE were yesterday (12th February), favoured with the interesting report of the debate in the Irish House of Commons, on Wednesday, the 5th, and Thursday, the 6th instant, on the Message of the Lord Lieutenant, communicating the resolutions of the two Houses of Parliament in England, recommending a legislative union between the two countries. This debate comprehends Lord Castlereagh's speech, in which the whole plan of the Union is detailed at length. We are happy in being enabled to lay this important business before the public, as the prevalence of the easterly winds has prevented the regular receipt of it by the ordinary course of the post.

The following are the leading points of the Union :—

In retrospect to past expenses, Ireland is to have no concern whatever with the debt of Great Britain; but henceforward the two countries are to unite as to future expenses, according to their relative ability. Accordingly it is proposed that Ireland shall contribute in the proportion of one to seven and a-half of all the sums raised in Great Britain. Whenever the debts of the two countries shall bear an almost equal proportion to this ratio, it shall be in the power of Parliament to consolidate them.

The Articles of the Union to be subject to revision at the end of twenty years.

Articles exported from Ireland to England, to pay on the import a duty equal to that paid in England by the British subject on the same article. The trade of the two countries to be free from all prohibitions, bounties, drawbacks, excepting those under the Corn Laws.

The Church Establishment of Ireland to become completely incorporated with that of Great Britain.

Ireland to send one hundred Representatives to the House of Commons, and four bishops and twenty-eight temporal peers to the House of Lords. The Irish peers, when elected, to be Peers of Parliament for life.

(48.) YESTERDAY the Duke of Portland presented to the House of Lords a Message from the King, communicating to the House the resolutions transmitted from the Parliament of Ireland, by which they adopt the principle of an incorporative union with this kingdom, and the Articles upon which they propose to effect it. As the Irish Houses have only echoed the wish and offers of the British Legislature, there is no impropriety in interpreting the conclusion of this desirable event, from which, we trust, a new era will derive of augmented happiness and glory to the common empire.

BRITISH PARLIAMENT.
House of Lords, Friday, 6th June.

(49.) BREACH OF PRIVILEGE.—The Earl of Carlisle rose and said, he always felt great difficulty in rising to address their lordships, but more peculiarly when what he was about to trouble the House with, might in the first instance be thought principally to concern himself, but more immediately, in his judgment, to affect the privileges, the honour, and the dignity of that House. Among the great landmarks of liberty which had been established at the revolution, one valuable one was the Act of the first William and Mary, cap. 2, sec. 2, which was considered as one of the great securities of the freedom of the people, in which it was expressly enacted, "That the freedom of speech and debates, and proceedings in Parliament ought not to be impeached or questioned in any Court or place out of Parliament." If he were to rest what he meant to complain of there, his lordship said, he should think he rested on sufficient authority, but he would go farther—

Lord Grenville interrupted the noble earl to observe, that as the noble lord was about to complain of a breach of privilege, it was always usual, when complaints of that nature were discussed by their lordships, to have the bar cleared, and that strangers should be desired to withdraw.

The Lord Chancellor instantly ordered the bar to be cleared, and the strangers of course retired. Not having heard the remainder of the Earl of Carlisle's speech, we cannot pretend to detail it; but our reporter was informed that the matter complained of was a representation in a newspaper on Monday last, of some pointed observations upon his lordship's speech in that House on the third reading of the Adultery Bill, stated to have been made from the bench by a noble lord who presides in one of our courts of justice. The earl, it is said, yesterday imputed the statement of these observations to the misrepresentation of the newspaper, as he could not conceive that the noble lord would have been so inattentive to the known privileges of Parliament, being himself a member of that House, as to have made any observations upon an argument given in the course of debate, while sitting on the bench of his own court, in which, if any person had attempted to answer him, he would have been instantly handed to a tipstaff; but that the noble lord would have been present in his place, and in that House made such observations, either upon his speech, or that of any other noble lord, that might have occurred to him. The earl, we understand, made several other strong remarks, and concluded with desiring that what he had said might be considered as a notice of a motion which he intended to bring forward on the subject next Tuesday. He accordingly moved, That the lords be summoned on Tuesday.—Ordered.

On the second reading of the Bill to prevent the effects of posthumous avarice, by prohibiting the future accumulation of wealth uselessly, in a manner similar to that adopted in a late well-known will (Mr. Thellusson's),

The Lord Chancellor said, that since he had introduced the Bill, he had taken pains to collect the opinions of all ranks of professional men of known abilities upon the subject, all of whom had concurred with him in sentiment, excepting only two gentlemen, both of them very eminent conveyancers. Those gentlemen, however, had stated to him the grounds of their objections, which were founded on a principle of political economy, but by no means to his mind satisfactory. On the contrary, when he came to examine them, his judgment, and that of others to whom he had made them known, were decisively against them. His lordship stated the grounds of the objections, the gentlemen holding that the accumulation of a large fortune by vesting it in the funds, or putting it out to interest in any other manner, and letting it remain for a great number of years, till it had swelled to an enormous sum, would ultimately be more advantageous to the public than dividing it at an earlier period, and letting it get into circulation. His lordship declared he held the converse of this proposition to be the truth, and that a fortune in circulation, even if spent in luxuries, waste, and dissipation, did more good to the public, and afforded more emulation to industry and better encouragement to arts and manufactures, than any useless accumulation of money could do. With regard, however, to any great or less objections of those gentlemen whose opinions he had consulted, his lordship said, he had committed them to writing, and compared them with the Bill; and he found that by omitting some of the technical expressions in it, putting in more common words, and shortening the Bill so as to reduce the whole to a single plain and simple proposition, every objection would be met. With that view, therefore, and as the Committee was the fittest place to make the alterations in, he moved that the Bill be committed for Monday next.—Ordered.

Adjourned to Monday.

House of Commons 19th April.
BILL TO PREVENT BULL BAITING.

(50.) SIR WILLIAM PULTENEY moved the order of the day for reconsidering the report of the Committee on this Bill.

The Secretary at War said, that if he had sooner known of such a Bill having been before the House, he should have opposed it, because he considered it a measure which the House ought not to entertain. It went to do away a practice that had subsisted as long as the country itself; and the evils of which, so far from being increased, there was every reason to suppose had been of late years considerably diminished. For his part he had never been present at a bull baiting in his life, and he believed there were many persons who had never heard of such a thing; no complaints had ever been made of the practice, and therefore he thought it a subject unworthy of legislative interference, which ought never to be exercised on trifling matters. These were not fit times for that busy meddling spirit, that *pruritus legis ferendæ* with which some gentlemen appeared to be actuated. It would now appear as if every man who, from local or personal motives wished to put a stop to any particular practice, had nothing to do but to bring in a Bill for that purpose, which, on account of the impropriety ought never to have been introduced into Parliament. His broad objection to this Bill was, that the evil it complained of, if such existed, was not of magnitude enough to call for legislative interference. This little petty meddling spirit of legislation was an evil of much greater extent than any complained of, and should never be countenanced by that House. A great part of this system was founded on the supposed condition of the poor. On the subject of the poor he was happy to inform those gentlemen present, that they should soon see a publication, which should only require to be seen in order that it might be read,—the work of a man who was one of the greatest ornaments of his country while he lived,

Qui, quid sit pulchrum, quid turpe: quid utile, quid non.
Plenius ac melius Chrysippo et Crantore dicit.

He meant the late Mr. Burke. The gentlemen who appeared so much the advocates of the poor, and used a language so like that of cant and hypocrisy, were running into an evil worse than that which they appeared desirous of preventing: they were for the depriving the poor of all their amusements, without even considering what had been the practices in this country, as well as in every other part of the world at all times. If gentlemen would look back to the ancients, they would find the religion of those people so interwoven with sports and amusements, that almost every day appeared a holiday with them. Let them also see what were the practices in Roman Catholic countries, where they would find that the poor enjoyed much more relaxation and amusements than they did in this country. He certainly believed that the poor of England enjoyed more physical comforts than those of any other country; but there was no country where such pains were taken, and such a war raised to deprive them of all the comforts arising from amusements. In the fine climates of Spain and Italy, it was usual for the poor, after the labour of the day, to amuse themselves with dancing the greatest part of the night to the music of the guitar. But should any such thing as a dance, or what was more commonly called *a hop*, occur in this country, the magistrates were all up in arms directly, and the sound of a fiddle is considered by them to be as abominable as the sound of an organ was formerly by the dissenters in this country. If a few strolling players were to come into a country village, their arrival was looked upon by the magistrates to be as dangerous as that of a set of wild beasts. Then if the poor, debarred of every means of recreation, should meet in public-houses, this must not be allowed them. If it be asked how they are to spend their holidays, the answer is—" Let them go home and read their Bibles." This was certainly a very good thing, but those who desired it to be done should set the example themselves. It was not, however, a recreation. But, happily for this country, the people had a species of hardy and athletic exercises, which contributed very much to give them a martial spirit; and it originated from the same spirit by which a person of higher rank was actuated to fight against the enemies of his country; because it was followed by a trial of skill and a certain degree of glory to the victor. The game of cudgel playing was one of those; and if two men found amusement in breaking each other's heads with sticks, it was very fair game to do so. Boxing was another amusement which, though it was much cried down and was so often attended with dangerous consequences to the combatants, he would never attempt to discourage. He did not think that it made the people savage or brutal. The sports of a people went a great way to form their national character. The people of England, who took delight in practices which some called brutal, were the very reverse of ferocious; they might sometimes be harsh, unmannerly, and rude, but he would assert that no people in the world had a greater horror of bloodshed nor a greater aversion to the use of deadly weapons. Let this conduct be compared with the gentleness and humanity of the French, who had never followed the savage custom of boxing: compare it with that of the Spaniards: and even in Holland a different spirit will be found to exist: —of this circumstances lately occurred, in which the most fatal consequences arose from a little affray with some Dutchmen, which with Englishmen would have ended in a black eye or in a bloody nose. It was well known that the English were not only as brave and as prodigal of their lives as any people in the world, but were always the first to forbear all manner of fury in success, and to spare the lives of the vanquished. He certainly admitted that the practice of bull baiting was very different from the manly, athletic exercises he had just mentioned, because there was some degree of cruelty in tormenting an animal, but even this had its use; it served to cultivate the qualities and keep up the breed of those useful animals called bull-dogs—a breed which he was sorry to see degenerating very much, so as to be nearly lost. England had long been famous for this breed of dogs, and they were mentioned by Gratius so early as the days of Augustus; even some of our ships had taken their names from these animals. But the practice of bull-baiting was objected to on the ground of its cruelty, and that too by the very men who gave their sanction to the game laws, and monopolized to themselves the noble practice of shooting. He would ask them if there was no cruelty in that practice? Certainly not, if every bird was killed on the spot; but he himself was shooter enough to know that for one bird that was killed, a dozen went off wounded. He would ask those gentlemen if there was no cruelty in hunting? What would the poor, who were already deprived of the liberty of shooting, say to those gentlemen of fortune who were endeavouring to cut them off all kinds of amusements? Why, that those latter were worse savages than they; that they were not content with having all nature before them, and monopolizing to themselves the right of killing game, but that they took delight in tormenting poor timid animals that ran away to save their lives—that they pursued these animals until their horses could scarcely put one foot before another. That that still was not sufficient to satisfy them;—but they panted for the honour of being in *at the death;* or in other words of gratifying their ferocious dispositions by seeing the entrails torn from the animal that had been so long a victim to their cruelty. He wished to caution the House not to afford the lower classes of people an opportunity of using such language as this. He was far from wishing to treat the magistrates of this country with any kind of disrespect; but he was sorry to observe that they were too much in the habit of using unnecessary and vexatious control over the lower classes of people; and like those persons who were always preventing children from enjoying their recreations and amusements, thought that every kind of control was useful to the poor. Many persons thought that the lower classes had nothing to do but to eat, drink, sleep, and work. This disposition, he feared, grew out of the system of the poor laws, which was the source of a very great and unfavourable change in the manners of the lower classes in the country. It was perhaps thought that if they partook of amusements they must spend their money and be a burden on the parish. For his part he held a different opinion, nor did he think these men had any right to prescribe to the poor the work they must perform, as they would do to their servants; and the principle they went upon was as mean and sordid as the laws were bad that gave rise to it. But whatever the principle in which the present Bill originated might be, he would always oppose that petty spirit of legislation which enters into that House on the suggestion probably of some little consequential man in the country whose hedges might have been damaged, or whose wife might have been frightened at seeing a bull bait. But the feelings of the lady who should make loud complaints to her husband against the brutes in human shape who had caused her so much alarm, were not at all affected at the cry of the hounds or the sight of the hunters, who were inflicting greater torture on other animals: all this was very fine. This Bill would have an injurious effect on the moral character of the people: it led men into the commission of all kinds of crimes, when those were made legally criminal which the people would never believe to be morally criminal. It would be disgraceful to the House to sanction such a Bill, and he would move to put off the further consideration of it for six months.

Sir William Pulteney defended the Bill, and said that in certain manufacturing counties the people were taken away from their work for weeks together by going to bull baits, and in places where the practice was unknown, the people were as brave as in any other part of England.

Mr. Canning rose to re-state some of the propositions, and exhibit in their genuine order some of the arguments of his right hon. friend, which had been misunderstood and misrepresented by the hon. baronet. The general scope of what was urged against the Bill could not, without great violence, be said to embrace harsh or invidious distinctions in favour of the poor against the rich. It could not be the object of his right hon. friend to degrade a class which he so highly valued, yet it could no more be his object to deprive of a long-tolerated amusement, a class of the community confessed by all to be entitled to every consideration from that House. The hon. baronet seemed to consider it an egregious absurdity to discuss the present question at large, he (Mr. Canning) admitted that it was a great absurdity to go at length into the discussion, because never in his mind was so absurd a question brought before Parliament. But if the Bill was thus absurd, it was the reason of all others the most pressing for discussing its merits unless, indeed, it should be contended that the measure ought not to be discussed at all. What his right hon. friend chiefly insisted on were two propositions, and if he understood these distinctly, they were, that 1st, Legislative interference is not necessary; and 2ndly, If it be necessary that the practice of bull baiting cannot be suppressed without appearing to make an unjust distinction in favour of the higher classes, whose sports and whose amusements are, in many respects, not less boisterous and brutal than those of the lower orders. Such proposition it was easy to comprehend in their application and force, and whatever gentlemen on the other side choose to say to the contrary, for one he was certain his right hon. friend meant not to arm the prejudices of one description of the people against the other. He was sure his right hon. friend meant not to pursue with vindictive comment, or hold up to public detestation, the favourite amusements of the gay and the opulent. But what severity was there in observing, that if gentlemen really intended to regulate and restrain the amusements of the lower orders, it would be well if the rich would begin with a self-denying ordinance. (Here the hon. member took a rapid view of the general argument of the Right Hon. Secretary, and inferred from his reasoning in this place, that the House would not act worthy of itself and of its dignity, in passing the present Bill.) He reminded gentlemen of what was the full attendance last year on the game laws, and supposed a case, that during the discussion of that subject last Session, a foreigner had come to hear the debate, and having asked what was the subject, was told "why nothing but a difference of opinion between some of the members whether they shall begin one month sooner or later to shoot a few birds that are variously dished up with a little bread-sauce." And suppose the same foreigner to be in the gallery at the moment he was speaking, what would again be his surprise to find that not a question of *War* or *Peace* —not whether we should grant subsidies to foreign princes—not a debate on laws for general national regulation, occupied the full attention of so large a body of the representatives, but a question respecting bull baiting! (A laugh.) The hon. baronet had expressed disapprobation of the practice of permitting hops in various parts of the metropolis; but whatever might be the antipathy of the hon. baronet to the amusement of dancing, surely there was some indulgence due to hops. As to cock fighting, he never attended such exhibitions; but it was easy to conceive that even that sport, if the cause of evils, was also the source of genuine enjoyment. On general grounds, therefore, on the ground that the practice of bull baiting conduced, as his right hon. friend had stated, to give an athletic vigour and tone to the character of the classes engaged in it, and that to this hour it is permitted throughout the whole kingdom of Spain — on the ground also that legislative interference, especially in minute affairs, is always impolitic, he should sit down, heartily approving of the motion made by his right hon. friend.

Mr. Sheridan said, that two more extraordinary speeches than those of the right hon. secretary and the hon. member who had just sat down he seldom, if ever, heard in that House. The former was not merely contented with general expressions of disapprobation of the amusements of the higher classes, but appeared to wish to excite the lower orders to rancorous opposition to the magistracy of the country, while the latter did little more than endeavour to enforce and illustrate similar doctrines. The hon. member said that nothing could be a greater absurdity than the Bill of the hon. baronet; now how did he make out this assertion? Was it the greatest absurdity possible to attempt to suppress a brutal and disgraceful sport? The greatest absurdity in this case was the right hon. secretary making a long speech to show the absurdity of a measure which if absurd, must be obviously so, and would therefore be most readily discovered in its true character, and of course exploded. But what was the full latitude of approbation of bull baiting which the hon. member avowed? Why one gentleman (the right hon. secretary) and another (his hon. friend), told the House that the practice was now fast dying a natural death, but "ah!" adds the other (Mr. C.), "I nevertheless hope I shall see many bull baitings." This was in the true style of a sportsman, for the hon. member would at all events come in at the death. Thus then it was manifested that gentlemen meant not to confine the sport of bull baiting to the lower orders, for most certainly it was now adopted into the circle of amusements for members of Parliament. With respect to much of the speech of the right hon. secretary, it was so fanciful and metaphysical that, however the country members behind him might be entertained by it, he (Mr. Sheridan) derived little, if any, gratification from it; though if considered as a whole, it could not but be deemed as abounding in truly Jacobinical doctrine. The allusion to the magistracy of the country had this tendency in a high degree, for what indeed could be so Jacobinical as to compare country justices to little children. Had such invective come from their (the opposition) side of the House, how loud would have been the right hon. and hon. members against (what they would call) sedition. Certainly every class in the community was in every respect entitled to enjoy all rational sports and all innocent amusements, but there might be some harm in giving wide dominion to the opinions of those gentlemen, who that evening, for the first time in their lives, stepped out of the beaten path, and, in seeking to amuse the poor, sought at the same time to subject the amusements of the rich to invidious comment. No doubt it was fitting that the poor should take recreation from labour and indulge in general sports; and it was not harsh to say, that while we are indulging ourselves in all amusements, they ought at least to be permitted to enjoy some. He trusted there was not a man in that house, or out of it, more heartily the friend of the poor than himself, and he entirely concurred in opinion with the right hon. secretary as to the impropriety of the magistrates interfering with hops and fairs, &c. But the principle was not carried far enough. The hon. member (Mr. Canning) alluded to the practice of bull baiting in Spain, but would he say that it is the effect of that sport, so prevalent among them, to raise the Spanish mind to heroism? Did he think that it was bull baiting which caused the superiority of the Spaniards in courage over the English? (a general laugh.) It was contended that the sport did not brutalize those concerned in it; that it is even not inconsistent with a humane disposition. Nothing could be less founded in truth than this. How was the fact? Why every instance of bull baiting was an instance of renewed ferocity in the manners of the people. Did not those engaged in the sport prepare the dogs for the pursuit by much previous instruction? and differing even from other barbarous games, was not the animal pinned, and the dogs let loose into his sides, while he is denied the means of defence. Yet this was the sport which fired the martial spirit, which aroused and confirmed the native courage of Englishmen! The contrary was the truth. However, if the right hon. secretary should ever be present at a baiting, no doubt he would let the bull loose, which certainly would be an effectual mode of raising the gallant pride of a warlike populace (a general laugh). It was idle to talk of the humane disposition of persons engaged in such pursuits. The practice of bull baiting, with all its circumstances, must be allowed to be the most beastly and brutal, the most unworthy of man that ever prevailed in society. The right hon. secretary had said that the breed of bull dogs was spoken of by one Gratius, so early as in the time of Augustus, but what did this prove? Not surely that the bull dog is a generous animal; the nature of the bull dog is the most worthless of any breed of the genus of animals to which he belongs. He is indeed the vilest animal that exists. So far from being courageous, he is sly, artful, and insidious, and having once got fast hold of the poor bull, he never lets him go, no more than a place-man lets go his place (a loud laugh). In alluding to what Mr. Windham said of gentlemen canting about the poor, Mr. Sheridan observed, that however the right hon. gentleman might think it fit to use such language, those who sat on the Opposition Benches, as they were called, instead of giving the poor of England bull baiting, would give them beef. Here the hon. member reverted to what was said of the magistrates, and called to the recollection of the House the interference of the officers of the police who entered a house in St. Giles's, about a twelvemonth ago, and having a magistrate's warrant, which was improperly granted, disturbed the people there assembled, interrupted the amusements of the poor unoffending persons who were that evening relaxing after the toils of many weary days, and provoked a riot, which ended but with the loss of three lives. This melancholy affair became afterwards the subject of legal discussion, and he had no hesitation in saying that the two unfortunate Irishmen who suffered in consequence were found guilty directly contrary to law. But it was nevertheless right that he should state that there were well grounded reasons for believing at one time that they would be reprieved, to procure which he had waited twice on the Duke of Portland, and did not doubt but that a reprieve would have been granted, had not that noble person been called in haste from town on urgent business. Here Mr. Sheridan renewed his objections to the sport of bull baiting, and said that an hon. friend of his intended shortly to bring in a Bill for preventing inhumanity to animals in general, especially to horses, which were seen every day in our streets treated with most vicious and unmerited cruelty. He concluded by declaring his cordial approbation of the Bill.

Mr. Canning explained.

Sir Richard Hill thought the question before the House worthy of legislative consideration. The legislature had frequently interfered with the sports of the public, as in the instance of bear baiting, which was now prohibited, and for the discovery of persons engaged in it, there was allowed a reward of 10s. The practice of bull baiting was general in many counties. In Staffordshire in particular, the lower orders spent much of their time, and all their wages, in feasts of this sort. Their days and nights were employed in pinning down the poor bull and preparing the ferocious dog. Was not the practice, therefore, worthy of legislative interference? He hoped the Secretary-at-War would not take this up as a party question, and that if he would not consent to peace being restored to mankind, he would at least let the brute creation be at peace. He spoke it from his own knowledge when he stated that there were several petitions in the Petition Office in favour of the Bill, but it was thought needless to present them, so much was the general humanity of the House relied on. He trusted, therefore, that the House would display a conduct worthy of its character, would listen to the call of humanity, and let the Bill go on.

Mr. Martin supported the original motion. The House could not more strongly express its humanity than by supporting the Bill.

The question being now called for, the House divided,

For Mr. Windham's motion . . 43
Against it 41
                            —
                Majority . . 2

The Bill of course was lost.

(51.) At three o'clock (on 2 July,) His Majesty went in State to the House of Peers to give his Royal Assent to the Union Bill with Ireland, the Duke of Richmond's Annuity Bill, and Sir George Pigot's Diamond Bill.

His Majesty was accompanied to the House by the Duke of Roxburgh, and the Gold Stick in Waiting; the King was dressed in a purple coat, embroidered waistcoat, and on returning wore a scarlet surtout; His Majesty was remarkably cheerful. He was received at the House by Earl Camden, who carried the Sword of State, and Lord Gwydir; the Marquis Townshend carrying before His Majesty the Cap of Liberty.

On this occasion the Life Guards, as usual, were drawn out, and also the whole of the police of Westminster, under the direction of Sir William Addington.

The spectators were not numerous.

The Dukes of Cumberland and Gloucester accompanied His Majesty in the House of Peers.

On the King's return to St. James's, His Majesty left town for Windsor, escorted by a party of light horse.

The park guns were drawn out to announce the event of the Union Bill having received the Royal Assent. Orders were given for three rounds to be fired, one of forty-two guns, and two of twenty-one guns each; but contrary orders being afterwards sent, the King was saluted, as customary, on entering and coming out of the House; and the guns, taken from the park, were deposited in the armoury-house without being fired.

It was expected that the King would have made a speech from the Throne on giving his Royal Assent to the Union, and that the Union Flag (which had been painted on the sudden for the purpose) would have been hoisted on Westminster Hall, but it was recollected that it was necessary that the Parliament of Ireland must give the Bill its fiat before it can be a complete measure.

BRITISH PARLIAMENT.
House of Lords, Tuesday, July 29.

(52.) His Majesty came in the usual state to the House at half after three, and being seated on the Throne, Sir Francis Molyneux, Gentleman Usher of the Black Rod, was sent to the House of Commons to desire the attendance of that Honourable House. The Speaker, and the rest of the members present, immediately attended, when the Speaker presented the Consolidated Fund Bill, and, as usual, addressed His Majesty on the subject of the large supplies that the Commons had cheerfully voted in the course of the Session. He touched, also, on the Union with Ireland, and other important topics.

The Royal Assent was then given to the Consolidated Fund Bill, and such others as remained; after which, His Majesty was pleased to make the following most gracious speech:—

"MY LORDS AND GENTLEMEN,—

"In putting an end to this laborious Session of Parliament, I must express the just sense I entertain of the diligence and perseverance with which you have applied yourselves to the various objects of public concern which came under your deliberation. It is with peculiar satisfaction I congratulate you on the success of the steps which you have taken for effecting an entire union between my kingdoms of Great Britain and Ireland. This great measure, on which my wishes have been long earnestly bent, I shall ever consider as the happiest event of my reign, being persuaded that nothing could so effectually contribute to extend to my Irish subjects the full participation of the blessings derived from the British Constitution, and to establish on the most solid foundation the strength, prosperity, and power of the whole empire.

"I have witnessed with great concern the severe pressure on my people from the continued scarcity of the season; but I trust that, under the blessing of Providence, there is now every reason to expect that the approaching harvest will afford a speedy and effectual relief.

"GENTLEMEN OF THE HOUSE OF COMMONS,—

"I return you my particular thanks for the zeal and liberality with which you have provided for the various exigences of the public service. I regret deeply the necessity of these repeated sacrifices on the part of my subjects, but they have been requisite for the preservation of our dearest interests; and it is a great consolation to observe, that, notwithstanding the continuance of unusual burdens, the revenue, commerce, and resources of the country have flourished beyond all former example, and are still in a state of progressive augmentation.

"MY LORDS AND GENTLEMEN,—

"The course of the campaign upon the Continent has, by a sudden reverse, disappointed the sanguine hopes which the situation of affairs at its commencement appeared fully to justify, and has unhappily again exposed a considerable part of Europe to those calamities and dangers from which it had recently been rescued by the brilliant success of my allies.

"Much as these events are to be regretted, it will always be matter of just satisfaction to me to reflect that, in the course of this important contest, my efforts, and those of my Parliament, have been unremittingly employed for the maintenance of our own rights and interests, and for animating and supporting the exertions of other powers in defending the liberties of Europe.

"Notwithstanding the vicissitudes of war, your constancy and firmness have been productive of the most important and lasting advantages in the general situation of affairs, and the determination manifested in your recent declarations and conduct, must afford me the best means of promoting, in conjunction with my allies, the general interests, and of providing under every circumstance for the honour of my Crown, for the happiness of my subjects, and for the security and welfare of every part of the British Empire."

BRITISH PARLIAMENT.
House of Lords, Nov. 11.

(53.) HIS Majesty opened the Session with the following most gracious speech from the Throne:

"MY LORDS AND GENTLEMEN,—

"My tender concern for the welfare of my subjects, and the sense of the difficulties with which the poorer classes particularly have to struggle, from the present high price of provisions, have induced me to call you together at an earlier period than I had otherwise intended. No object can be nearer my heart, than that by your care and wisdom, all such measures may be adopted as may, upon full consideration, appear best calculated to alleviate this severe pressure; and to prevent the danger of its recurrence, by promoting, as far as possible, the permanent extension and improvement of our agriculture.

"For the object of immediate relief, your attention will naturally be directed, in the first instance, to the best mode of affording the earliest and most ample encouragement for the importation of all descriptions of grain from abroad. Such a supply, aided by the examples which you have set on former occasions, of attention to economy and frugality in the consumption of corn, is most likely to contribute to a reduction in the present high price, and to ensure, at the same time, the means of meeting the demands for the necessary consumption of the year.

"The present circumstances will also, I am persuaded, render the state of the laws respecting the commerce in the various articles of provision the object of your serious deliberation. If, on the result of that deliberation, it shall appear to you that the evil necessarily arising from unfavourable seasons has been increased by any undue combinations, or fraudulent practices, for the sake of adding unfairly to the price, you will feel an earnest desire of effectually preventing such abuses; but you will, I am sure, be careful to distinguish any practices of this nature from that regular and long-established course of trade, which experience has shown to be indispensable, in the present state of society, for the supply of the markets, and for the subsistence of my people.

"You will have seen, with concern, the temporary disturbances which have taken place in some parts of the kingdom. Those malicious and disaffected persons who cruelly take advantage of the present difficulties, to excite any of my subjects to acts in violation of the laws and of the public peace, are, in the present circumstances, doubly criminal, as such proceedings must necessarily and immediately tend to increase, in the highest degree, the evil complained of, while they at the same time endanger the permanent tranquillity of the country, on which the well being of the industrial classes of the community must always principally depend.

"The voluntary exertions which have on this occasion been made in the immediate repression of those outrages, and in support of the laws and public peace, are therefore entitled to my highest praise.

"GENTLEMEN OF THE HOUSE OF COMMONS,—

"Under the circumstances of the present meeting, I am desirous of asking of you such supplies only as may be necessary for carrying on the public service, till the Parliament of the United Kingdom of Great Britain and Ireland may conveniently be assembled.

"The estimate for that purpose will be laid before you, and I have no doubt of your readiness to make such provision as the public interests may appear to require.

"MY LORDS AND GENTLEMEN,—

"I have directed copies to be laid before you of those communications which have recently passed between me and the French Government respecting the commencement of the negotiations of peace. You will see in them fresh and striking proofs of my earnest desire to contribute to the establishment of general tranquillity. That desire on my part has hitherto been unhappily frustrated by the determination of the enemy to enter only on a separate negotiation in which it was impossible for me to engage consistently either with public faith, or with a due regard to the permanent security of Europe. My anxiety for the speedy restoration of peace remains unaltered ; and there will be no obstacle nor delay on my part to the adoption of such measures as may best tend to promote and accelerate that desirable end, consistently with the honour of this country and the true interests of my people ; but if the disposition of our enemies should continue to render this great object of all my wishes unattainable, without the sacrifice of these essential considerations, on the maintenance of which all its advantages must depend, you will, I am confident, persevere in affording me the same loyal and steady support which I have experienced through the whole of this important contest, and which has, under the blessing of Providence, enabled me, during a period of such unexampled difficulty and calamity to all the surrounding nations, to maintain unimpaired the security and honour of these kingdoms."

House of Peers, Wednesday, December 31.

(54.) THIS day His Majesty came down to the House soon after three o'clock, attended by the usual Officers of State, and having taken his seat upon the throne, the Usher of the Black Rod was sent with a message to the Commons, to acquaint them therewith ; soon after which several Members of that House, with the Speaker at their head, appeared at the bar ; the latter of whom, on presenting the Exchequer Loan Bill, according to custom, addressed the King with respect to the Supplies which had been voted in the present session. In the course of his speech, he alluded to the principal topics which had occupied the attention of Parliament, and concluded with a panegyric on the approaching Union with Ireland. The Royal Assent was then given to the " Bread Regulation," the " Habeas Corpus Suspension," the " Population," and twenty other public Bills ; the forms of which being gone through, His Majesty addressed the two Houses of Parliament in the following speech :—

" MY LORDS AND GENTLEMEN,—

" I cannot close this session of Parliament without returning you my particular acknowledgments for the distinguished industry and zeal with which you have applied yourselves to the interesting object which, at the commencement of the session I most especially recommended to your attention. It has been my earnest wish that nothing should be omitted which could tend to relieve the pressure occasioned by the present dearth of provisions, and to insure a sufficient supply till the produce of the next harvest can be brought into use.

" The diligence with which your enquiries have been conducted, has afforded you the best means of ascertaining the true circumstances of our present situation ; and the extensive measures which you have wisely adopted, in consequence, for diminishing the consumption of grain, and procuring an increased supply, will, I doubt not, be found productive of the most salutary effects.

" Much, however, must depend on the disposition which will, I am confident, be manifested by all those who have the means of carrying into execution my solemn recommendation and injunction, issued at your desire, for the adoption of all practicable economy in the use of those articles which are necessary to the subsistence of the poorer classes of my subjects.

" The time fixed for the commencement of the Union of Great Britain and Ireland, will necessarily terminate your proceedings on this important subject ; but I am persuaded that the consideration of it will be resumed with the same zeal and temper, on the first meeting of the Parliament of the United Kingdoms.

" The early period which I have appointed for that meeting, will afford a speedy opportunity of completing whatever you may have necessarily left unfinished, and of considering what measures may tend further to alleviate the pressure on my people, or to prevent the danger of its recurring.

" GENTLEMEN OF THE HOUSE OF COMMONS,—
" I thank you for the readiness with which you have granted the Supplies necessary, under the present circumstances, for the public service.

" MY LORDS AND GENTLEMEN,—
" The detention of the property of my subjects in the ports of Russia, contrary to the most solemn treaties, and the imprisonment of the British sailors in that country, have excited in me sentiments in which you and all my subjects will, I am sure, participate.

" I have already taken such steps as this occasion indispensably required ; and it will afford me great satisfaction, if they prove effectual ; but if it shall be necessary to maintain, against any combination, the honour and independence of the British empire, and those maritime rights and interests on which both our property and our security must always depend, I entertain no doubt, either of the success of those means which, in such an event, I shall be enabled to exert, or of the determination of my Parliament and my people, to afford me a support proportioned to the importance of the interests which we have to maintain."

His Majesty with his attendants immediately after retired, when the Lord Chancellor desired the King's proclamation to be read, wherein it was specified that an Union should take place between this and the Irish Parliament, and that their first meeting should be on the 22nd of January next.

(55.) YESTERDAY (6th August) arrived a mail from Dublin, with letters and papers of the 2nd instant. On Friday last the Lord Lieutenant of Ireland went in state to the House of Peers, and gave the Royal Assent to the Union and 83 other Bills.

On the following day the House of Peers met at twelve o'clock, and proceeded to the election of 28 Peers as Representatives on the part of Ireland in the Imperial Parliament ; when the following noblemen, standing highest on the list, were declared duly elected :—

Earl of Clanricarde. Earl of Roden.
  „   Westmeath.   „   Altamont.
  „   Bective.   „   Glandore.

Earl of	Longford.	Viscount	O'Neill.
„	Earne.	„	Bandon.
„	Dysart.	„	Donoughmore.
„	Leitrim.	„	Carleton.
„	Lucan.	Baron	Cahier
„	Londonderry.	„	Glentworth.
„	Conyngham.	„	Callan.
„	Landaff.	„	Somerton.
Viscount	Wicklow.	„	Longueville.
„	Northland.	„	Rossmore.
„	Oxmantown.	„	Tyrawley.

Soon after the election was concluded, his Excellency arrived at the House of Peers, and being seated on the throne, and attended by the Speaker and a number of Members of the House of Commons, put a final period to the Irish Parliament, with the following judicious speech from the throne:—

"MY LORDS AND GENTLEMEN,—

"The whole business of this important session being at length happily concluded, it is with the most sincere satisfaction that I communicate to you, by His Majesty's express command, his warmest acknowledgments for that ardent zeal and unshaken perseverance which you have so conspicuously manifested, in maturing and completing the great measure of a Legislative Union between this kingdom and Great Britain.

"The proof you have given on this occasion of your uniform attachment to the real welfare of your country, inseparably connected with the security and prosperity of the empire at large, not only entitle you to the full approbation of your Sovereign, and the applause of your fellow-subjects, but must afford you the surest claim to the gratitude of posterity.

"You will regret with His Majesty, the reverses which His Majesty's Allies have experienced on the Continent; but His Majesty is persuaded, that the firmness and public spirit of his subjects will enable him to persevere in that line of conduct which will best provide for the honour and the essential interests of his dominions, whose means and resources have now, by your wisdom, been more closely and immediately combined.

"GENTLEMEN OF THE HOUSE OF COMMONS,—

"I am to thank you, in His Majesty's name, for the liberal supplies which you have cheerfully granted for the various and important branches of the public service in the present year.

"His Majesty has also witnessed with pleasure that wise liberality which will enable him to make a just and equitable retribution to those bodies and individuals, whose privileges and interests are affected by the Union; and he has also seen, with satisfaction, that attention to the internal prosperity of this country, which has been so conspicuously testified by the encouragement you have given to the improvement and extension of its inland navigation.

"MY LORDS AND GENTLEMEN,—

"I have the happiness to acquaint you that the country in general has, in a great measure, returned to its former state of tranquillity. If in some districts a spirit of plunder and disaffection still exists, these disorders, I believe, will prove to be merely local, and will, I doubt not, be soon effectually terminated.

"The pressure of scarcity on the poorer classes, much relieved by private generosity, and by the salutary provisions of the Legislature, has been long and unusually severe; but I trust that, under the favour of Providence, we may draw a pleasing prospect of future plenty, from the present appearance of the harvest.

"I am persuaded that the great measure which is now accomplished, could never have been effected, but by a decided conviction on your part that it would tend to restore and preserve the tranquillity of this country, to increase its commerce and manufactures, to perpetuate its connection with Great Britain, and to augment the resources of the empire.

"You will not fail to impress these sentiments on the minds of your fellow-subjects; you will encourage and improve that just confidence which they have manifested in the result of your deliberations on this arduous question; above all, you will be studious to inculcate the full conviction, that, united with the people of Great Britain into one kingdom, governed by the same Sovereign, protected by the same laws, and represented in the same Legislature, nothing will be wanting on their part but a spirit of industry and order, to insure to them the full advantages under which the people of Great Britain have enjoyed a greater degree of prosperity, security, and freedom, than has ever yet been experienced by any other nation.

"I cannot conclude without offering to you, and to the nation at large, my personal congratulations on the accomplishment of this great work, which has received the sanction and concurrence of our Sovereign on that auspicious day which placed his illustrious family on the throne of these realms. The empire is now, through your exertions, so completely united, and by union so strengthened, that it can bid defiance to all the efforts its enemies can make, either to weaken it by division, or to overturn it by force. Under the protection of Divine Providence, the United Kingdoms of Great Britain and Ireland will, I trust, remain in all future ages the fairest monument of His Majesty's reign, already distinguished by so many and such various blessings conferred upon every class and description of his subjects."

NAVAL AND MILITARY INTELLIGENCE.

(56.) It appears by the statement of Mr. Robson in the House of Commons, that the British disposable force now at home, as extracted from the journals, consists—of Cavalry, 23,581; Guards, 11,792; 23 battalions of Foot, 19,371; Invalids, 6099; Cornish Miners, 633; Fensible Infantry, 8775; Militia, 39,404; Scotch ditto, 6026; Dutch troops at the Isle of Wight, 5000; amounting to 121,181, besides Artillery and Flying ditto, Engineers, Marines, &c., together with Volunteer Cavalry, 16,000; India House, 2000; and other Volunteers paid by his Majesty, amounting to

130,000 more, exclusive of those not paid, making in all (not including the Volunteers who do not receive pay, Artillery, Marines, &c. &c.) 269,181.

(57.) THE distribution of the British Navy, 1st January, 1800, exclusive of the hired Armed Vessels, which are chiefly employed in protecting the Coasting Trade of Great Britain:

STATIONS, &c.	Line.	50 Guns.	Frigates.	Sloops.	Total.
In Port and Fitting	50	8	97	133	268
Guard Ships	3	...	1	...	4
In the English and Irish Channels	23	...	24	57	104
In the Downs and North Seas	3	...	7	22	32
At the West India Islands, and on the passage	3	...	15	17	35
At Jamaica	7	1	16	16	40
In America and Newfoundland	2	1	5	7	15
East India, and on the passage	9	7	8	15	39
Coast of Africa	...	...	1	1	2
Coast of Portugal, Gibraltar, and Mediterranean	19	2	26	22	69
Hospital and Prison Ships	26	2	...	...	28
Total in Commission	145	21	200	290	656
Receiving Ships	7	1	8	...	16
Serviceable and Repairing	5	0	...	...	5
In Ordinary	22	2	26	39	89
Building	15	2	3	...	20
Total	192	26	239	329	786

Captured during the War:

Of the Line, including Dutch Ships of 54 and 56 guns	83
Frigates of 28 to 44 guns	111
Ships of from 20 to 26 guns	59
Sloops of war, of from 14 to 18 guns	83
Cutters, Gun Vessels, &c., 12 guns and under	81
Total—Men-of-war	417
Privateers of all Nations	715
Grand Total	1,132

(58.) IT appears, by the Adjutant-General's returns, that the number of troops in the pay of Great Britain on the 24th of December, 1800, amounted to 160,082. The Marines being in the Admiralty Department are not included; but that Corps, consisting of 23,370, increases our effective military force to 191,452, exclusive of the numerous Volunteer Corps, which do not receive pay from Government. The military establishment of Ireland, as stated by Lord Castlereagh, on the 10th of February, consists of—Regulars, 45,819; Militia, 27,104; and Yeomanry, 53,557; amounting to 126,500, which makes the military establishment of the United Kingdom 317,952 men. Taking the naval establishment, exclusive of Marines, 100,000 men, our force will be found to consist of 417,952 men.

(59.) THE English marine having always the advantage over that of the French, it must follow that the tactics of the latter are either unjust in their principle, or defective in their application. It is necessary to observe, that the superiority of a marine force, when in action, must depend on three things: 1. The better condition of the vessels; 2. The greater naval skill of the officers; and, 3. The better use of the artillery. The French vessels are acknowledged to be the best sailors. The English admit this, by using the French prizes in preference, even when they have more of their own than they can employ. England has but one author who wrote on naval tactics, and he was not a seaman; all their further knowledge on this subject is drawn from French authors. It is impossible, therefore, that the English can be better tacticians than the French officers. It may be said that their sailors are superior to those of the French navy; but on the mechanical management of a vessel the issue of an action can depend but in very few instances. It appears that the superiority of the English marine does not rest on the better condition of their vessels, or the greater skill of their officers; it must therefore consist in the different use which they make of their artillery. In order to decide this question, it must be remarked how the artillery is employed in the two marines. The French fire always at the masts and rigging; three-fourths of this space is a void, and of course three-fourths of the bullets are lost in the air. From the vague elevation which is given to the guns, the masts, though wounded in different places, are seldom brought down, but last during the action. The yards presenting themselves but obliquely, are less endangered, and the hurts received by the cordage are easily repaired. It is evident, therefore, that, by firing in this manner, the French cannot sink the vessel, dismount the guns, or kill any great number of the crew; on the contrary, the enemy's crew, finding themselves so little exposed to danger, display all their force and vigour, and keep up the undiminished vivacity of their fire. The English always point their guns at the hull of the vessel. It is thus that they succeed in striking between wind and water, in dismounting the guns, and in killing a great number of men. In the first case, a part of the crew must be taken from the batteries to work the pumps, than which nothing can be more fatiguing or more depressing, as when men are in danger of sinking, they are but little inclined to fight. The guns which are dismounted cannot be replaced at the time, and the carnage made among the crew, whilst it thins their number, tends also to diminish the courage and the efforts of the survivors. When the balls are aimed at the body of the vessel, those which rise a little higher strike the masts all nearly in the same place, which is precisely the way to bring them by the board. It follows, therefore, that the English employ a preferable mode in the pointing of their cannon. On the 1st of June, 1794, the English had two vessels dismasted; the French had *eleven*. In the battle of the Nile, the former had one, and the latter had six entirely dismasted; and it is to be remarked, that the dismasted vessels have always the greater number of killed and wounded.

From the conduct of the French in action, it appears that their only object is to disable the enemy's vessel; and even in the battle of the Nile, when our ships were all at anchor, this habit still prevailed. But in order to show the advantage of cutting off the men, instead of disabling the vessel, it is only necessary to read the reports of the English captains who have been taken, and which all state, that their surrender was occasioned by the loss of men. If the superiority of the English marine is not owing to the manner in which they point their artillery, from what cause then does it proceed? Why is it that their uniform success is not interrupted by any of the chances of war? The French have reduced their naval tactics to a system. The English dispense with all study on the subject, and have not even a marine school. The facility with which they triumph over their enemies has induced them to regard all theory unnecessary. It will be said, perhaps, that the English have better sailors, and in greater numbers than the French; but in an action, a certain number are appointed to work the vessel, and the remainder to serve at the guns; for the latter service, a sailor is no more fitted than any other person. The French have gunners; the English have none. Are, then, the English sailors more courageous than the French? They may be so, if courage be allowed to consist, in a great degree, of the confidence which a man has in his means of victory, and of the slightness of the danger which he has to encounter. Thus the habit of conquering makes them enter into action with a courage and an enthusiasm which men cannot be supposed to feel who are accustomed to nothing but reverses and disasters. Do the English soldiers resemble their sailors? No. The French troops are to them, what the English sailors are to those of France, and precisely for the same reason.

It appears from these observations, that the superiority of the English marine consists chiefly in the manner of pointing their guns, and that the superior efforts of their officers and seamen in action is only a necessary consequence of the first position. *If we were* to employ against the English marine *its own means of victory*, it would not continue to be the principal support of a Government which forms the greatest obstacle to the triumph of the cause of Liberty.—*The "Moniteur" of the 21st July.*

(60.)   *Admiralty Office, Jan.* 21.
COPY of a Letter from Sir Hyde Parker, Knt., Commander-in-Chief of His Majesty's Ships and Vessels at Jamaica, to Evan Nepean, Esq., dated in Port Royal Harbour, the 4th of November, 1799.

"SIR,—I have a peculiar satisfaction in communicating to you, for the information of my Lords Commissioners of the Admiralty, that His Majesty's late ship "Hermione" is again restored to his navy, by as daring and gallant an enterprize as is to be found in our naval annals, under the command of Captain Hamilton himself, with the boats of the "Surprize" only. Captain Hamilton's own letter with the reports accompanying it (copies of which are inclosed), will sufficiently explain to their Lordships the detail of this service, and the bravery with which the attack was supported, and leaves me only one observation to make on the very gallant action which adds infinite honour to Captain Hamilton as an officer for his conception of the service he was about to undertake. This was, Sir, his disposition for the attack; which was, that a number of chosen men, to the amount of fifty, with himself, should board, and the remainder in the boats to cut the cables and take the ship in tow. From this manœuvre he had formed the idea, that while he was disputing for the possession of the ship, she was approaching the "Surprize," who was laying close into the harbour, and in case of being beat out of the "Hermione," he would have an opportunity of taking up the contest upon more favourable terms. To the steady execution of these orders was owing the success of this bold and daring undertaking, which must ever rank among the foremost of the many gallant actions executed by our navy in this war. I find the "Hermione" has had a thorough repair, and is in complete order. I have, therefore, ordered her to be surveyed and valued, and shall commission her as soon as the reports are made to me from the officers of the yard, by the name of "Retaliation."

"I have the honour to be, &c., &c.,
"H. PARKER."

"*Surprize*," *Port Royal Harbour, Jamaica, Nov.* 1, 1799.
"SIR,—The honour of my country and the glory of the British Navy were strong inducements for me to make an attempt to cut out, by the boats of His Majesty's ship under my command, His Majesty's late ship "Hermione" from the harbour of Porto Cavallo, where there are about 200 pieces of cannon mounted on the batteries. Having well observed her situation on the 22nd and 23rd ultimo, and the evening of the 24th being favourable, I turned the hands up to acquaint the officers and ship's company of my intention to lead them to the attack; which was handsomely returned with three cheers, and that they would all follow to a man. This greatly increased my hopes, and I had little doubt of succeeding. The boats containing one hundred men, including officers, at half-past twelve on the morning of the 25th (after having beat the launch of the ship, which carried a 24-pounder and twenty men, and receiving several guns and small arms from the frigate) boarded; the forecastle was taken possession of without much resistance; the quarter-deck disputed the point a quarter of an hour, where a dreadful carnage took place; the main-deck held out much longer, and with equal slaughter: nor was it before both cables were cut, sail made on the ship, and boats a-head to tow, that the main-deck could be called ours. They last of all retreated to the 'tween decks, and continued firing till their ammunition was expended; then, and not until then, did they cry for quarter. At two o'clock the "Hermione" was completely ours, being out of gun-shot from the fort, which had for some time kept up a tolerable good fire. From the Captain, Don Romond de Chalas, I am informed she was nearly ready for sea, mounting 44 guns, with a ship's company of 321 officers and sailors, 56 soldiers, and 15 artillerymen on board. Every officer and man on this expedition behaved with an uncommon degree of valour and exertion; but I consider it particularly my duty to mention the very gallant conduct, as well as the aid and assistance at a particular crisis, I received from

Mr. John McMullen, surgeon and volunteer, and Mr. Maxwell, gunner, even after the latter was dangerously wounded. As the frigate was the particular object of your order of the 17th of September, I have thought proper to return into the port with her. Enclosed I transmit you a list of captures during the cruise, also two lists of killed and wounded.

"I have the honour to be, &c.,
"E. HAMILTON."

"A List of Killed and Wounded on board the Spanish frigate "Hermione," late His Majesty's ship "Hermione," when captured by the boats of His Majesty's ship "Surprize," under the command of Captain Edward Hamilton, in Porto Cavallo, October 25, 1799, and general statement of the complement on board,—

Prisoners landed at Porto Cavallo the same day, out of which there were 97 wounded, mostly dangerous	228
Escaped in the launch, which was rowing guard round the ship, with a 24-pounder	20
Remain prisoners on board	3
On shore on leave, 1 lieutenant, 1 captain of troops, 4 pilots, and 1 midshipman	7
Swam on shore from the ship	15
Killed	119
Total	392

(Signed)   E. HAMILTON."

"A List of Killed in the boats of His Majesty's ship "Surprize," in cutting out a Privateer Schooner of 10 guns and two Sloops from the Harbour of Aruba, on the 15th October, 1799,

Mr. John Busey, Acting Lieutenant, killed.

(Signed)   E. HAMILTON, Captain."

"A List of Officers and Men Wounded on board the Spanish frigate "Hermione," on the attack made by the boats of His Majesty's ship "Surprize," under the orders of Captain Hamilton, in the Harbour of Porto Cavallo, the 25th October, 1799,—

Edward Hamilton, Esq., Captain, several contusions but not dangerous; Mr. John Maxwell, gunner, dangerously wounded in several places; John Lewis Matthews, quartermaster, dangerously; Arthur Reed, quarter-gunner, dangerously; Henry Milne, carpenter's crew, dangerously; Henry Dibleen, gunner's mate, slightly; Charles Livingston, able seaman, slightly; William Pardy, able seaman, slightly; Robert Ball, able seaman, slightly; Thomas Stevenson, able seamen, slightly; John Ingram, private marine, slightly; Joseph Titley, private marine, slightly.

"(Signed)   E. HAMILTON, Captain.
"(A copy.)   H. PARKER."

(61.)   *Admiralty Office, August 9.*
COPY of a Letter from Earl St. Vincent, K.B., &c., to Evan Nepean, Esq., dated on board the "Royal George," at Sea, the 4th instant.

"SIR,—I did not think the enterprise of Sir Edward Hamilton or of Captain Campbell could have been rivalled until I read the inclosed letter from Sir Edward Pellew, relating the desperate service performed by Acting Lieutenant Coghlan, of the "Viper" cutter, on the 29th of July, which has filled me with pride and admiration; and, although the circumstance of his not having completed his time in His Majesty's navy operates at present against his receiving the reward he is most ambitious of obtaining, I am persuaded the Lords Commissioners of the Admiralty will do all in their power to console him under his severe wounds, and grant him promotion the moment he is in a capacity to receive it.

"I am, Sir, &c.,
"ST. VINCENT."

"*Impetueux," Palais Road,
August* 1.

"MY LORD,—I have true pleasure in stating to your Lordship the good conduct of Lieutenant Jeremiah Coghlan, to whom, for former gallant behaviour, you had given an acting commission to command the "Viper" cutter from this ship.

"This gallant young man, when watching Port Louis, thought he could succeed in boarding some of the cutters or gun-vessels which have been moving about the entrance of that harbour, and for this purpose he entreated a ten-oared cutter from me, with twelve volunteers; and on Tuesday night, the 29th instant, he took this boat with Mr. Silas H. Paddon, midshipman, and six of his men, making with himself twenty; and, accompanied by his own boat and one from the "Amethyst," he determined upon boarding a gun-brig, mounting three long 24-pounders and four 6-pounders, full of men, moored with springs on her cables, in a naval port of difficult access, within pistol-shot of three batteries, surrounded by several armed craft, and not a mile from a 74 and two frigates bearing an admiral's flag. Undismayed by such formidable appearances, the early discovery of his approach (for they were at quarters), and the lost aid of the two other boats, he bravely determined to attack alone, and boarded her on the quarter; but unhappily, in the dark, jumping into a trawl-net, hung up to dry, he was pierced through the thigh by a pike, and several of his men hurt, and all knocked back into the boat.

"Unchecked in ardour, they hauled the boat further a-head, and again boarded, and maintained against 87 men, 16 of whom were soldiers, an obstinate conflict, killing 6 and wounding 20, among whom was every officer belonging to her. His own loss, 1 killed and 8 wounded; himself in two places, Mr. Paddon in six. I feel particularly happy in the expected safety of all the wounded. He speaks in the highest terms of Mr. Paddon, and the whole of his party, many of whom were knocked overboard, and twice beat into the boat, but returned to the charge with unabated courage. I trust I shall stand excused by your Lordship for so minute a description, produced by my admiration of that courage which, hand to hand, gave victory to a handful of brave fellows over four times their number, and of that skill which formed, conducted, and effected so daring an enterprize.

"'Le Cerbère,' commanded by a Lieut. de Vaisseau, and towed out under a very heavy fire, is given up as a prize by the squadron, to mark their admiration, and will not, I know, be the only reward of such bravery; they will receive that protection your Lordship so liberally accords to all the young men in the service who happily distinguish themselves under your command.

"I enclose Lieut. Coghlan's letter, and have the honour to be, &c.,
"EDWARD PELLEW.
"Earl of St. Vincent, C.B., &c."

"*His Majesty's cutter 'Viper,'*
Tuesday morn, 8 o'clock.

"DEAR SIR,—I have succeeded in bringing out the gun-brig "Le Cerbère," of three guns (24-pounders) and four 6-pounders, and eighty-seven men, commanded by a Lieut. de Vaisseau. Pray forgive me, when I say from under the batteries of Port Louis, and after a most desperate resistance being made, first by her, and afterwards by the batteries at both sides, and a fire from some small vessels which lay round her; but nothing that I could expect from a vessel lying in that inactive situation was equal to the few brave men belonging to your ship whom I so justly confided in, assisted by six men from the cutter, and Mr. Paddon, midshipman, who I am sorry to say was wounded in several places, though I hope not mortally. I am sorry to state the loss of one man belonging to the cutter, who was shot through the head; and four of your brave men with myself wounded in different parts of the body: the principal one I received was with a pike, which penetrated my left thigh. Mr. Patteshall, in the cutter's small boat, assisted with two midshipmen from the "Amethyst," in one of their boats. The loss of the enemy is not yet ascertained, owing to the confusion.

"I remain, &c,
"J. COGHLAN.

"N.B.—There are five killed and twenty-one wounded, some very badly."

"A Return of Killed and Wounded in a Ten-oared Cutter belonging to the "Impetueux," under the command of Lieut. Jeremiah Coghlan, on the 29th of July.

"Viper" cutter—1 seaman killed; Lieut. Jeremiah Coghlan, Mr. Silas H. Paddon (midshipman), 2 seamen, wounded.
"Impetueux"—4 seamen wounded.
Total—1 killed, 8 wounded."

(62.) YESTERDAY forenoon (4th April), arrived at the Admiralty a foreign messenger from Leghorn, with despatches from Lord Keith, Commander-in-Chief in the Mediterranean. He brought the very unpleasant tidings of the loss of the "Queen Charlotte," of 110 guns, his Lordship's flag-ship, which took fire just before daybreak on the morning of the 17th March, while under an easy sail, between the island of Gorgona and Leghorn. The accident was occasioned by the fire of a match, which was kept lighted for the purpose of firing signal guns, and communicated to some hay which lay on the half-deck. The fire spread very rapidly, and bursting through the portholes and the hatchway of the ship, soon caught the shrouds; and notwithstanding every exertion, she burnt to the water's edge, and then blew up. Upwards of 700 lives are lost; as the boats of the ship could not contain one-fourth of the complement of men. Lord Keith was himself on shore at Leghorn.

(63.) LOSS OF THE "QUEEN CHARLOTTE."—We have the painful duty to state the loss of His Majesty's ship "Queen Charlotte," of 110 guns, Capt. Todd, which was blown up off the harbour of Leghorn, on the 17th of March, when the Commander, and, we fear, above 800 of the crew, perished by the explosion. Vice-Admiral Lord Keith, whose flag was flying on board of her was, at the time, with some of the officers, providentially on shore. Twenty commissioned and warrant officers, two servants, and one hundred and forty-two seamen were the whole of the persons who escaped destruction. The only consolation that presents itself under the pressure of so calamitous a disaster is, that it was not the effect either of treachery or wilful neglect,. as will appear by the following statement:—

Circumstances immediately preceding and attending the loss of His Majesty's ship "Queen Charlotte," off Leghorn, on the 17th March, 1800.

Mr. John Baird, carpenter of the "Queen Charlotte," reports that about twenty minutes after six o'clock yesterday morning, as he was dressing himself, he heard throughout the ship a general cry of "Fire!" on which he immediately ran up the fore ladder to get upon the deck, and found the whole half-deck, the front bulk-head of the admiral's cabin, the main-mast's coat, and boat's covering on the booms, all in flames, which from every report and probability he apprehends was occasioned by some hay, which was lying under the half-deck, having been set on fire by a match in a tub, which was usually kept there for signal guns. The main-sail at this time was set, and almost entirely caught fire, the people not being able to come to the clue-garnets, on account of the flames. He immediately went on the forecastle, and found Lieutenant Dundas and the boatswain encouraging the people to get water to extinguish the fire. He applied to Mr. Dundas, seeing no other officer on the fore part of the ship (and being unable to see any on the quarter-deck, from the flames and smoke between them), to give them assistance to drown the lower-decks and secure the hatches, to prevent the fire falling down. Lieutenant Dundas accordingly went down himself, with as many people as he could prevail upon to follow him, and the lower-decks' ports were opened, the scuppers plugged, the main and fore-hatches secured, and the cocks turned, and water drawn in at the ports, and the pumps kept going by the people who came down, as long as they could stand at them. He thinks that, by these exertions, the lower deck was kept free from fire, and the magazines preserved for a long time from danger; nor did Lieutenant Dundas or he quit this station, but remained there with all the people who could be prevailed upon to stay. till several of the middle-deck guns came through that deck. About nine o'clock, Lieutenant Dundas and finding it impossible to remain any longer below, went out at the fore-mast lower-deck port, and got upon the forecastle, on which he apprehended there were then about one hundred and fifty of

the people drawing water, and throwing it as far aft as possible upon the fire. He continued about an hour on the forecastle, and finding all efforts to extinguish the flames unavailing, he jumped from the jibboom and swam to an American boat approaching the ship, by which he was picked up.
(Signed) JOHN BAIRD.

Leghorn, March 18, 1800.
The "Queen Charlotte" had just completed her equipments, and was to proceed to sea in the course of a few days for Genoa, having on board a vast quantity of shells, grenades, and mortar cartridges, for the siege of that place. She was launched in 1790, in immediate succession off the slip of the "Royal George," and was allowed, both as a prime sailer and for her other superior qualities, to be the finest ship that ever displayed English colours. At her main she bore the triumphant flag of Earl Howe, on the memorable 1st of June, 1794.

The Lords Commissioners of the Admiralty, on Friday, ordered letters to be immediately dispatched to the known relatives of those officers of the ship who were fortunately saved from the wreck.

(64.) IT is with concern we state the loss of the "Marlborough," of seventy-four guns, Captain Sotherby, on the 4th instant, near Belleisle. She was cruising in company with the "Captain," of seventy-four guns, and struck on a reef of sunken rocks. After remaining on them for several hours she got off by throwing some of her guns overboard, and run into deep water, where she anchored; but the water gained so fast upon her that the remainder of the guns were thrown overboard, and the mast cut away. The water still continuing to gain on the pumps, it was rendered indispensably necessary to quit the ship, in order to preserve the lives of the crew. Signals were accordingly made to the "Captain," who bore down and took out the crew. The ship, it is supposed, sunk soon afterwards.

(65.) THE sum of 200,000*l.*, it is said, has been fixed as the compensation to be given to the officers and men of Admiral Mitchell's squadron for the Dutch ships taken by them at the Helder.

(66.) MONDAY se'nnight a court martial was held on board the "Gladiator," in Portsmouth harbour, on Thomas M'Carty, a seaman belonging to His Majesty's ship "Melpomene," for desertion. The charge being completely proved, he was sentenced to be hanged.

SHIPPING NEWS.

(67.) THE officers and crew of His Majesty's ship "Charon," Captain Bridges, now laying at Sheerness, have subscribed one day's pay towards erecting the Grand Naval Pillar. An example so laudable it is thought will be soon followed by every ship in His Majesty's service.

(68.) IT appears that a great number of convicts which were chartered on board the "Hillsborough" to Botany Bay died on their passage.

(69.) THERE are at present in the Downs upwards of fifty transports employed on foreign service.

(70.) THERE were for London, in the lately arrived West India fleet, ninety-eight vessels. The cargoes of these ships comprised 32,942 hhds., 2,042 tierces, 864 barrels of sugar; 1,209 puncheons, 50 hhds. of rum; 5,702 casks, 26,545 bags of coffee; 340 bales, 6,003 bags of cotton; 726 bags of ginger; 154 pipes, 137 casks wine; 243,570 staves; besides a considerable quantity of tortoiseshell, ivory, indigo, molasses, dyers' woods, cocoa, &c.

(71.) IN consequence of the prevalence of the easterly winds there has been no arrival of any provision vessels from Ireland during the last six weeks.

(72.) ANOTHER West India packet has been taken, to the very great inconvenience of the merchants. We cannot add that we feel much regret upon the subject, for having for several years past taken notice of the very unfit vessels employed in this service, which are neither armed for defence nor can sail, and seeing that no measures have ever been taken to procure better, it is to be hoped that the repeated captures, and the inconvenience suffered, may at last remedy the evil.

(73.) THERE are at this time eight London mails for Hamburgh on board several packets lying in Yarmouth Roads, waiting a favourable wind to sail for Cuxhaven.

Yesterday morning arrived a mail from New York, brought to Falmouth by the "Jane" packet, in fifty-five days; we cannot learn that she has brought any particular news or passengers from America.

(74.) YESTERDAY morning arrived a mail from Lisbon, brought to Falmouth by the "King George" packet in seventeen days.

THE UNION WITH IRELAND.

(75.) THIS afternoon (July 2nd), His Majesty will go in state to the House of Peers, to give the Royal Assent to the Union Bill. The park guns will be fired on the occasion. There is certainly no event during the present reign to be compared to it in point of national advantage and general prosperity.

(76.) IT is stated in letters from Ireland, that in consequence of the Union the value of land has risen to twenty years' purchase,—a rate for many years past unknown.

The same accounts state, that the agent of an English company, and himself a gentleman of large property, is now on a tour through Ireland in order to lay out 250,000*l*. in the purchase of land, and has actually purchased an estate on the Irish coast, with a harbour, which harbour he means to improve and render useful. Another British company has undertaken an extensive colliery. A Manchester house has purchased land near the city of Dublin, whereon to erect a cotton manufactory; and several porter breweries are about to be established on British capital.

(77.) THERE is to be a new Great Seal in consequence of the Union with Ireland, a plan of which has been presented to the king for his approbation. The crown, instead of the ordinary one of England, is imperial, and the fleurs-de-lis, we understand, are wholly omitted.

(78.) THE alterations in the new great seal, now finished, and in the custody of the Lord High Chancellor are, that the arms of France are entirely expunged: the arms of England, of Scotland, of Wales, and of Ireland, are quartered, and the arms of Hanover are placed upon the centre of the four quarters.
His Majesty, in the new seal, instead of being styled "King of Great Britain, France, and Ireland," styles himself simply "Britannicorum Rex," King of the British.

(79.) TWENTY thousand pounds collected by subscription were paid for Cumberland House, now fitting up for the Irish Union Club. The shares are of 1000*l*. each. The managing Committee are Lord Mathew, Mr. Cavendish Bradshaw, and Mr. Concannon.

(80.) THE UNION.—On the 1st of January the flags and banners of the United Kingdom are to be hoisted and displayed on all His Majesty's forts and castles within the United Kingdom, and the Islands of Guernsey, Jersey, Alderney, Sark, and Man; and also on board all His Majesty's ships of war then lying in any of the ports or harbours of the said United Kingdom, or of the islands aforesaid.

POLICE CASES.

(81.) MANSION HOUSE.—YESTERDAY a man and his wife with a dancing bear and a monkey, were brought before the Lord Mayor, having been found going about the city as a nuisance. These uncommon prisoners drew a great crowd round the Mansion House; but the Lord Mayor, finding this animal not so furious as represented, after asking the poor old Italian some questions, suffered them all to depart, strictly charging him not to dance his bear any more in the city, which he faithfully promised to attend to.

(82.) MANSION HOUSE, Dec. 30.—This morning the sale was stopped at Billingsgate of above five hundred weight of salmon and several boxes of herrings, they being quite spoiled, and not fit for consumption. Part of them was produced before the Lord Mayor, and the salesman who was disposing of them.
Mr. Goldham told his Lordship that many of these fish were out of season, and could not lawfully be sold.
The salesman confessed the justness of Mr. Goldham's charge; but said, if he did not sell them other salesmen would. He begged his Lordship would let him have the herrings to boil down for the oil, and he would answer that no more of them should be sold.
The Lord Mayor refused, saying he had it not in his power; and ordered all the fish to be sunk in the middle of the river. He told the salesman that every fish which came to Billingsgate Market out of season would be seized according to law.

(83.) A PERSON, who called himself a Midshipman, was on Wednesday examined and committed by the Lord Mayor for *pressing* a young man in the city without having a city warrant.

(84.) PUBLIC OFFICE, BOW-STREET.—BEFORE Henry Wigstead, Esq.—Late on Monday evening, Thomas Veuch, a baker, of Brompton, at whose shop we stated a few days since that fifty quartern loaves short of weight were seized, was brought before the above magistrate by summons, when the charge being fully proved on the evidence of the constables who attended the magistrate on the seizure, and the defendant pleading guilty, he was convicted in the mitigated penalty of 3*s*. for each ounce, amounting to 12*l*. 3*s*., which is directed by Act of Parliament to be distributed among the poor of the parish, which the magistrate gave directions should be laid out in coals, and likewise that the bread seized should be distributed among the poor of the parish.

(85.) PUBLIC OFFICE, BOW-STREET.—On Tuesday, a gentleman, from Twickenham, attended at this office, and stated that a basket maker of Twickenham, named Cole, was in the continual habit of using disrespectful expressions against His Majesty and the Government of this country, and advising people to take pattern by the French, &c.; in consequence of which Mr. Bond granted a warrant, and two of the officers apprehended and brought him to this office, where he underwent a private examination before Mr. Ford, who committed him to Tothill-fields Bridewell.

(86.) On Monday a Foreigner was brought to town from Gravesend, where he had been arrested, on suspicion of being a spy from the French Government, by one of the Bow-street officers, who carried him before Mr. Ford at the Alien Office, where he underwent a strict examination, the result of which was his being committed to the custody of a messenger.

(87.) TUESDAY evening three men, who were taken into custody for hissing at His Majesty on his way to the House of Peers, underwent an examination before Sir William Addington, at his house in Greek-street, Soho, who committed them to Cold Bath Fields Prison. Two of them are journeymen shoemakers.

LAW COURTS.

Court of King's Bench, February 8.

(88.) Mr. Erskine moved the Court for a rule to show cause why a criminal information should not be filed against Samuel Ferrand Waddington, Esq., for having been guilty, if he was rightly instructed, of one of the darkest crimes which an individual can commit against society at large. This was forestalling, and that in an article which could not be denied to be an actual and indispensable necessary of life. He was sure he would not be deemed wrong in this assertion, when he informed the Court that this article was hops, an ingredient without which beer could not be brewed so as to keep and be wholesome, and it was needless for him to state that beer was the common beverage of the great mass of the people of this country; and with those of the most industrious and laborious classes it might very fairly be said to be one of the staffs of life. He was extremely sorry to think that a crime of this baneful nature, and of so long standing in this country, should be looked upon by many of our fellow-citizens as not punishable. It had been complained of so long ago as the reign of Edward VI, and a statute had then been framed to prevent it. Since that a variety of judicious statutes had been passed for the same salutary purpose, which in more modern times the Legislature had thought proper to repeal, leaving the offence when in future committed to be punished as a misdemeanour by the common law of the land. The repeal of those judicious statutes had, however, led many persons to suppose that this offence against the dearest interests of society was no longer *in esse*, and had increased a practice which struck deeply at the root of the common happiness of the subjects of this realm. By the justices and barons of the Exchequer, in the reign of Edward VI, it was determined that salt was a victual, or, in plainer terms, a necessary of life. That hops are entitled to the same consideration there could be no doubt, as it is a bitter which is absolutely necessary to be used in the brewing of beer; and not only so, but the Legislature has positively and strictly enacted that it shall be the only bitter which shall be made use of in the manufacture of that universal beverage. From affidavits which he had then before him, Mr. Erskine said, he was instructed to say that from the year 1798 hops had advanced in price to a very enormous and alarming degree; that this enhancement of price was actually given to overgrown speculations in that article. To show what is looked upon as forestalling the article of hops, Mr. Erskine cited a case in 3 Coke, where it was held to be forestalling, and a crime against the common law to sell corn in sheaves. In like manner, by parity of reasoning, purchasing hops on the poles amounts to the same thing. It is in fact much stronger, for no single man whatever in so general an article as grain could purchase all the corn in England. Particular speculations might enhance the price in particular spots, but in others it would be lower, and every day's practice proved to us, that in an article so general as corn the market price would find its own level. It was extremely different, however, where an article was so much limited in its growth as that of hops, the produce of which was confined to two or three counties. In this case it may be within the power of the purse of one individual, or of a purse formed by conspiracy, to bring about the most mischievous and injurious consequences to the general welfare of the community. My Lord Coke had always held the opinion that forestalling was one of the most mischievous crimes against the community, because it was a grievous oppression of the poor; and of that opinion he doubted not the Court would be on this and every similar occasion. This subject was of the highest importance, Mr. Erskine said, to the general welfare of the kingdom, and he flattered himself that the present application and the consequent conduct of the Court upon it, would prove most salutary in rooting out so baneful a practice, not only in this but in every other necessary of life. It was a practice the most shameful that could be imagined, and of the most deadly tendency. It was high time it should be put a stop to, and he had no doubt but the Court would convince the public mind that no men or set of men, let their rank or station be what it might, should offend against the law with impunity. In order to show that the gentleman against whom the present application is made has offended against the law, Mr. Erskine read the affidavit of Mr. Knipe to the following purport. "That in 1798 Mr. Waddington had informed him he was just come from Kent, where he found there was a fine speculation to be made in hops: that he had 80,000*l.* in hand, and that he was determined to purchase hops to the utmost extent of that sum, so as to create a scarcity." Mr. Erskine then stated, that Mr. Waddington had not contented himself with purchasing a single hop garden here and another there, but that he or his agents had, like a swarm of locusts, made a round sweep of whole counties. He then read from the affidavit of Mr. W. Richardson, "That the same course had been pursued by Mr. Waddington down to 1799." And, said Mr. Erskine, I have reason to believe that even the crop of hops for next season is forestalled in the same manner.

Lord Kenyon declared that he was extremely happy this subject had been brought before the Court, the matter was of immense moment to the public, and the offence complained of was of uncommon magnitude; he was sorry to say it had become too prevalent, and its evil consequences could not be too speedily put an end to. He was of opinion, that as the offence had been committed in more than one county, the rule should be for leave to file an information or informations.

Mr. Justice Grose said he was sorry to find any one had been so far misled as to suppose this offence was not punishable. Such an opinion unhappily had gone abroad, but it was absurd and unfounded; and he had, within a few days past, informed a grand jury that this was an offence punishable at common law, and it was their duty wherever they met with it to give it their most serious attention.

Lord Kenyon said that he remembered a few years ago being on the Oxford Circuit, when, from the prevalence of this offence, the whole county was on the verge of open insurrection; that he informed the grand jury this was an offence punishable at common law; and in consequence of the prudent measures by them adopted, the discontents in a very short time totally subsided, and the county was restored to peace and harmony.

Rule granted for an information or informations.

COURT OF KING'S BENCH.
The King v. Armstrong.

(89.) ON the motion of Mr. Erskine, the rule that was obtained on a former day to show cause why a criminal information should not be filed against Mr. Armstrong for sending a challenge to Major-General Coote was made absolute, no cause being shown. The defendant had very prudent and discreet advice from his counsel not to show cause against the rule, and he had followed it. That was a circumstance of which he should certainly remind their lordships in a subsequent stage of these proceedings. The counsel observed, that His Majesty had seen this matter in so serious a light towards the army that he had publicly signified his approbation of the conduct of General Coote, in having instituted this prosecution, and had directed it to be published throughout the whole army.

Guildhall, London, July 4.
Sittings before Lord Kenyon and a Special Jury of Merchants.
The King against Rusby.

(90.) THIS is as momentous a cause as ever presented itself in a court of justice. It concerns every man in the kingdom, and calls most loudly for the interposition of the legislature of the country.

Mr. Knap opened the pleadings, from which it appeared, that on the 8th of November last defendant, Mr. Rusby, bought of Shrimpton and Co., ninety quarters of oats, in the market called the Corn Exchange, at 41s. per quarter, and did unlawfully regrate thirty quarters of the said oats to William Hardy for the price of 43s. per quarter.

Mr. Erskine said this was a prosecution against the defendant, and although certainly he neither could nor ought to claim more than justice against him, and if he did he should receive no more at their hands; yet he had a right to say, that this was a case that deserved all their attention and all their consideration. There was nothing, perhaps, that was more the subject of regret than the present high price of provisions; and perhaps when we came to consider the cause of it we should not have to look for it in the elements, but in the mal-practices of those who committed offences against the public trade of the kingdom. The remedy was not to be found in legislative institutions; the remedy was not to be found in sweeping away with a rude and sudden hand statutes that had been growing up for ages for the protection of trade, much less by rash unadvised experiments, some of which he understood were making at that moment. But it struck him that the best way by which these evils were to be remedied was, by putting in force those laws that yet remained,—by going up to the source and fountain of the law of the country, to see what it was, and whether it was sufficient for all the purposes of justice,—and if it was insufficient, it would give the Legislature an opportunity of seeing whether they ought not to build up again that fabric which was destroyed at once. It would be found that the common law has this great advantage belonging to it, that it was founded on broad, sound, intelligible principles; that judges and juries had an opportunity of moulding it to the purposes and ends of justice; whereas certainly it very often happened when statutes were made to repress any particular offences, the precision necessary, and wholesomely necessary, produced very great difficulties; and sometimes cases might occur that might not be within the evil, and yet be within the statute, and might put it out of countenance. The offence here charged against the defendant, he apprehended, did not require the aid of any statute to punish it. He conceived the offence was founded in the very principles of trade and commerce, and the offence was as ancient as the country and its laws. The three offences of forestalling, engrossing, and regrating, were by Lord Coke, in the 8th institute all comprehended, under the word forestalling, as an offence against trade. He considered this offence to be this. A man might come into a market and buy what was to be sold there, and he might buy for his own consumption, or for the purpose of commerce, to sell it again; no doubt he might. But the offence here charged was, that the market was not allowed to take a fair course; that when corn was brought to it by those who grew it, or by those who had bought it in the first stages, certain people came to market for the purpose of setting an artificial price on it, and by their own artifices and manoeuvres, or in combination with others, to buy that corn, and to sell it in the same market at an advanced price, by which the consumer had not the same advantage he would have had if that had not taken place; for, as Lord Coke justly observed, in proportion to the number of hands it went through, the price would be increased to the consumer. Having stated these preliminary observations, Mr. E. said, he would tell the jury in a few words what this case was. He understood there was a set of persons who had thrust themselves into the corn market of this great city, between the corn factors, who represented the sellers, and the buyers. Those persons were numerous, and had possessed themselves of stands in the market. The mode of doing business was this. The corn remained in bulk, either in the vessels in which it was brought into the different ports of the kingdom, or in lighters. Samples were put into bags and delivered to the corn factors, and great care was taken by the statutes that factors should not be sellers of corn, and they were obliged to take an oath, as the representatives of the sellers, that they would expose it for sale fairly. The seller fixes the price at which the factor is to sell, and the quantity to be sold was generally marked on the bag. If this, therefore, were suffered to take its natural course, the market would be pretty even. Without the intervention of these jobbers here complained of the market would find its own level, and settle at its fair price. But the jobbers come, and this is the practice: they go round to the different stands, and say to the corn-factor, what do you sell this at? The factor tells them the price They say to the factor, we will give you this price at all events, if you cannot get a better. After this comes the consumer, and if the factor gets a greater price, no harm is done; but if he does not, if the factor is about to receive no more from the consumer than the jobber offered him, the jobber, in consequence of his pre-emption, steps in and has the preference; the consequence is, the consumer must pay a higher price. The jobbers instantly take it away, and put it on their own stands, by virtue of their fraudulent pre-emption. The consumer does not get it, of course, from the factor, because it is whipped away by the jobber; and then he exposes the same sample for sale and sells it at an advanced price; and he will not let it go till it comes up to a certain price. Now, could any man contemplate that practice without saying it was an offence against the public trade. With regard to engrossing, what quantity would be considered as engrossing must be matter of fact to be left to a jury. That, perhaps, was not to be measured by the simplicity of ancient times, but must be measured by circumstances. But what made it a misdemeanour in one age, made it so, and must make it so, in all ages; and that was, by making the commodity pass through different hands it increased the price. Besides, the statutes on this subject, which were repealed by the 12th of the present King, in which Mr. Burke took the lead, he observed, that the 31st of the King repealed the 15th Cha. II, c. 7, sec. 4; but the words in parenthesis in that section still remained untouched. The prosecutors in this case had many difficulties to encounter in every corner, but he trusted that the sanctity of an oath would enable them to lay this transaction before the jury. It was not immorality that was here complained of, but an offence for which the defendant must answer. If the defendant conceived he was doing that which was lawful, the Court would consider that when he received judgment on the conviction of a jury; their conviction would have a mighty operation, because it would be a proclamation of the law, and a promulgation of the penalties. It would bring back the market to that state of equity at which it ought to be fixed, and the poor would be relieved from their accumulated distresses. He thought the prosecution would be attended with the best consequences. Mr. Snell, who is a corn-chandler, would tell the jury, that on the 8th of November last he came to the market, and looked at a sample of oats marked 90, which was placed on Messrs. Shrimpton's stand. They asked 44s. per quarter for it. Mr. Snell did not purchase it. He saw Mr. Rusby, who is a jobber, and is in company with Thomas and William Smith, contract for it at 41s. per quarter, and carry it to his own stand; and very soon after it was sent to the stand of Prest and Nattras, who sold thirty quarters of it for the defendant at 43s. per quarter to a Mr. Hardy. Prest and Nattras also sold the other sixty quarters as the defendant's agents. This was the nature of the case; and after the jury were in possession of the evidence, they would do justice between the public and the defendant.

(Witnesses were here called in support of the prosecution, who gave evidence in corroboration of the statement of the counsel.)

The counsel for the defendant, in the course of a very able speech, among other things, observed that he should satisfy the Court and the jury that this offence was not committed by the defendant Mr. Rusby, but by Thomas Smith, his senior partner. Smith thought it was not a good bargain and wished speedily to get quit of it again, and therefore immediately carried the sample to the stand of Prest and Nattras. Rusby and William Smith, the other two partners, dissented from it. Rusby in particular protested against it, and that circumstance he should prove by Thomas Smith himself. And surely, though the act of one partner was the act of another as to the partnership, yet it would not be said that the act of one was the act of another in a crime.

Lord Kenyon here observed, that there was a case in Lord Raymond's Report, where Lord Holt had laid it down, that the act of one might be held to be the act of another in misdemeanour. If a servant threw a quantity of rubbish into the street, which was a nuisance, the master was answerable. The case was this: the servant of a builder having thrown a quantity of rubbish in the street, and having left no light near it, a coach was overturned in the night, and it was held *respondeat superior*.

The counsel said, if one partner accepted a bill of exchange it bound the whole partnership, but if one partner forged a bill that could not affect his partners.

Lord Kenyon said, certainly not.

The counsel said, he had heard about one hundred times from his learned friend on the other side, in cases of libel, and where it did not apply—*Actus non facit reum nisi mens sit rea*. Thomas Smith conceived that this was a falling article, carried it to the stand of Nattras and Prest. Rusby resisted the re-sale and Smith carried the re-sale into execution against that resistance.

(Thomas and William Smith were then called on the part of the defence, and deposed to the effect stated by the counsel for the defendant.)

Mr. Erskine, on the part of the prosecution, made a very eloquent reply, in the course of which he observed, that the poor of England were more industrious and more virtuous than those of any other country, and he would venture to affirm that since the origin of civilization among mankind there never existed a poor in any nation so amply protected by the virtues and humanity of their superiors.

The substance of Lord Kenyon's charge to the jury:—

Gentlemen of the jury,

I have not often been present when a cause of more consequence has been decided. Causes often come here where large sums and great wealth, real or personal, are disposed of, and where the interest of individuals is deeply concerned ; and I have always found in that box that attention and abilities that were adequate to the decision of them. But the cause now presented to you is one in which all ranks of people, rich and poor, but more particularly those of the lower classes of society, are deeply interested. Some may have the comforts and conveniences of life, but it is fit that all should have the necessaries of life ; and if, in consequence of the intrigues and combinations that are formed in any quarter of the kingdom, that part of the community without which the superior ranks cannot exist have not those necessaries, they are put in a situation in which the wisdom of no country will ever place them. The legislature of all nations, and the administration of justice in all countries, are never better employed,—I had almost said are never so well employed,—as when they condescend to look at those who are at the greatest distance from them. Humanity calls for it; the duties of religion call for it ; and if there are any minds not affected by religion and humanity, yet their own interests call most clamorously for it. Gentlemen, the law has been stated to you, and although the Act of Parliament which has been on the Statute Book about 150 years is certainly repealed, and in my opinion it was in an evil hour repealed, yet, thank God, the power which repealed it was not informed of, or did not intend to repeal, the provisions made by the common law. That which is called common law existed undoubtedly after society was formed. In very ancient times one cannot trace it with much accuracy or precision ; but we have reason to suppose that wisdom had considerably advanced before the Conqueror came over, or before the beginning of the Statute Book, about the time of Henry the Third. Among our Saxon ancestors we may suppose the common law had its origin. However, without minutely tracing it to its sources, there is no doubt now but that the common law provides, for the three offences called forestalling, engrossing, and regrating. And I believe, since the exigencies of the times require it, all the judges have in their charges to grand juries told them, that although the statute law upon this subject has been repealed, yet that this is an offence by the common law. Nobody has controverted it. It has been very properly admitted by the counsel who conducted the case on the part of the defendant, and the single question is, whether this offence exists, which we all agree ought to be remedied. The question is, whether this offence has been committed by the party who is now before you as a defendant. Gentlemen, speculators have said that no such offence can exist, for that the nation would be prejudiced by considering it to be an offence. A very learned man compares it to witchcraft. I wish the life of Dr. Adam Smith, who is a great name in the country, had been prolonged,—there is a loss of part of the public stock when a virtuous and good man dies. I wish we could have had that sagacious author here, to have heard this transaction, as it has been laid open by the witnesses, and then to have told us whether forestalling, engrossing, and regrating were as imaginary as witchcraft. Suppose he had been told that cheese and candles, fish and meat, &c., had been brought to market to answer the exigencies of the day, of the next day, and perhaps of the third day, and that a man with a large purse had come and bought it all up, and had afterwards, at a profit of five per cent., sold it to the poor, whose daily labour could not go farther than to supply their daily necessities. Such a transaction, I am afraid, is no uncommon thing. I should after this have been glad to have asked that excellent person, whether he was now convinced that this was really an offence. Surely that which enhances the degree of this offence is the present situation of the poor ; and that man must be devoid of all feeling who does not feel deeply for their distress. The learned advocate says it is not an offence committed by his client. Mr. Nattras, who I believe spoke the truth in the beginning of his evidence, before the transaction was fully opened, said he believed that Rusby delivered to him the sample. When he was called up the second time, he did not know from whom he had received it. Gentlemen, we are obliged to hear all the witnesses on both sides, and we are obliged to hear a different number of witnesses on different sides. But all juries adopt the rule, that witnesses *non numerentur, sed ponderentur.* You are bound to hear and to attend to all the witnesses. But I protest I do not believe what Mr. T. Smith swore, when he tells you there were words between him and Rusby on account of this transaction. Why should there have been any words on account of this transaction, which was not to be distinguished from many others that had gone before, and which were of daily occurrence? It requires a degree of credulity to believe this evidence, to which I am not liable. It is almost the perfection of the human heart to exhibit friendship, and to do all that we can possibly do for our friend. But that ought always to be kept within certain bounds, and ought never to lead us to transgress the laws of God or man. A man at all times, and particularly when he is speaking under the solemnities of an oath, ought to have a most sacred regard to truth. We are not monks and hermits taken from our cells, knowing nothing of the world, but we have been bred up, I hope, in those scenes of life which exhibit more knowledge and more virtue than some other places which I mentioned before, and which I shall not repeat again, though I am proud to have mentioned them, and I am proud to have stood acquitted in the eyes of all my country. In consequence of the hint which I gave to the very learned counsel for the defendant, he put this case on the ground I think on which it ought to stand. He knows that for his abilities, personal character, and everything that belongs to him, I have the most unfeigned respect. The defendant is liable for acts committed by his partners, as in this case, where his interest was concerned, and you cannot shut the door against the truth. Was not his interest concerned in this case, when, in consequence of this second sale in the market, there was a profit of 5 per cent. Supposing that it ever took place, it was equally for the benefit of the whole partnership, and I am bound to believe that it did take place. Where are the books? Mr. Nattras told you he had not brought his book, but that he had brought a copy of it as far as regarded this transaction. When the book was produced and the paper compared with it, was it a copy? It was not a copy, and the alterations in the original entry in the book is extremely suspicious. Gentlemen, you will consider the whole of the evidence. This is a most momentous case at the present moment. What would you say to this case if it were stated to you that a rich man planted messengers at all avenues, and bought up everything that was coming to town, and raised the price of provisions 50 per cent? A precedent made in a court of justice to stop the torrent of such affliction to the poor, is certainly useful to the public.

The jury immediately found the defendant Guilty.

Lord Kenyon, addressing himself to the jury, said, "You have conferred the greatest benefit on the country, I believe, that any jury almost ever did."

There was another indictment for the same offence, which stands over. His lordship observed "That if the same virtue and public spirit which had commenced this prosecution should induce the prosecutors to prefer another indictment against Thomas Smith, from the evidence he had given, he would stand unprotected."

HISSING AT THE KING.

COURT OF KING'S BENCH, WESTMINSTER, JULY 10.
Sitting before Lord Kenyon and a Special Jury.
The King v. Dutton.

(91.) THIS was an indictment against the defendant, John Dutton, which charged that he, with several others, riotously and tumultuously assembled about His Majesty's carriage as he was returning to his palace from the Theatre of Drury-lane, on the 15th of May last, and hissed, hooted, &c. The defendant pleaded Not Guilty.

As Mr. Attorney-General's speech on the part of the Crown is extremely short, we shall state it *verbatim*.

"Gentlemen of the jury.—The offence with which the defendant is charged, is one which, taken simply by itself, is an act of high indecency to whatever person it may be applied; but when it is applied to a person in the situation of the Sovereign of the country, to whom we all owe, for our own sakes, the highest respect, it is an offence of deep malignity. Upon any occasion it would be such an offence; but gentlemen, at the moment when it happened, at a time when the hearts of all his Majesty's loyal subjects expanded with affection, rejoiced that he had escaped the hands of a man who now appears to have been an unfortunate lunatic, at such a moment, for any man, and especially a man of the description of the defendant, a person resident on the spot, and who must necessarily have been acquainted with all the circumstances, assembled with a number of other persons to insult the King returning from the theatre after an event such as has been stated to you, such as you all know to have happened, is a crime of such malignity, that I could not suppose any person to be guilty of it. And I must confess, that the improbability that men could be found so lost to all sense of that duty which they owe to their king, to their country, and to themselves; at such a moment to insult a person in such a station, and under such circumstances, made me hesitate for a moment whether this charge ought to be preferred. A grand jury of the country has found that there is ground for that charge. It will be proved to you, gentlemen, that a number of persons were thus forgetful of all they owed to their country and to themselves, and that they did dare to insult His Majesty in this situation. It will be also distinctly proved to you, that the defendant John Dutton, was one of these persons. Gentlemen, he was seized in the very act. Under these circumstances, much as I am astonished to find that there should be men so lost to all sense of their duty, I thought it became me to prefer an indictment to a grand jury. That grand jury has found that to be a true bill. You are now sworn to determine between the defendant and his country, whether he is or is not guilty of this heinous offence thus laid to this charge.

The first witness was John Francis Wood, who gave evidence on the trial of James Hadfield, and was called solely for the purpose of showing that this insult was offered to His Majesty by the defendant on the same evening that an attempt had been made on His Majesty's person by the firing of a pistol.

Thomas Mayhew said he was one of the patrols under the magistrates at Bow-street. He was on duty on the 15th of May last, and saw a number of persons assembled about His Majesty's carriage, as he was returning to his palace from the theatre. They were running along-side of the carriage hissing and hooting. There might be a dozen or twenty of them, and there might be eight or ten hissing. He said he saw the defendant among them. He was one of the foremost active and riotous. It was then generally known all about the streets that an attempt had been made on His Majesty's life in the theatre. The defendant and others continued in his view to pursue the carriage about twenty yards. He was stationed at the corner of Southampton-street, in the Strand. He apprehended him, and on looking at the defendant said, he had no doubt but that he was the person.

The defendant, on being asked if he had anything to allege in his own defence, said, he had been eighteen months in London, that he was about to return again to the country, and wished to see the King before he went.

Lord Kenyon, "Gentlemen of the jury, you have heard the evidence, and it is now your province to decide whether the defendant is guilty or not guilty."—Guilty.

Hanging in Effigy.
Court of King's Bench, December 6.
The King v. Emerton.

(92.) This was a criminal information against the defendant for having hanged in effigy the Rev. Mr. Cotterel, rector of Hadley. This gentleman, it was stated by Mr. Garron, counsel for the prosecution, had been a clergyman for six and thirty years, had brought up a numerous and amiable family; in all the relations of public life had been a pattern of perfection, and except in this instance, had been universally loved, esteemed, and respected. Having had, however, to exercise the unpleasant task of a commissioner of the income tax, he had undeservedly incurred the resentment of the defendant. Mr. Emerton's schedule was so improbable that it was necessary to summon him before the commissioners, and to surcharge him considerably. This took place on the 20th of March, on the 26th there was erected a gibbet, about ten feet high, on Mr. Emerton's nursery-grounds, close by the Northern-road, and a figure hanged by it, which was an exact likeness of Mr. Cotterel. A day or two after this gibbet was taken down, and another erected, considerably higher, on a spot, if possible, still more conspicuous, and the venerable parson was suspended from it in effigy. The figure had hitherto been dressed in black, but on the ensuing Saturday night, by the defendant's direction, it was painted white; for what other purpose than to ridicule religion, by exhibiting the person in his surplice? Till the 6th of April was the faithful pastor thus insulted in the eyes of his flock, and rendered ridiculous to every one travelling that way who frequented road. A greater violation of propriety; a greater outrage upon decency; a more cruel, unfeeling, unprincipled act could not possibly be conceived. He understood, the learned counsel said, it was to be pretended this was all a mistake; that the figure taken for Mr. Cotterel was a gawking erected to scare the birds from eating the defendant's seeds. He could prove, however, that Mr. Emerton vowed revenge against Mr. Cotterel, that he went to an undertaker and bought an excellent black coat of him, and that no one who knew the original, was at a loss to know whom the effigy was meant to represent. He was told, too, that the figure was to be shown to his lordship and the jury, and that by making Mr. Cotterel stand up beside it, his learned friend was to demonstrate that there was no resemblance between them. But if the skeleton of Abershaw were produced, could any one now discover to whom it belonged.

The facts of the case as thus stated being clearly proved. Mr. Erskine rose and made a very witty speech in favour of the defendant. He maintained that the figure had no resemblance to the prosecutor, and that his client was a very bad maker of figures, appeared from the wretched figure he made to-day. This gawking had been sent to his house, but instead of taking it for a person in his robes, he thought it was a bundle of trees which he had ordered from his nurseryman. Therefore all that his friend had said about the surplice, must be rejected as a surplusage. He was afraid, however, he must allow that his client, in a moment of irritation, had committed the offence imputed to him. He had shown himself ignorant of the garden of human life, he had neglected to weed anger from his heart, and had mistaken the fruits of resentment for the essence of pleasantry. Verdict, Guilty.

Mr. Cotterel then stepped forward and declared that he did not feel, and never had felt, the least resentment against Mr. Emerton. His friends had insisted upon this prosecution being raised that his character might be vindicated, and since that had been effectually done, he hoped things would go no farther.

Lord Kenyon, "Christian charity beareth all things, endureth all things."

Clerkenwell Sessions.
Forestallers.

(93.) A most important cause to the public was on Saturday tried; Thomas Hill and William Hill, two butchers in Newport Market, were indicted for forestalling, by buying cattle at Knightsbridge, on the road to Smithfield Market. The fact was clearly proved, and it appeared to have been a common practice for butchers to meet droves of cattle coming to market, and buy them up. The enormity of the practice was fully impressed upon the jury by the Chairman in his address to them. They were both found Guilty. In consideration of the defendants being the first example since this sort of prosecutions fell into disuse, and the offence itself not being sufficiently promulgated, the Court only sentenced them to pay a fine of £20 each, and to be imprisoned three months.

Dixie and Chambers were tried for defrauding Lord Mount Edgecumbe of a guinea, by pretending to have been sufferers by the late fire in Panton-street. They were sentenced to be imprisoned one year, and put in the pillory.

Middlesex Sessions, September 15.

(94.) This day the Sessions for the county began at Hicks's Hall, Clerkenwell, when several persons were tried for trifling assaults.

(95.) Two more causes againt the clergy for non-residence, were tried on Tuesday in the Common Pleas. In one the plaintiff was nonsuited on account of a flaw in the proceedings; in the other he gave up the cause. Upwards of 800 actions have been brought by the same plaintiff, whose name is Wilson.

December 10.

(96.) "The Admiralty session was held at the Old Bailey, when T. Potter, one of the crew of a smuggling vessel, was sentenced to be hanged, and to be afterwards anatomized, for the wilful murder of H. Glynn, late a boatswain belonging to His Majesty's Customs at Plymouth, and who was shot whilst rowing towards the smuggler, for the purpose of boarding her, in the execution of his duty. He was executed on the 18th.

(97.) Forgeries.—Thomas Crump was indicted for uttering a sixteenth share of a lottery ticket, numbered 9392, in the present English lottery now drawing, with intent to defraud Peter Richardson, Elizabeth Goodluck, and George Arnull, the number of said share being altered from 9390 to 9392.

The following circumstances appeared by the evidence of several of the clerks belonging to the office of Richardson and Goodluck, at Charing Cross:—On the evening of the 1st of February last, the prisoner went to that office and purchased ten shares, among which was the share in question; he had them all registered; paid 6d. a number for the registry, and gave his true name and place of abode, in order that intimation might be sent him in case any of the numbers should turn up a prize. The manner in which the numbers were registered was of one clerk reading them out to another, who entered them down in a book. The number in question was entered down 9392 instead of 9390, which was the proper number of that share; and it was positively sworn that there was no ticket at the office of Richardson and Goodluck of the number 9392, although that number was put down in their book, as it was alleged, by mistake. All the noughts on the lottery tickets had two strokes marked, one over and the other under them, and the cause assigned for doing so was that they might not be changed into a 6 or a 9. It was easy to mistake a mark like this for the figure 2; but it was candle-light when the clerk read out the ticket in question to him who registered it. On the 4th of March, the ticket 9392 was drawn a prize of 1000l. It was known at Richardson's office that this number was registered there, though it had never been in their possession; and they sent no notice to the prisoner as they were bound to do. For this the clerks who gave evidence could assign no reason. On the 5th of March, the prisoner came and demanded payment for the sixteenth. It was then perceived that the nought had been altered to the figure 2, by means of a line drawn between it and the stroke under it. This line was of a different colour from that of the other parts of the ticket, on account of being made with a different kind of ink. When the prisoner was told the ticket had been altered, he replied it was in the same state in which he had received it at their office, and insisted on being paid the share of 1000l. An altercation having then ensued between the prisoner and the clerks, Mr. Richardson was sent for, and upon seeing the share he immediately discovered the alteration. He then observed to the prisoner that he presented an instrument which would be attended with serious consequences to him if he demanded payment for it; that he must be cautious what answers he made; that the alteration in the share was such as could not impose upon the office; and that he should keep it in his possession. He then begged of the prisoner to go and bring his friends, in order that the matter might be satisfactorily explained, and know what the number really was. The prisoner replied that he knew the number to be 9392; that he had bought it as such at their office; that it had not since been altered; that he had the number with several others printed on a card; and that he would not be hummed in that way. Mr. Richardson told him that if he persisted in demanding payment for the share he would have him taken to Bow-street, but recommended it to him to call the next morning with his friends. The prisoner replied that as Mr. R. threatened to take him to Bow-street, he certainly would go there. Mr. R., on his cross-examination stated the reason why notice had not been sent to the prisoner of the number registered having been drawn a prize, to be that of there having been strong circumstances to induce him to think that a mistake had been made in registering the number. It was he himself who prevented the letter of notice from being sent to the prisoner, knowing that he had not sold the number registered in his name; and besides he did not wish to trifle with the feelings of a set of poor fellows who formed the club, on whose account the prisoner had purchased the tickets, knowing what a disappointment it must be to them to tell him that a prize had been drawn in their favour which they could not share. It was acknowledged by all the witnesses who belonged to the lottery office that the prisoner appeared perfectly confident. It was proved by a person from the Stamp Office that the ticket in question was originally 9390, and not 9392; that it was shared by Richardson, and that 9392 was shared by Hornsby and Co. Such a share as that produced in Court would not have been passed at the Stamp Office, on account of the line drawn between the nought and the stroke underneath.

The prisoner, when asked what he had to say in his defence, observed, that when he purchased the share the number as it now stood was called over by the clerk, and was so registered. He left the rest to his counsel, who called the following witnesses to shew that the alteration was not made by the prisoner.

— Harrison said, that he and the prisoner were journeymen in the tin manufactory of Mr. Moore at Lambeth. He was along with prisoner when he purchased the shares, and witness chose the share in question himself, but he could recollect none of the numbers except the first of the nine. The prisoner gave a true description of himself at the time the shares were registered: and printed cards of the numbers, among which was the number 9392, were distributed among the members of the club three weeks before the drawing of the lottery.

Mary Crump, a servant in the house of Mr. Cleland, Adelphi-terrace, and sister to the prisoner, said, that on Saturday evening, the 1st of February, he called on her, and shewed her ten shares of lottery tickets, which he said he had just purchased. She repeated all the numbers to her brother, and he took them down on a piece of paper. She read them over again, and they corresponded with the numbers he took down. She could swear positively to the number 9392; and her reason for recollecting it so well was, that when she read it she made this remark to the prisoner. "Thomas, this is the date of the year when you and I first came to London." They had come to London in the year 1792. Her brother gave her the list he had just written out, and she gave it to Edward Stinton, who was a member of the club, in order to have it printed.

Edward Stinton said, he was butler in the same house where the last witness lived as servant. He received a list from her on Sunday, the 2nd of February, which list he gave to be printed on cards for the satisfaction of the club. This list contained the number 9392.

Thomas Glassington said, he was publisher of the "Morning Herald." He had been applied to by Mr. Stinton, in the beginning of February last, to get some cards printed; they were printed by Mr. Brown, the printer of the paper, and the numbers on the cards corresponded with the copy given him by Stinton.

Another witness, who was a member of the club, swore, that on Monday, the 3rd of February, he took an account from the shares themselves, and one of the numbers was 9392. The prisoner bid every member take lists for their own satisfaction.

Three or four respectable persons were then called, and gave the prisoner an excellent character for honesty and propriety of conduct. Among these was Mr. Moore, the owner of the manufactory where the prisoner worked, who said he had been with him seven years as an apprentice, and had been since employed by him as a journeyman. He had always entertained the highest opinion of him, and never had any reason to change his mind.

Mr. Justice Grose told the jury that the indictment was founded on an Act of Parliament of last year, for raising a sum of money by lottery; in this Act the offence the prisoner was charged with was declared a felony; but as the words "without benefit of clergy" were not added, the punishment was not capital—it was a clergyable felony. The principal question to decide was, whether this alteration in the number existed at the time the prisoner bought the share. The jury should take notice of the confidence with which the prisoner conducted himself when he went to ask payment, and if a reasonable doubt existed in their minds, his good character ought to weigh in his favour.

The jury, without retiring, found the prisoner Not Guilty.

(A considerable degree of interest prevailed in Court towards the conclusion of this trial; but we were happy to observe that there were no marks of indecent exultation when the verdict of acquittal was given.)

(98.) Handcock v. Baker and Others.

THIS was an action to recover damage for an assault. The case proved was nearly as follows:— The plaintiff's wife having cried out *Murder!* and called for assistance from her chamber window, the defendent and others broke into the house to her, where they found the wife almost naked, with marks of violence upon her neck, and drenched with water, thrown upon her by the husband; on which they carried him to the cage. There was a struggle between the parties, and some blows were struck, about which there was contradictory evidence. The jury of course gave a verdict for the defendants.

(99.) A WATCHMAN, named *Night*, was tried for assaulting Mr. Hunt, an apothecary, as he was going his rounds at eleven o'clock at night. The cause of the rencontre was that of the defendant singing out, "Past eleven o'clock, cloudy morning." The prosecutor passing by at the time, and being a little *in his cups*, as was admitted by his counsel, wished to correct the watchman for improperly describing the time of the night. These good intentions of the prosecutor were disregarded by the defendant, who, after some words had passed between them, struck the other a blow with his staff.

Evidence was called on the part of the defendant to shew, that the prosecutor struck him first; but the jury giving more credit to the evidence on the part of the prosecution, found the defendant *guilty*.

PROVINCIAL TRIALS.

(100.) SEVENTY inn-keepers in Leicestershire were last week convicted in the mitigated penalty of 10*l.* each, with costs, for selling ale in unstamped measures.

(101.) ON Wednesday last, a case of rather a novel nature was brought before the sitting magistrate in the Council Chamber at Edinburgh. A person offering to enlist in the Marines, was discovered to be a woman, named Margaret Grant, who, it seems, has been in the practice of dressing herself in man's apparel, and had enlisted twice before, defrauding the parties of the enlisting money. After undergoing an examination, she was remanded to the City Guard. She was dressed in a blue jacket and trousers, wore her hair loose, and had a round hat.

(102.) AN information has been laid before the Mayor of Bridgewater against Robert Bell, of North Petherton, gardener, for forestalling, by purchasing six tons of potatoes now growing, and to be delivered to him between Michaelmas and Christmas next. A similar information was made before the same justice against William Sprouting, of Bridgewater, victualler, for purchasing ten tons of potatoes now growing, to be delivered between Christmas and Lady-day next; the complainant was bound over to prosecute.

(103.) UPWARDS of twenty butchers were, on Monday, fined by the magistrates of Maningtree, for flaying hides below the knee and gambril.

(104.) A CAUSE of much importance to the clergy was tried at Durham assizes last week, which produced a great sensation there. A prosecution was brought forward against the Vicar of Norham, for a non-residence of nine months, viz., from the end of September, 1798, to the beginning of July, 1799. The witnesses for the prosecution proved, that the Vicar found the parsonage house at his induction in so ruinous a state, that it was deemed necessary to rebuild it; that immediately upon his receiving the sum awarded for dilapidations, he entered into contract with a builder to erect a new house, in the space of one year from its commencement; that the builder began the work, as soon as the weather would permit, in the following spring, 1799; that the first intimation the Vicar received of this prosecution, was by being served with a writ in the ensuing September, while residing in the village (the only one he could procure), which was extremely poor and mean; that he lived in this miserable place during the summer months. The same witnesses likewise proved, that he had always kept a resident curate, who was much beloved in the parish; that the Vicar himself was an excellent parish priest, faithfully discharging the various duties of his profession, and was highly esteemed. The vicarage was stated to be worth nearly two hundred pounds per ann., and that the rebuilding of the house was a great pressure upon his income. It was also admitted, that his intention of constantly residing therein was generally known. Notwithstanding all these, and many other strong circumstances were proved by the prosecutor's witnesses, who live in the parish, the Judge (Baron Graham) was of opinion, that whatever malice might appear on the part of the prosecutor, whatever merit on the part of the Vicar, though he was proved to be actually building a house for the purpose of residence, yet, as he was not personally abiding in his parish during the nine months sued for by the prosecutor, he was subject to the penalty of 10l. for each month that he was absent. The jury found their verdict accordingly.

SUFFOLK ASSIZES.

(105.) At these assizes, held before Sir Archibald Macdonald, and Sir Beaumont Hotham, Knts., which ended on Saturday last, the following prisoners were tried:
James Orman Clark, capitally convicted of burglariously breaking into the dwelling-house of George Suggate, at Halesworth, on the 4th of May last, and stealing thereout 31 watches and sundry other articles, to the value of £200, and upwards. He received sentence of death, and was left for execution. The above young man, about 23 years of age, was a midshipman on board Admiral Duncan's fleet in the battle of Camperdown, and both on that occasion, and afterwards, under Admiral Mitchell, at the Helder, conducted himself in a very gallant manner. These services he mentioned at the time of sentence being passed upon him, and earnestly pleaded for mercy through the intercession of the worthy Chief Baron, who gave him no hopes, but feelingly lamented that he had disgraced a profession so glorious and honourable to his country. The prosecutor, with great liberality and humanity, likewise interceded in his behalf immediately after conviction.
Margaret Catchpole was identified and convicted of having broken out of Ipswich gaol, on the 28th of March last, where she was confined after being sentenced to death, for horse stealing, at the summer assizes, 1797, but had been reprieved on condition of being transported for seven years; she again received sentence of death, but was reprieved before the judge left the town.

CHELMSFORD.

(106.) A REMARKABLE occurrence happened towards the close of these assizes: J. Taylor had been arraigned and tried on the charge of uttering a forged note in the name of Bartholomew Browne, for £820 10s., with intent to defraud the bank of Cricket and Co., at Colchester, of which the jury found him guilty; but just as Baron Hotham was about to put on his black cap, and to pass sentence of death upon the prisoner, one of the barristers not retained on the trial, happening to turn over the forged note, saw it signed Barthw. Browne, and throwing his eyes immediately on the indictment, perceived it written therein Bartholomew Browne. He immediately pointed out the circumstance to Mr. Garrow, counsellor for the prisoner, who rose up and stated the variance as fatal to the indictment, in which the judge concurred, and discharged the prisoner; but as he was still liable to a new indictment, and immediately arrested for debt, his friends paid the latter to save him from the former.

(107.) A CURIOUS cause was tried at Aylesbury Assizes, in which Mr. Groom, a farmer, in Buckinghamshire, was plaintiff, and the Earl of Sandwich, master of the King's hounds, and Mr. Gordon, defendants. Mr. Groom attempted to stop His Majesty and his party in the chase, from passing over his grounds; and failing in doing so, he brought his action against the master of the King's hounds, but he was nonsuited. The trial lasted five hours.

SENTENCES AND PUNISHMENTS.

(108.) YESTERDAY morning, April 4, John Slater, for returning from transportation, Thomas Hashwell, for coining, Charles Edlin, for a burglary, Valentine Middleton, for a highway robbery, and W. Lee, for a burglary, were executed before the new gaol, in Horsemonger-lane, Borough, pursuant to their sentences at the last Kingston assizes. They all behaved with becoming propriety, and were the first malefactors that have suffered on the new-erected platform at the new gaol.

(109.) TUESDAY, 15 July, the session ended at the Old Bailey, when John Brown, Mary, the wife of John Beckwith, Mary Beckwith, Mary Ann Fielding, Charles William Price, and Mary Smith, *alias* Hall, severally received judgment of death. Twenty-four were ordered to be transported for seven years; sixteen were ordered to be imprisoned in Newgate; twenty-four were ordered to be imprisoned in the House of Correction at Clerkenwell; thirteen were ordered to be publicly whipped, and two privately.
Wednesday, the Recorder made his report to His Majesty of the prisoners under sentence of death in Newgate, who were convicted in May sessions last, when John Newman, William Mead, and Richard Franklyn, were ordered for execution on Wednesday, July 23rd.

(110.) YESTERDAY morning, 5th June, eight malefactors were executed at the front of Newgate. Dawson, who was convicted of forgery, seemed to die with great unconcern, though a different behaviour might have been expected from a person who had been well educated.

(111.) LAST Saturday se'nnight, James Murray, under sentence of condemnation for a highway robbery (who was to have been executed on Wednesday last), made his escape out of the gaol of Leicester, by a most extraordinary exertion, and a series of good fortune almost beyond credibility. Soon after six o'clock on Saturday morning, the turnkey let him into the felon's yard. Murray, with the assistance of a stool placed at the top of the pump, jumped to a window above, and thence to a spout, each several feet above his head; having gained the summit, he quickly descended into an adjoining yard belonging to a butcher; the servant being gone a milking, had left the key under the door, this enabled him to go out without noise into the high street (one of the most public in the town), down which he walked with great seeming composure, passed three or four persons who recognized him, but in the moment of surprise let him pass. Thence he went into the swine market, where his chains were observed; but by some extraordinary fatality, no person attempted to stop him. In the meantime one person who had seen him in High-street, went and told the gaoler he was at large. An immediate alarm was given, without being able to discover what was become of him. Murray, it appears, got clear of the town, and effected his escape to a village some miles from Leicester, where he hid himself in a barn, but being discovered by some boys, he offered them a shilling to fetch a blacksmith; dreading, however, an alarm, during their absence he got out and secreted himself among some standing corn. What he had anticipated was soon verified, the clamour became general; several persons returned with the boy. Quite exhausted with fatigue, he determined to surrender himself, and immediately came forward, declaring that since it appeared he must die, he would surrender without further trouble; but in this dread moment his good fortune did not desert him; the parties suffered a sense of duty to give way to the emotions of pity, and instead of hurrying him back to an ignominious death, they liberated him from his chains, relieved the wants of nature, changed his dress, gave him money, and sent him away; and from that time he has not been heard of.

(112.) YESTERDAY Probert stood in the pillory at Charing-cross, in pursuance of his sentence, for setting fire to his house in Compton-street, about two years since.

(113.) SEPT. 30.—YESTERDAY the prisoners who had been capitally convicted during the September sessions, were put to the bar and received sentence of death; 5 for burglaries, 2 for sheep stealing, 2 for highway robberies, 1 for horse stealing, 1 for forgery, 1 for feloniously firing a pistol, 1 for counterfeiting shillings and sixpences, and 1 for taking a bill out of a letter in the Post Office; after which the Court was adjourned.

(114.) DUBLIN, SEPT. 30.—ON Saturday last, Patrick Lacy, pursuant to his sentence, stood in the pillory one hour, opposite the Exchange, for concealing bank notes in the tops of his boots, to a considerable amount, with intent to negotiate them.

(115.) ON Nov. 12, were executed before Newgate, Thomas Chalfont, for secreting a letter, which came within his power, as a sorter at the General Post Office, and stealing thereout a 10l. bank note, the property of Messrs. Bedwell and Co.; Thomas Newman, for stealing a gelding, the property of George Arnold; John Price and John Robinson, for a burglary in the dwelling-house of Mr. John Lambe and Co., and stealing a quantity of silk; and William Hatton, for maliciously firing at J. Doonah (a watchman), with a loaded pistol.

(116.) DEC. 10.—THE recorder passed sentence of death at the Old Bailey, on J. Coward, for stealing three heifers; Elizabeth Deering and J. Mills, for stealing in a dwelling-house; John and Mary Oakes, and Margaret Miller, for highway robberies; J. Reynolds, W. Barnes, and D. Rawley (a boy), for burglaries; J. Fisher, for stealing sugar in a wharf; and G. Thomas, for forgery; D. Grant, for receiving stolen sugar, was sentenced to be transported for 14 years; twenty-eight persons were ordered to be confined for 7 years; twenty-seven to imprisonmemt, whipping, and fines; and Mary Ann Bellows, a girl 11 years old, was ordered to the Philanthropic Society. B. Pooley, a letter carrier, found guilty at September sessions, of having taken a bill for 200l. out of a letter, and whose case, in consequence of his counsel having objected to the indictment, on the ground that the note not having been duly stamped, he had not stolen anything of value, had been referred to the twelve judges, was pardoned; but he was ordered to be detained to answer other charges.

(117.) YESTERDAY, Sir William Scott made a report to His Majesty of James Thomson, who was capitally convicted at the Admiralty session held at the Old Bailey, in December last, of felony and piracy, when he was respited on condition of serving in the navy.

(118.) ENSIGN OBRIE, of the 9th Foot, arraigned for killing Lieutenant Smith, of the same regiment, in a duel at Netley Camp, was ordered, together with his second in the unhappy affair, to be imprisoned for the space of six months, and each to pay a fine of 6s. 8d.

(119.) ON Saturday last, the magistrates fined thirty-seven butchers, bakers, and shopkeepers, in the town of Ashburton, for selling by short weights and measures.

(120.) THE driver of the Twickenham stage coach was on Monday sentenced to one month's imprisonment, at Hick's Hall, for driving his coach so close to his right hand side of the road, as not to leave room for a gentleman who was riding on horseback to pass the coach on the side which, by the custom of the road, was the side which he was sanctioned in taking. The gentleman was not hurt; but the leading horses of the coach run against his horse, and he was obliged to turn about and to ride round to the other side of the road. Mr. Mainwaring, in passing sentence, observed, that in his opinion, the sentence of the Court was extremely lenient, and that carelessness of this kind in the drivers of coaches of any sort, deserved most severe punishment.

HIGHWAY ROBBERIES.

(121.) TUESDAY, as Mr. Levien, of the City, was returning to town from Slough in a post-chaise, he was stopped in Butcher's Grove, on Hounslow Heath, about two o'clock, by two highwaymen, who robbed him of his watch, six guineas, and some loose money. He drove with all speed to the office in Bow Street, where he arrived about three, and communicated what had happened to the magistrates, who were then sitting. Three patrols were instantly dispatched to the turnpike gates of Paddington, the Gravel Pits, and Holland House; and at the former gate, between four and five o'clock, the two offenders came, when one of them, leaving his horse, was secured in a field, after throwing a pistol away; and his companion, riding down the Mary-le-bone Road, was pursued and taken near Portland Street, but not until he had made great resistance, and received several wounds; and in whose possession, on being searched, were found Mr. Levien's watch, and the money of which he had been robbed, together with a pistol, powder, and some bullets. Their names are Thomas Smith and Sylvester Smith, persons well known, and who, after an examination of some length at Bow Street, were committed for re-examination on Friday next.

(122.) A GENTLEMAN and a lady were robbed yesterday forenoon, on their way to town from Clapham, by two highwaymen.

(123.) EARLY yesterday morning, as one of the Dover stages was returning to London, near Shooter's Hill, it was attacked by three footpads. The guard being imprudently on the box without his blunderbuss when the coach was stopped, he moved towards the roof of the coach to get it, which the robbers perceiving, discharged at him a pistol containing two balls, both of which entered his body, and wounded him in a dangerous manner. The robbers then secured the blunderbuss, and the passengers were obliged to submit quietly to be robbed of everything of value. The guard was conveyed to Welling, with very little hopes of recovery.

(124.) On Sunday morning last the Warrington mail was robbed by a man on foot, about two or three o'clock, between Winwick and Red Bank Hill, who, after a struggle with the post-boy, pulled him off his horse, which the robber then mounted and rode away with the mail towards Winwick Green. The usual reward of 200l. was immediately offered for his apprehension. From the circumstance of a pistol, cap, plate, and feather being found near the spot, it is supposed that the robber belongs to the Queen's own Regiment of Dragoons; it is also supposed he had his own horse near the place, as the post-boy's horse was left at a short distance, and a man of the above description passed through the toll-bar at Lane-head. This is the third time the same mail has been robbed within twelve months.

(125.) SOME days ago a French priest was attacked by a footpad on the Edgeware Road, who, not content with the few shillings he had about him, insisted on his coat, alleging it was superior to his own; the exchange was no sooner completed than the priest ran, so did the thief, vociferating to him to stop, but in vain, fearing he meant to ill use him. On reaching a public street, the thief gave up the pursuit, and the priest, putting his hand in his pocket, found at once the cause of this renewed attack, discovering he had got 50l.

(126.) One of the desperate gang of footpads, whose depredations have so long alarmed society at Shooter's Hill, was, on Tuesday evening, secured in a ditch between that place and Welling, after a very narrow escape with his life in stopping a patrol from Bow Street, in a carriage, who twice fired at him with a carbine and horse pistol, and only slightly grazed his arm. He was immediately taken before Mr. Bond, in Bow Street, who committed him for re-examination. One of his companions, from the officer's report, is supposed not to have been quite so lucky, being believed to be shot in the back, and probably dead in an adjoining wood, which the patrol were directed to traverse on Wednesday in hopes of finding him.

(127.) WEDNESDAY night last, about eight o'clock, as Counsellor Bellew, attended by his servant, was returning to town on horseback, he was called upon to stop by some footpads near Santry Hall. Depending upon the fleetness of his horse, he immediately pushed him forward, whereupon two of the freebooters fired: a ball grazed the Counsellor's neck, and another lodged in his shoulder. The robbers took from him his watch and some cash. When retiring, the desperadoes asked the servant who the gentleman was? They were told he was Counsellor Bellew, the brother of Sir Edward Bellew, whereupon they returned his watch. The ball, we hear, has been since extracted, and Mr. B. is in a fair way of recovery.

(128.) On Saturday night, about nine o'clock, Mr. Francis, of Hampstead, was stopped in St. Mary-le-bone Fields by two footpads, who threw him down, and rifled his pockets of a considerable sum in bank-notes.

(129.) On Monday night last about nine o'clock, Mr. Bates, of Cecil Court, St. Martin's Lane, and another gentleman, were stopped in a post-chaise near the workhouse at Islington, by three footpads, who robbed them of a watch and some money.

(130.) On Monday afternoon, about 4 o'clock, as Mr. Medina, of Newington, was going from thence to Highgate in a carriage, he was stopped by a single highwayman, who presented a pistol to his breast, and robbed him of his money and a gold watch.

(131.) On Sunday morning last, about three o'clock, Carpmeal, one of the Bow Street officers, and Mr. West, hop factor, of the Borough, and a lady, were attacked in a post-chaise a little on this side Shooter's Hill by three footpads, one of whom stood at the horses' heads while the two others came up to the chaise and opened the doors, when, perceiving Carpmeal presenting his pistols at them, they instantly retreated behind the carriage ; one of them at the same moment discharging his pistol at Carpmeal, the ball of which splintered a piece off the chaise, but did him no injury ; the villain who stood at the horses' heads discharged his pistol into the chaise, though without effect ; and the horses springing forward at the moment, he let go his hold, and made off before the carriage could be stopped. Five balls had lodged in different parts of the chaise.

(132.) On Friday last, between one and two o'clock, two French priests were stopped about the middle of Maiden Lane, leading from Battle Bridge to Highgate, by two footpads, armed with pistols, who demanded their money ; but the priests not understanding English, and one of them making some resistance, when they attempted to take his watch, the chain of which broke in the struggle, one of the robbers discharged his pistol at him, the ball of which entered his hand, which it shattered in so dreadful a manner, that immediate amputation of the middle finger was found necessary. Some persons in the adjoining fields hearing the report of the pistol, made towards the spot, when the villains ran off.

VARIOUS CRIMES AND OFFENCES.

(133.) MR. TOWNSEND, the Bow-street officer, was yesterday robbed of his hat in the Chapel Royal.

(134.) SEVENTY persons, most of whom are capitally indicted, are to be removed this morning from the county gaol in Horsemonger-lane, Southwark, to Kingston, for trial, on Wednesday and the following days.

(135.) ELIZABETH LOVELL, the Gipsey fortune-teller, was committed for trial for stealing six silver tea-spoons, the property of Mr. Weldon of Oxford-street, into whose house she obtained admission under pretence of telling the servant's fortune, as mentioned in a former paper.

(136.) On Tuesday night, Mr. Cross, of the Crown Inn, at Portsmouth, was robbed of upwards of five hundred ounces of plate. It was stolen out of his bed-room while he was asleep : and a gentleman, who was also in bed, was robbed of 110*l*. and a gold watch.

(137.) THERE can be no question, if the public statements have been accurate, but that the soldier did his duty in shooting the unfortunate deserter, who was attempting to escape from his custody, on Monday. There can be no question but that he himself would have become the object of a very severe punishment if he had acted otherwise. There may be some doubt, however, whether it may not be wise to order that in great towns fire-arms only shall be delivered upon similar occasions.

(138.) THE wife of a gardener, coming from Chiswick in a small cart, on Saturday morning, was stopped near Kensington Gore by two footpads, one of whom she knocked down with the handle of her whip, and drove on unmolested.

(139.) LETTERS from Colchester and Ipswich are full of accounts of burglaries, footpad robberies, &c. At the latter place, half-a-score different handbills are in circulation offering rewards for apprehending depredators.

(140.) ONE the late "Moniteurs" announces the arrest and imprisonment, at St. Hypolite, of Sans Peur, the ex-Prior Cologna, whom it states to be one of the most ferocious brigands of the South. The mistress of this priest, together with her father, were arrested at the same time. Sans Peur had already been condemned to death, and search has been making for him these six years past. He regularly said mass every day, armed with a brace of pistols, and having a sabre and a double-barrelled gun upon the altar!

(141.) On Wednesday evening an affray occurred at Deptford, in consequence of an impress taking place for the navy. A lieutenant and a midshipman of a ship-of-war, laying off Deptford, having *pressed* several men, one of the name of William Jones resisted, and attempted to effect his escape. In the scuffle he received several wounds from the lieutenant, who struck him with his hanger, of which wounds he languished until Friday, when he died at St. Thomas's Hospital. A coroner's inquest brought in a verdict of wilful murder against the lieutenant and midshipman.

(142.) A REMARKABLE attempt was made on Saturday night, about ten o'clock, to commit a robbery upon a dog. This faithful animal it seems is the property of one Person, of Church-street, Bethnal-green, who, working at a factory at Bow, does not return home above once in a month, but has, for a long time past, made a practice of sending his mother half-a-guinea a week by his dog, who has always brought the deposit safe in his mouth. Talking lately of the circumstance in a public-house, a person was induced to stop the animal on Saturday night near his mother's house, when, in making the attempt, he was so much bitten that it is thought he will lose the use of one of his fingers ; and, by the interference of a neighbour, who knew the dog's errand, was obliged to relinquish his fraudulent design.

(143.) WE are sorry to hear of the frequent thefts which are continued to be committed by persons employed in the General and Penny Post Offices, in purloining letters which are supposed to contain bank notes. Not a week passes but numerous frauds of this nature occur. We insert this article as a caution, rather than as a charge of a want of vigilance in the supervisors of this department of Government.

(144.) THE city street hustlers have adopted a new expedient for the purpose of ascertaining what game are worth powder and shot, or, in their own language, "who will pay for drawing." One of the party steps into a banking-house where they appear to be a little busy, and marks those who are receiving considerable sums, and likewise where it is deposited. Such persons are immediately followed out. The signal is given to the rest of the gang, who are waiting in the street, and the first convenient opportunity is embraced for plundering them. If the booty obtained consists of bank notes, all under 20*l.* are circulated by purchasing trifling articles of different tradesmen; when the notes are for large sums, they are immediately disposed of, at a loss of twenty per cent., to a well-known dealer in such articles on Saffron-hill.

(145.) THE five bank notes of 1000*l.* each, which were advertised a few days since in this paper as being recovered, are the property of a banking house whose clerk was robbed of them, in January, 1799, by some street-hustlers, who waylaid him in Lombard-street. A negociation has been carried on almost ever since by an attorney of the name of N——, who was em-employed by these rascals, as it was found dangerous to attempt to negociate notes of so large an amount. At first it was offered to restore them for 500*l.*; that sum being refused the negociation was broken off. On being renewed the attorney demanded 400*l.* more for his trouble. The banking house, finding what a gang it had to deal with, at length paid 900*l.* for the restoration of the property.

(146.) THE quantity of forged notes now in circulation has so increased that the Bank of England have been under the necessity of employing an additional number of inspecting clerks, for the purpose of detecting the bad notes from the good notes. The former chiefly consist in one and five pound notes.

(147.) SOME smugglers, a few nights ago, experienced a serious loss, owing to their signal lights not being properly attended to, near Rottingdean, where a boat, containing 150 tubs of contraband spirits was, on being rowed on shore, seized by the revenue officers in waiting. The crew of a large boat, laden with 450 tubs and packages, to effect their escape, were compelled to throw their cargo overboard, but which, for the most part, was afterwards recovered, by boats belonging to the Custom-house at Shoreham.

(148.) THE churchyard of St. George's in the East was, on Monday morning last, robbed of four bodies. The villains left behind them a scaling-ladder, which was so constructed that it might be carried in a common-sized pocket.

(149.) THERE must be a great diminution in the revenue from the vast number of smugglers, particularly in Sussex and Kent; and it is supposed that one-half the spirits in those counties are smuggled into them, as well as a great quantity of tobacco and other articles.

(150.) THE public has read with horror, from time to time, the trials of barbarous wretches who take apprentices from parishes without giving them sufficient diet, attending to their morals in the smallest degree, or to their health. Avarice and cruelty seem to devote these unhappy children by indentures to famine and to murder. For our own part, we suspect that the present laws are defective, unless the parishes are to blame. Why are not apprenticed children obliged to appear every Sunday at church, and to be examined by proper persons. Cleanliness and proper clothing would thus be extorted from their masters, and these unfortunates would at least have an opportunity to complain of their hunger or their stripes. We presume to recommend this interesting subject to a public, distinguished beyond any competition with other ages or other countries, for humanity and benevolence.

(151.) MARGARET CATCHPOLE, who made her escape from Ipswich gaol, is re-taken. She made for the coast, in hopes of getting on board some smuggling vessel; her dress was that of a complete sailor, for while in prison she had prepared a smock-frock and pantaloons from the sheets of her bed, and had so disguised herself with a queue, round hat, &c., as to be taken for a smart young man.

(152.) NON-RESIDENCE.—It is of the last importance to the welfare of the State that residence in its fullest sense should be performed by the clergy. The amazing increase of Dissenters throughout these kingdoms, which is chiefly owing to this neglect, may be attended with the very worst consequences. The bishops, we are convinced, have the residence of the clergy very much at heart; and the worthy Chief Justice, on a late trial, hinted at the magnitude of the evil, in terms the most direct and pointed. It is hoped, therefore, that the clergy will not be induced by any private selfish motives to omit so important a duty as is this of residence in their parishes, nor delay till they are compelled by the Legislature (which must be soon) to do what they ought to do, from a conscientious regard to the duty which they owe to their God and their country.

(153.) MR. ERSKINE goes down to Chelmsford on a special retainer of 300 guineas, to defend Mr. Williams, a young Cantab, in an action brought against him by Mr. Pepper, a captain of a yeomanry corps in Essex, for assaulting him in discharge of his military duty in keeping the ground clear previous to a review of his corps.

(154.) A SERVANT of the Rev. Rowland Hill very lately died, and his master preached his funeral sermon to a numerous audience; in the course of which he mentioned the following anecdote :—" Many persons present were acquainted with the deceased, and have had it in their power to observe his character and conduct. They can bear witness that I speak the truth when I assert, that for a considerable number of years past he has proved himself a perfectly sober, honest, industrious, and religious man ; faithfully performing, as far as lay in his power, the duties of his station in life, and serving God with constancy and zeal ; and yet this very man, this virtuous and pious man, was once a robber on the highway. More than thirty years ago he stopped me on the public highroad, and demanded my money. Not at all intimidated, I argued with him. I asked him what could induce him to pursue so iniquitous and dangerous a course of life ? ' I have been a coachman, sir,' said he, ' but am now out of place, and not being able to get a character can obtain no employment, and am therefore obliged to resort to this means of gaining subsistence.' I desired him to call upon me ; he promised me he would ; and kept his word. I talked further with him, and offered to take him into my service. He consented, and ever since that period he has served me faithfully, and not me only, but he has faithfully served his God. And instead of finishing his life in a public ignominious manner, with a depraved and hardened mind, as he probably would soon have done, he has died in peace, rejoicing in hope, and prepared, we trust, for the society of just men made perfect. Till this day this extraordinary occurrence has been confined to his breast and mine ; I have never mentioned it even to my dearest friend."

(155.) THAMES POLICE.—THE following remarks taken from Mr. Colquhoun's last publication, appear materially interesting :—

There are two classes of men who are at present great nuisances in the maritime affairs of the river Thames. Those in the first class, consisting of about 100 individuals, are denominated *crimps*.

These men profess to procure seamen for outward bound ships. They frequently lend small sums to the thoughtless mariners, or allow them to run scores at the ale-houses which some of them keep, or get them into their debt for board and lodging. When seamen are wanted, application is made to these crimps. In many instances, where ships have lost men, and are upon the point of sailing, they take the advantage of the captains, who are often strangers, by insisting on an extravagant sum of money being deposited. No other means exist whereby seamen can be procured; the time presses, the ship is on the point of sailing, and the ship masters have no other alternative but to comply. Men are, of course, procured, who frequently run away before three days elapse, when they are required by 2 Geo. II, cap. 36, to sign the agreement, under which the penalties of the law attach for desertion, and the money is then lost, as the crimps pretend the seamen have received it ; although many instances occur where the strongest suspicion is excited that the desertion arises from a preconcerted plan between the crimps and the mariners, that they may, after the ship for which they are intended sails, be enabled, through the same medium, to commit frauds upon others ; but even when this is not the case, the only means of recovering the money from the crimps being by an action-at-law, the process of which is dilatory and tedious, and where an expense must be incurred, in the first instance, to an amount frequently equal to, or more than the sum advanced, strangers decline this mode of seeking justice. The crimps are aware of this, and continue their impositions and frauds with impunity. With a very few exceptions, the chief part consist of men of very loose and abandoned characters, and some who pretend to follow this profession, have actually been discovered to be thieves upon the town, and persons who have been imprisoned on charges of felony, and punished for various offences.

The evil is of great magnitude, since, independent of the money of which shipmaster's are frequently defrauded, commerce and navigation are obstructed in a very considerable degree by the machinations of such miscreants.

The second class of persons who are found in general to be great nuisances, are those who pretend to be *dealers in seamen's wages, and purchasers of prize money*.

The known improvidence of the general run of seamen, seems to require an additional degree of protection against that fraud and pillage, and those gross abuses to which their total ignorance of the means of protecting themselves, their situation, their habits of life, and their thoughtless disposition, expose them.

Unguarded and unprotected as these careless, though useful members of the state are at present, it is scarcely a matter of wonder that they should attract the notice and arrest the attention of those harpies who prey upon the public in a great metropolis, and who are ever to be found in all the principal commercial towns, ready to advance money on assignments being made by seamen of wages due, or to purchase prize money, under circumstances greatly to the disadvantage of the seamen with whom they connect themselves, always injurious to their families, and defeating in the result every means which might be established to secure a provision against old age and infirmities.

The purchasers of seamen's wages and of prize money, are in the habit of going to Gravesend and to the Nore, when fleets arrive, and, having provided boats, they go on board the ships for the purpose of bringing the men on shore that they may avoid the *press*. They charge them an exorbitant price for landing their chests and bedding, and afterwards for concealment. By entertaining them, and furnishing lodging, liquor, and clothes, the seamen get suddenly into debt. They are then arrested, and when locked up, and in distress, compelled to give a will and power to the crimp to receive their wages, prize money, and everything belonging to them in case they should die. The crimp next procures the sailors another ship, for which the captain pays them two guineas crimpage, and a certain sum in addition is paid by the men. When the sailors go upon their new voyage, the crimp receives their wages, prize money, &c., and makes what use of their property he pleases. Instances have been known where a seaman has brought home

40*l*., and in a fortnight after he has been 14*l*. or 15*l*. in debt. Nothing can exceed the oppression which these poor people suffer, by which the crimps make large sums of money, and live in profusion and extravagance.

It is also the practice of these miscreants, besides charging 1*s*. 6*d*. in the pound for the money advanced, to furnish clothes and other necessaries, charging, in many cases, from 50 to 100 per cent. on the actual cost, by which the seamen are suddenly plunged into debt ; and the more so, as men coming from long voyages are generally in want of every necessary ; and in this manner their hard earnings, notwithstanding their high wages, are speedily squandered, to the great injury of themselves and families.

An estimate of the annual plunder on each branch of trade :—

East Indies	25,000
West Indies	232,000
British American Colonies	10,000
Africa and Cape of Good Hope	2,000
North and South Fisheries	2,000
United States of America	30,000
Mediterranean and Turkey	7,000
Spain and Canaries	10,000
France and Netherlands	10,000
Portugal and Madeira	8,000
Holland	10,000
Germany	25,000
Prussia	10,000
Poland	5,000
Sweden	3,000
Denmark	5,000
Russia	20,000
Guernsey, Jersey, Alderney, Isle of Man	2,000
Ireland	5,000
Coasting Trade	20,000
Coal Trade	20,000
Total	461,000
Ship Owners of 13,444 Ships and Vessels lose in Tackle, &c.	45,000
	£506,000

The cant term for sugar, is sand ; ditto for coffee, beans ; ditto for pimento, pease. Rum and other liquors, vinegar. Receivers of the banks of the Thames are called copemen.

DUELLING.

(156.) THE daily Union duels in Ireland are nothing to the late family moonlight diversions at Acton.

(157.) MR. GRATTAN AND MR. CORRY.—The following statement of the affair of honour which took place between the Right Hon. Isaac Corry and Henry Grattan, Esq., is authenticated under the signatures of Major-General Cradock and Captain Metge.

In consequence of what passed in the debate in the House of Commons early on Monday evening, the 17th inst. (February), Major-General Cradock, on the part of Mr. Corry, waited on Mr. Grattan, in the Speaker's chamber, and proposed a meeting immediately on the rising of the House ; to which Mr. Grattan assented. At daylight the gentlemen proceeded to the field, and the ground being taken, the parties fired according to agreement by a word, when Mr. Corry was wounded in the left arm. The gentlemen presented their second pistols, but neither firing on the word, they remained in that situation. After a short pause, the seconds demanded what was the matter, and having given the word again the gentlemen presented a second time, but without firing, each calling on the other to fire : it being evidently the intention of each party not to fire the second shot at the other, Mr. Corry, under these circumstances, proposed aloud to Mr. Grattan, that both should give their honour to fire together upon the word being given again, to which Mr. Grattan agreed : and at the word they both fired together accordingly, after which they quitted the ground, the sheriff having been sometime on the field, using his efforts to prevent the proceedings. In passing from the ground, Mr. Grattan inquired with anxiety of General Cradock, whether Mr. Corry was much hurt. In consequence of such inquiry, and their mutual conduct in the field, General Cradock observed to Mr. Metge that it was to be regretted that the parties had separated without some exchange of compliments ; to which Mr. Metge replied, it was his entire wish that it should take place. Mr. Grattan then proceeded to the house where Mr. Corry was engaged with his surgeon, and they exchanged mutual civilities.

JOHN FRANCIS CRADOCK.
JOHN METGE.

(158). YESTERDAY a meeting took place near Ilford, betwixt R——d L——ce, Esq., and F——d G——n, Esq., when after a discharge of three pistols each, and the latter gentleman being wounded in the shoulder, the seconds interfered, and adjusted the dispute.

(159.) A CIRCUMSTANCE occurred on Friday last, which if it applied to any other than the person to whom it does, would be considered as extraordinary indeed.

Lord Camelford having invited Mr. Peter Abbott to dine with him at his house in Baker-street, on the above day, the conversation turned after dinner on a subject of gallantry, in the course of which something dropped from Mr. Abbott which appears to have given great offence to the noble lord. Nothing, however, passed at the time to give room to suppose that he was offended. He offered to take Mr. Abbott home in his carriage, which was accepted. His lordship had previous to getting into it desired his servant to drive out of town on the Acton road, and he had procured a couple of swords and a brace of pistols to be put into the carriage. When they had got a little distance from town, Mr. Abbott expressed some uneasiness at seeing no lamps, and frequently inquired whither his lordship was taking him. No direct answer was received, but when the carriage reached Acton Green, Lord Camelford told Mr. Abbott that some expressions he had used after dinner, conveyed such a reflection on his character, that he could not suffer them to pass unnoticed; he had accordingly provided himself with swords and pistols, and he insisted on Mr. Abbott's fighting him. There was some struggle between them, but the latter having disengaged himself and got out of the carriage, ran to a farm-house at some little distance from the road, where he perceived a light. Lord Camelford followed him into the house, and some violence ensued. Mr. Abbott, however, got back to town safe, and having consulted with his friends on the steps necessary to be taken, Townsend, the Bow-street officer, was sent with a warrant to apprehend Lord Camelford at his house in Baker-street, on Monday morning last, and having done so, his lordship was carried to Bow-street, and underwent a private examination before Mr. Ford. Some difficulties occurred in respect to the necessary bail to allow of Lord Camelford's discharge, when Lord Valentia and a captain of the navy appeared as bail for him, and the several parties were bound over for his appearance to answer for the assault; Lord Camelford himself in 4,000*l*., and his two sureties in 2,000*l*. each.

PRIZE FIGHTS.

(160.) A MORNING paper of yesterday gives the following shocking detail of brutality respecting a boxing-match, fought on Tuesday, near the gibbet on Wimbledon-common, between a fellow of the name of Gamble, an Irishman, and James, formerly belonging to the Horse Guards, for the stake of 100 guineas. There were depending on this match bets to the amount of 5000*l*.

"The combatants set-to about ten o'clock in the morning; Gamble having for his second Benjamin Stanyard, and Bartholomew for his bottle-holder. James's second was Joe Ward, and his bottle-holder Hall. The two champions fought with astonishing fierceness for the space of fifty minutes, during which they had thirty rounds, when victory declared itself in favour of the Irishman, who was so determined that he fought *seven rounds after his collar-bone had been broken!!!*"

"James vomited a great deal of blood at almost every round towards the conclusion, and was taken for dead from the stage!

"Another battle is shortly to take place between the victorious Gamble and a Bristol man, who lately fought with success, in order to ascertain whether England or Ireland be the most capable of supplying at this time the best pugilist!"

(161.) THE pugilistic contest which is expected to take place on the 20th of the ensuing month (October), between Belcher and Mendoza, excites much attention in the sporting world. The bets are nearly equal.

(162.) BEFORE ten o'clock yesterday morning, above sixty post-chaises and hackney-coaches, containing in the former two or three and in the latter four or six well-dressed gentlemen, passed Hyde-park Turnpike, to be present at the pugilistical conflict between two gentlemen—not of Verona, but of England and Ireland—by names Belcher, a noted pugilist from Bristol, and Gamble, an Irishman. The number of light carts, horsemen, and pedestrians were, as a French general observes, "incalculable." It was wished that His Majesty's press gangs could have been upon the spot.

The battle took place on Wimbledon-common, for 100 guineas a side. The combatants set-to at a quarter before twelve o'clock. Bets to a considerable amount were made on the spot, and the amateurs of boxing never hoped to be better entertained since the days of Broughton and Slack. In this, however, they were much disappointed, for, after one round, the superior skill and dexterity of the Bristol hero was so apparent that any odds was offered against the Irishman. Five rounds more ended the contest, during which Gamble received several knock down blows, and then gave in. The whole time of fighting did not occupy more than a quarter of an hour.

After this battle was over, another took place between a fellow of the name of Caleb Baldwin and an Irishman, a pupil of Gamble's, who shared the fate of his tutor, though not without hard fighting. This defeat of the two Irishmen will long be remembered as a sad disaster among their friends; but it is perhaps a fortunate circumstance for the peace of some parts of London; for had both the Irishmen proved successful, a triumphal entry into the metropolis was planned, and St. Giles's would have been in an uproar for some time to come.

VOLUNTEERS.

(163.) THE total number of Volunteers to be reviewed in Hyde Park to-morrow, amount, according to the returns made to the Commander-in-Chief, to 12,053, being an increase on the last year's muster of nearly 3,000.

The order of review for the Volunteer Corps that are to assemble in Hyde-park on His Majesty's birthday, was published on Friday, by order of His Royal Highness the Commander-in-Chief. The same ground nearly is to be taken as last year, and troops are to form on four sides of a square, the right being placed at the Serpentine River, where it issues out of Kensington Gardens. Under the Duke of York, the Earl of Harrington is to command the line; the four sides of the square are to be commanded by General Burrard, Lord Chatham, Lord Charles Somerset, and General Garth. His Majesty will be on the ground at nine in the morning precisely, and the different corps are directed to assemble between six and seven. A 12-pounder, stationed in the centre, is to give the signal for the different manœuvres. The corps are to fire three volleys from centre to flanks, with pieces elevated, as is usual in firing a *feu de joie*, and are then to give three English cheers, hats and hands waving in the air, drums beating and music playing "God save the King." The different regiments are to pass afterwards in review before His Majesty; and having passed him by three hundred yards, may proceed directly to their quarters or halt in the park, and take up some convenient position at a distance from the main body. Many injunctions are given to preserve order and regularity; and all carriages whatever are prohibited from entering the park. Eighty-six corps are enumerated, and the total number is estimated at 12,053.

(164.) THE RANELAGH CUP.—On Tuesday evening the Volunteers of the metropolis, and the adjacent villages, had a complete trial of skill in Ranelagh Gardens. The cup and cover were of the same value as last year, but being made longer in the pedestal, appeared considerably higher, handsomer, and larger; it held about two bottles. On the centre was engraved the prince's crest, and the motto "Ich dien," and underneath the following inscription:—

"This cup, given by the Proprietors of Ranelagh, in honour of the birthday of His Royal Highness the Prince of Wales, was shot for by Gentlemen, Members of the Volunteer Corps."

Soon after four, the Volunteers began to muster from the following corps, to the number of three hundred and fifty men:—

Royal Westminster.	Portsea.
St. Pancras.	Tower.
St. Margaret and St. John's.	Chelsea.
	St. Saviour's.
Covent Garden.	Dowgate.
Somerset House.	St. James's.
Limehouse.	Kensington.
Kentish Town.	Temple.
Chiswick.	Mary-le-bone.
Pimlico.	St. Andrew's.
Royal Exchange.	Knight Marshal.
Hans Town.	Poplar and Blackwall.
Cornhill.	Fulham.
St. George the Martyr.	Christchurch, Surrey.
Bloomsbury.	Cheap Ward.
St. Olave's.	St. Martin's.
Billingsgate Ward.	St. Clement's Danes.
Finsbury.	St. George's, and other
Islington.	Associations.

A spacious bank had been erected (in that part of the garden where Mount Ætna stood), to which, at five o'clock, was affixed, at the distance of ninety-six yards, a target of eighteen inches diameter, and Captain Silk, of the St. Martin's, appointed umpire. The Volunteers were divided into companies of fifty each; the first division consisted chiefly of the Pimlico, among whom was Wright, the winner of last year, and of whom great expectancies had been formed, but the only ball placed by the whole division was Tubbs's, who continued victor of that, and the succeeding company; but, before the end of the next, two shots were placed by Turner and Brown, which were thought equal, and the opinions concerning their merits various, until No. 197, when Stevenson obliterated all their hopes. At half-past seven the firing closed, and the target being measured, the umpire adjudged the victory to Mr. Stevenson, of the Barners-street division of the Mary-le-bone Association, who was immediately led into the Rotunda, preceded by the band, playing "See the Conquering Hero," where the cup, brimful of claret, was delivered to him by Mr. Charles Ashley.

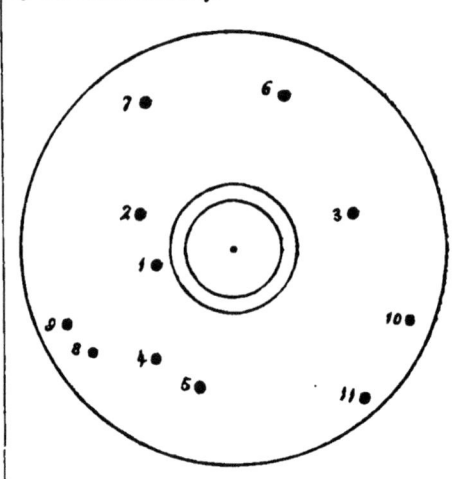

References to the target, with the exact distance of each ball from the centre:—

No.		Ins.
1. Stevenson, Marybone	..	2¼
2. Turner, Islington	..	3¼
3. Brown, Bloomsbury	..	3½
4. Sturt, St. Pancras	..	6¼
5. George, St. Martin's	..	7
6. Bedford, St. George's	..	7¼
7. Freer, Christchurch	..	7½
8. Gill, Kentish Town	..	7¾
9. Adams, St. Andrew's	..	7⅞
10. Tubbs, Pimlico	..	8
11. Wheatley, Limehouse	..	8¼

Exclusive of the Volunteers, there was an assemblage of upwards of fifteen hundred ladies and gentlemen, who, after the conclusion of Rossi's fireworks, formed themselves into sets, and continued dancing until daylight.

(165.) REVIEW OF THE VOLUNTEER CORPS.—Yesterday being the anniversary of His Majesty's birthday, the morning was ushered in by the ringing of bells, and other demonstrations of loyalty and affection. About seven o'clock the Volunteer Corps of the Cities of London and Westminster, and their vicinity, began to assemble in Hyde Park, in order to be reviewed before His Majesty, who entered the park exactly at nine o'clock, at which instant a gun was fired, announcing his arrival.

The morning was dreadfully perverse. It rained incessantly during the whole time of the review; and besides the personal inconvenience to the officers and troops, and to thousands of male and female spectators, whom their loyalty had assembled upon this occasion, it destroyed the effect of one of the grandest spectacles imaginable.

His Majesty was attended in the Park by His Royal Highness the Prince of Wales, the Dukes of York, Clarence, Cumberland, Prince Augustus, and the Duke of Gloucester. Several General Officers, and many of the most distinguished characters in the country, followed in His Majesty's suite.

The whole of the army having passed His Majesty, whose minute attention to each corps in succession was generally observed and admired, they waved their caps and hats, and gave three British cheers. The manœuvres and evolutions were executed with considerable precision, considering the state of the weather, which wetted the muzzles of the musquets. The review ended soon after eleven, and the King waited on the ground till almost every corps had passed out.

Some of the cavalry were thrown from their horses, but none were materially hurt. The ground was completely cleared at a quarter past one o'clock.

His Majesty appeared in high spirits, and several times expressed his perfect satisfaction at the numbers and discipline of men, whose unbought loyalty must prove his firmest support and most glorious safeguard.

(Another account.) The celebration of this day, on which His Majesty entered into his 63rd year, commenced with the grandest sight ever exhibited in Hyde Park. At six o'clock, all the volunteers corps in London and its immediate vicinity, to the number of 12,000, were under arms and assembled in the field before eight, Notwithstanding the immense crowd of spectators, and their impatient curiosity, the ground was most excellently kept by the City Light Horse, the London, Westminster, and Surrey Cavalry. His Majesty arrived at nine, attended by the Prince of Wales, the Dukes of York, Cumberland, and Gloucester, Prince William of Gloucester, Earls Harrington and Chatham, Lord Cathcart, and all the General Officers, &c., and then the review commenced. Although it poured a torrent of rain the whole time, he continued, without even a great coat, equally exposed as his subjects, The only observable difference from his usual conduct, on similar occasions, was, that as he passed the line he did not keep his hat off quite so long as in fine weather. The formation of the line, and the various orders of the day, were executed with precision, and the firing, under every disadvantage, was excellent. The evolutions ended about two. His Majesty and the Princes returned to Buckingham House, then all the corps filed off, after having endured a most soaking rain for upwards of eight hours.

(166.) On Tuesday morning there was a full parade of the Reading Association, in which they went through their usual manœuvres with great spirit. At 3 o'clock they adjourned to the George Inn, where an excellent dinner was given by the privates to the officers. The corps had referred the management of the entertainment to a committee, who performed the pleasing task with a regularity, attention, and politeness which we have never seen exceeded. Many new and loyal toasts were drank, several patriotic tunes were played by the band, and many excellent songs were given; no similar meeting was ever more rationally cheerful or more emblematic of that harmony which ought to pervade all ranks of people at this critical time.

(167.) Two of the Loughborough Volunteers having given in their resignation, and surrendered their arms, the corps have voted them cowards and dastards, that they be sent to Coventry, and their names advertised three times in the Leicester paper.

RIFLES.

(168.) The rifle corps is about to be considerably augmented. The example of other nations renders this necessary. At the same time, it would be infinitely better if the powers of Europe were to agree to banish from use this species of troops. They can produce no real advantage to either party, but introduce into warfare a destructive kind of mutual annoyance, that approaches very near to deliberate murder. It begets very bad moral habits, and is totally different from killing in the heat of action. All humane writers have disapproved it, and in this case it should be abandoned.

HIGH PRICE OF CORN AND DEARNESS OF PROVISIONS.

(169.) BREAD.—Yesterday (31 Dec., 1799), the principals of the Bakers' Company waited upon the Lord Mayor at the Mansion House to set the assize of bread; and it appearing by the returns of the mealweighers that 10,492 quarters and 6 bushels of wheat sold from the 16th to the 21st December, upon an average of 96s. 1¾d. per quarter, and 13,077 sacks of flour sold, from the 21st to the 27th inst., upon an average of 88s. 10d. per sack, his lordship was obliged, according to Act of Parliament, to give the bakers a whole assize, which advances the quartern loaf to 1s. 3d., to commence to-morrow.

(170.) The report of the Committee of the House of Commons in respect to bread, corn, &c., was yesterday printed. It contains much useful information. The result of the enquiries that have been made appears to be, "that the standard wheaten bread should continue to be made; but that the bakers should be prohibited from selling it until twenty-four hours after it is baked." It is a fact, proved by the clearest evidence, that one-half of the bread in London is consumed the day on which it is baked. If bread were kept for twenty-four hours the saving would be from one-third to one-eighth part of the whole consumption.

(171.) A BILL just passed into law, for regulating the price of bread, enacts "That it shall not be lawful for any baker or other person residing within the cities of London and Westminster and the Bills of Mortality, and within 10 miles of the Royal Exchange, after the 26th day of February, 1800, or residing in any part of Great Britain after the 4th March, 1800, to sell, or offer to expose to sale, any bread, until the same shall have been baked 24 hours at least; and every baker, or other person, who shall act contrary hereto, or offend herein, shall, for every offence, forfeit and pay the sum of 5l. for every loaf of bread so sold, offered, or exposed to sale."

(172.) On 20th Feb., resolutions were moved in the House of Peers by his Grace the Archbishop of Canterbury, respecting the scarcity of grain, and an agreement was signed by the great majority of that House, that not more than one quartern loaf per week for each individual in their respective families should be permitted to be consumed; in which agreement the House of Commons most readily concurred."

Bread, and Recommended Substitutes, with Improvements of that in present use.

(173.) SCARCITY, like all other ills, must be boldly contended with in order to be overcome. The new Bread Law will doubtless tend to diminish the consumption of that necessary article: the recommendation to limit each person to a quartern loaf a week, however expedient to be followed, will have very limited operation. A consideration of the necessities of others seldom restricts the enjoyments of the many; and even the best disposed conceive that their individual indulgence cannot operate upon a nation's wants, without considering that the population of a country consists of an aggregate of individuals.

We have seen statements which appeared to us to prove, that the infinite possible saving to be effected, would, even at the present period, be the last advantage derivable from universally making the standard Wheaten Bread. The practice has been tried with success in most parts of Britain, and the only reason we have heard why it has not been adopted in the capital is, that the bran is wanted for pigs and poultry; although grains, and many other things not adapted to human sustenance, are better adapted to pigs than bran, and poultry seldom or perhaps never use it.

It has been ascertained that the entire flour, so strangely obnoxious to some millers and bakers, possesses an oil of high medical virtue, which is lost to society by the present practice. We would not in this instance attribute public inconvenience to the interested machinations of even the convicted delinquents, much less condemn a numerous and respectable body, upon possibly foundless rumour; particularly as many persons of distinguished worth, who, however influenced the sources of their information, are admittedly dispassionate, still doubt the unrefuted reports which direct our judgment. But, waving this consideration, however important we are induced, by an intimate knowledge of its superior excellence in point of health, flavour, lightness, and appearance, to recommend the practice first adopted by Dr. Maunsell, of Limerick, of making bread composed of at least one third boiled potatoes, and the rest of wheat flour; and venture to predict, that nineteen times out of twenty in which the experiment shall be fairly made, it will obtain a decided preference.

Potatoes, though not so abundantly propagated as they ought to be amongst an enlightened people, can yet be bought for a fourth part of the price of flour; such bakers, therefore, as adopt this method, may make rapid fortunes by selling the quartern loaf at 1s., whilst the rest charge for it, as at present, one-third more, provided the existing laws permit the practice. If they do not, the wise and patriotic energy of Lord Auckland, and the other members of each House of Parliament, who brought the important and necessary discussion forward, will, we trust, speedily legalize the measure.

It is stated, that a pound and a half of rice, boiled till soft in five quarts of water, and, whilst warm, mixed with 14 lbs. of flour, will add 7 lbs. to the quantum of bread.

Potatoes boiled, and, whilst warm, mixed by milk with an equal quantity of wheat flour, make paste for pies, &c., and lighter and better than that formed entirely of flour with butter, suet, or dripping.

(174.) THE recommendation made by the Archbishop of Canterbury in regard to bread, goes not only to a certain allowance in the consumption of each person, but to the disuse of all kinds of pastry, until the tenth day of October next. An agreement to this effect has been signed by the Members of both Houses of Parliament.

It is singular that some of the leading members of opposition should affect to doubt, or at least to ask, what is the character and true definition of Jacobinism. It would exceed the limits of our columns to describe and fix the features of this ever-varying monster. It takes every shape to elude and distress the country which it visits.

While the Government, and almost every respectable individual in the kingdom, are occupied in alleviating the evils of scarcity, in checking consumption, in finding substitutes, and above all, in ascertaining the causes and procuring the remedy; while every good man is struggling against a physical evil, and for the safety of the country, the Jacobin is contriving to unite it with moral evil, and to convert it to the public ruin.

Threatening letters have been sent, during the last fortnight, to some of the most eminent persons connected with the corn trade by those Jacobins, who, from the scarcity, neither fear nor feel inconvenience or danger, but hope for riot, commotion, and mischief. The style of the first letters was the coarse imitation of vulgarity and ignorance, which is the characteristic of incendiary menaces. The last letters are couched in precise and even elegant terms. The vigilance, not more than the good sense of the people, makes us scorn these vile and infamous artifices; but, we trust, the authors of the crime will not long escape the vengeance of the Law.

The persons against whom the charge of monopoly is made in these letters, have perhaps been the most useful to the country, by importing foreign corn for the public alleviation. The severity of the season has alone prevented all those importations from arriving.

(175.) WE are told that one cause of the high price of corn is, the consequence of the practice of selling by sample, instead of the corn being fairly brought to market. The middle-man buys the corn, but desires the farmer to keep it for him until he wants it; or, in other words, until he finds the price suits his expectations.

(176.) YESTERDAY the Lord Mayor ordered the price of bread to be raised half an assize, which will make the price of the quartern loaf 17½d. to-morrow.

(177.) THE use of flour for pastry is prohibited by the Royal Family during the present scarcity. Rice is used as a substitute.

(178.) ONLY three ships of coals were brought to market in the course of last week; they sold at the enormous price of 4l. per chaldron.

As the persons concerned in furnishing the metropolis with coals do not choose to supply it at a reasonable rate, it is submitted whether the turf dug from the intended excavation in the Isle of Dogs would not make an excellent substitute.

(179.) SEVERAL of the nobility have adopted the plan of allowing their servants board wages in lieu of bread. We have no doubt but the saving in the consumption of it will be very great, though the plan will not be very profitable to the masters. The waste of bread in large families is known to be prodigious.

(180.) RICE BREAD.—As the article of bread is now a serious object in housekeeping, it may be an acceptable piece of information to the public to learn, that many families have adopted the use of rice in making bread, in the proportion of one-fourth. The rice is previously boiled for ten or twelve minutes in three times its weight of water, which is put to it cold. Thus, ten pounds and a-half of flour, the quantity used in three quartern loaves, when made into dough, with a pound and a-half of what the baker calls sponge, will knead up with three pounds and a-half of whole rice so prepared, and the produce will be six loaves instead of four. Hereby a saving will be made of threepence in the quartern loaf, valuing the rice at sixpence per pound, after paying the baker amply for his trouble, and the consumption of the oven will be reduced nearly one-half. The bread is very palatable, lighter, and whiter than wheaten bread.

(181.) NOTHING can be more proper than that the fares of hackney coaches should be raised while the price of fodder is so dear. We trust, however, that a clause should be introduced into the Bill now before Parliament, compelling the coach-masters to keep better cattle and cleaner coaches.

(182.) GREAT fears were, on Saturday, entertained of disturbances in the markets, on account of the high price of provisions. They were general over the town. The City and Westminster light horse, and the horse guards, were ordered to hold themselves in readiness to act, should occasion require; a detachment of the latter patrolled the streets at the west end of the town till a late hour at night.

(183.) YESTERDAY the Lord Mayor ordered the price of bread to be raised one whole assize, which will make the price of the quartern loaf to-morrow 18d.

(184.) IT is near three months since some regulations were in agitation to obtain a better supply of fish, and yet the markets are neither cheaper nor is the quantity greater. That it ought to be otherwise is undeniable. At this season turbot might be caught in great abundance. Our ships of war upon the Dutch coast almost live upon fish. Admiral Duncan's fleet had at times such quantities of turbots and soles served out that the men used to throw the latter overboard.

We have, upon a former occasion, suggested the idea of the Marine Society employing vessels to procure fish, as the same system of forestalling is in some degree practised in respect to fish as of cattle, to keep up the price. It is a fact, that the increased price of butcher's meat is an additional expense to Government of near 2,000l. a-day for the navy only. We therefore recommend that Government should furnish vessels to the Marine Society. It is in vain to expect that those who look for great profits will ever countenance any plan to introduce greater supplies of fish; but the Marine Society would. Unless this business is undertaken by some popular society or body of men, who have no other view than the general good, impediments will be constantly thrown in the way and defeat the object.

(185.) WE regret, that notwithstanding the exertions of government, the price of provisions continues to increase. With the most anxious solicitude for the comforts of the poor, every method has been adopted which wisdom could suggest to defeat the regraters and forestallers. The farther rise of bread cannot fail to excite the most serious attention, more especially, if true, that upwards of twenty ships laden with corn, have remained in the river more than a fortnight for want of warehouse room to receive their cargoes.

(186.) IF the *millers* were actuated by a proper regard for their country, respecting the new Bill, they would not shew that, with them at least, it goes so much *against the grain*.

(187.) THE noble and learned judge who is at the head of the criminal justice of the kingdom, as soon as the jury had returned a verdict of Guilty, in the case of the regrater, informed them that they had conferred a benefit upon the country greater than any jury had ever done before. We subscribe entirely to the opinion of the Chief Justice. A greater crime never yet existed, nor is there any to be compared with it in the extent of its mischievous operation. It is many months since we ventured to express our opinion respecting the doctrine of Dr. Adam Smith upon this important subject. That great man, who has been too implicitly followed by the zeal of his disciples, would have been the first to retract his advice, if he could have witnessed the practical evils which have so abundantly flowed from its adoption. Not only has the crime itself, in a great degree, been qualified or concealed from the eyes of the offender, but the wrongs of the people have been aggravated by the insult of hearing their sufferings denied, and their alarms compared to superstition and witchcraft. It is to be hoped that by this conviction the whole race of middle-men will be driven from every market, and that no addition of price will be allowed, under any form or pretence, to be added between the seller and the consumer.

The practice of selling by sample is perhaps the greatest evil that ever man endured. Were the whole of the commodity brought in bulk to market, not only would the purchaser see the state of it at once, but the seller would rather content himself with just and moderate profits, than be at the expense of removal and return.

(188.) ARTICLES of daily consumption, such as fish, fruit, &c., cannot be resold without a crime. He who buys them for anything but his own consumption is a forestaller, and ought not to be tolerated. The French markets are admirably regulated. A particular spot is appropriated to every commodity, and nothing is allowed to be sold in detached shops, which are all regrates by profession. The hours of sale are fixed by law, as well as the removal of purchases; and a register is kept of them by a public officer in the markets. It is to be hoped we shall not long have to deplore the present wretched system, which exposes the people to every species of imposition, and dashes the cup of plenty from their mouths.

(189.) IF a man would buy a piece of plate, or a carriage, a tolerable bargain, he looks out for it second hand. How lucky is he who can purchase a bit of fish, or a joint of meat third or fourth hand, though every hand it passes through is an addition to the price he must pay for it! It will be found on oath, that corn has been sold six times at the same market, perhaps to be sold in as many new ones. Could we know how many wretches have been the proprietors of every morsel of bread we put into our mouths, how many speculators have owned the joint upon our table, how many remorseless hands have screwed so tight the machine of scarcity and extortion, it would be more disgusting than the evil itself. But how else to come at a remedy?

(190.) THE verdict given against Mr. Waddington, at Worcester, for forestalling hops, joined to those which have lately been given against the regraters of corn, will, we hope, go some length towards destroying these iniquitous practices.

(191.) Warrants have been issued for the apprehension of twelve regraters and forestallers at Sheffield.

(192.) A QUAKER, who is a large miller, in the neighbourhood of Dartford, has been hanged in effigy on that road, by the mob.

(193.) As the price of oats and straw are now reduced to the usual standard in times of plenty, we trust that the charge of inn-keepers, and particularly of posting and stage-coaches, will also be reduced without delay. Sixteen-pence a mile posting is now an immoderate profit, and ought no longer to be submitted to.

(194.) ON Saturday several large waggon loads of bread were sold at Brentford, and other places, at only one shilling a loaf. Although we cannot recommend this plan of buying cheap bread, of which it is impossible to know the quality of the ingredients, yet it is evident that the price of bread ought to be much cheaper than it now is, and that the high price of flour bears no proportion to that of wheat.

(195.) SINCE the reduction of the price of bread, great numbers of the bakers in and about the metropolis have, in defiance of the Act of Parliament, sold bread new baked, and some have even delivered it to their customers quite warm. Others have sold hot rolls. We hope that as the Act is still in force, they may be made to pay the penalty.

(196.) IT is very necessary to guard the public in its just indignation against the regraters, from confounding these pernicious criminals with the importers of corn. Two more distinct and opposite classes of men cannot be found in society. The first starves, but the second nourishes the people. The speculation of the one is to stint, of the other to fill the market; and if we are not absolutely at the merciless mercy of the former, it is because we are assisted and relieved by the enterprise of the last.

(197.) WE observe with pleasure that a general spirit prevails in all parts of the country to put the law in force against forestallers, regraters, &c. Butter factors, pig jobbers, higlers, and all description of middlemen, as they are called, are narrowly watched, and prosecuted if found offending—and none of these are permitted to purchase in markets till the inhabitants are supplied. Baron Hotham concluded his charge to the grand jury at Norwich, with noticing the practice of forestallers and regraters, declaring that those who dragged forth those pests to society, to justice, deserved the commendation of every part of the community.

(198.) INGROSSING AND FORESTALLING. — Amongst the laws of Ethelstan, in the Saxon times, there was an ancient law for preventing ingrossing and forestalling, by which no person was to sell any commodity of more than twenty-pence in value, out of the neighbourhood of any town; but within the gates of the town, in the presence of the municipal officer of the town, or some other trusty person, or the King's commissioner, in places most frequented by the people, and every merchant openly in the sight of the public.

At the time of the Conquest, all cattle are prohibited from being purchased, unless within cities and in the presence of three trusty witnesses, nor any other necessaries, without security and warranty, &c., nor shall any market or fair be permitted except within the cities and towns of our kingdom.

In the 25th of Edw. III, Robert Hadham was committed to prison, removed from every office under the King, and fined for selling corn in sheaves, before it was threshed and measured. This sale, as recorded (Rot. 13 Buck. Hadham's case, Hil. 25, E. III), was contrary to the law and custom of England.

By the 25th of Henry VIII, cap. 2, the Lords of the Council, Justices, &c., or any seven of them, have power to set prices on victuals; and the same to be proclaimed under the Great Seal. —Query if this law be repealed.

(199.) THE artificers, &c. of the dockyard at Portsmouth, have published a paper in which, after reprobating all idea of rioting or violation of property, they subscribe the resolution "That we and our families will abstain from making use of any butter, cream, milk, and potatoes, when the market price of butter shall exceed 9d. per pound, cream in proportion, milk at 2d. per quart, and potatoes at 6d. per gallon."

(200.) THE ancient laws which are now resorted to against regraters, &c., were the common law of the Anglo-Saxons; but they were then, as they are now, too tedious and expensive; the proceeding by indictment also gives too much time to strike the necessary terror in the marble hearts of the offenders. Therefore very early in the history of the statute law (Edward I), summary Acts were made, vesting the power of punishing the criminal in the hands of the magistrates, two forming a quorum in a summary. Our ancestors reasoned wisely when they perceived that the enormity injured society immediately, therefore let the punishment and the terror of it fall upon the head of the criminal immediately. In almost every King's reign, until Edward VI, those laws were extended and confirmed; and in the 5th and 6th of this King, they were all collected together, and formed one grand bulwark to dispense plenty to the people. For a long series of years those black crimes were known only by name; and during the long reign of Elizabeth, not one complaint on conviction took place,—a convincing proof of itself that the crimes did not exist at that period.

Thus those salutary laws continued till the year 1772, the 12th of George III, when "in an evil hour," as Lord Kenyon and the other judges deem it, all those wise, humane, and just laws were repealed, after having stood the test of time from 1272 to 1772, exactly five hundred years. It was the last act but *one* that was passed, in a very thin House, by the same Parliament that entered into the American War.

(201.) THE inhabitants of Newbury have resolved to discontinue the use of butter, until the price shall have fallen to 1s. per pound.

(202.) ON Wednesday, one of the artificers in Portsmouth dockyard was *horsed* by his comrades for purchasing potatoes, butter, and milk, at a price above those stipulated in their late agreement. Having carried him with every possible indignity, they turned him out of their *fraternity*.

(203.) RIOTS IN LONDON.—We are concerned to learn that the mob continued to commit several acts of violence after our paper was put to press on Monday night. About eleven o'clock the mob proceeded to the house of Mr. Rusby, in Blackfriar's-road, one of the gentlemen who was sometime since convicted in the Court of King's Bench for regrating corn. It is evident, from the proceedings of this party, that they must have had some person among them to direct their movements, above the common order of the lower class of people. Their march was very systematic and cautious. Two men preceeded them along the road, who broke every lamp as they passed, for fear of being recognized. The men knocked at the door next to Mr. Rusby's, and inquired which was his house. They were told that he was lately come into the neigbourhood, and they could not say which was his house. The mob said, if they would not tell, they should revenge themselves on that house, and the signal was given to begin breaking the windows. Upon this the mob was informed that Mr. Rusby's house was next door. They knocked at it, and Mrs. Rusby looked out of the window and inquired what they wanted. She prayed in God's name that they would not hurt her children, who were in bed; they said they had no intention to do so, but they enjoined her and her children to be dressed within a prescribed period, or they must take the consequences, as they were determined to demolish the house. In this interval, Mr. Rusby escaped out of a back door, and as soon as Mrs. Rusby was dressed, the mob opened a line for her and her children to pass out. They then entered the house, broke the windows and all the furniture. This outrage caused so much alarm, that notice was sent to the War Office, and a detachment of the Guards and a party of the horse were ordered out, who soon cleared the road. This took place between one and two o'clock. The parish association was also under arms about three, but by that time all was quiet.

Another party of the mob proceeded about ten o'clock from Mark-lane, over London-bridge, into the Borough, where they attacked the house of Citizen Weaver, a cheesemonger, in the Borough. It appears that they had notice that this shopkeeper had within the last few days caused a large quantity of hams and cheeses to be thrown into the Thames, on account of their having been kept so long as to become unsaleable. The populace, therefore, proceeded to inflict vengeance on his house, the windows of which were demolished, as well as the greater part of the furniture.

Being given to understand that the mob intended to return to his house yesterday evening, Mr. Weaver went early in the morning before a magistrate, and made an affidavit of the circumstances of the transaction, of which the mob had had notice. This affidavit was immediately printed, and stuck up about the Borough; and declared, that the hams and cheeses had come from Embden, but being long on the voyage, they had been damaged. He had bought them in order to retail to the poor at reduced prices, but before they could be sold, they became nearly putrescent.

Notwithstanding this notice, the mob began to assemble about dusk, near Mr. Weaver's house in the Borough; and about eight o'clock near 5,000 persons were collected. The City Light Horse Volunteers, the Surrey Yoomanry, and the Southwark Volunteers soon appeared under arms, and although they took every means to persuade the mob to disperse, they were not attended to, as it was perceived that those gentlemen did not wish to go to extremities. All they could do was to keep the mob from attacking Mr. Weaver's house.

Finding the mob would not disperse, application was made at the War Office for a party of Dragoon Guards, who, as soon as they arrived, gave no quarter, and in a few minutes not twenty people were to be seen together. At ten o'clock the streets were quiet, and we have reason to hope that we shall hear no more of similar excesses, which, from whatever causes they may proceed, cannot be tolerated.

The Exchange Gates, during the early part of yesterday morning, were shut, to muster the ward associations; and all the different corps in and about London were ordered to be under arms at five o'clock in the afternoon. They not only patrolled about the metropolis, but round every part of it, keeping up a regular link of communication.

(204.) MANY riots occurred in London and some of the provinces in consequence of the high price of bread and other provisions. The mob were particularly embittered against the regraters and forestallers who were considered as increasing the evil by their avarice.

Combe, Mayor.

(205.) A COURT of Lord Mayor and Aldermen, held at the Guildhall of the city of London, on Tuesday, the 16th day of September, 1800:

Resolved unanimously, That it is the opinion of this Court, from the best information it has been able to procure, that had not the access to the corn-market been yesterday impeded, and the transactions therein interrupted, a fall in the price of wheat and flour much more considerable than that which actually took place, would have ensued; and this Court is further of opinion, that no means can so effectually lead to reduce the present excessive prices of the principal articles of food, as the holding out full security and indemnification to such lawful dealers as shall bring their corn or other commodities to market. And this Court does therefore express a determination to suppress at once, and by force if it shall unhappily be necessary, every attempt to impede by act of violence the regular business of the markets of the metropolis.

(*Dublin, Sept.* 16.)

(206.) THE Lord Mayor and Court of Aldermen being determined, as far as in them lie, to bring to speedy and condign punishment all and every person and persons who shall be found acting as factor or middleman for the sale of provisions within the said city or liberties thereof, or interfering in any manner between the buyer and seller of such provisions, brought or intended to be brought for sale to any of the public cranes or markets thereof, have issued a proclamation offering a reward of 20*l*. (over and above any penalties given by any law) to any person who shall within three calendar months, give information against any person or persons guilty of said offence, or any of them, so that they may be prosecuted to conviction.

The Lord Mayor and Court of Aldermen require the several clerks of the markets and peace officers, and all others, to be aiding and assisting in bringing before them all persons who shall be found committing any of the offences aforesaid in law.

(207.) WE understand that the cow-keepers have held several meetings of late, in order to enhance the price of milk 1*d*. per quart. This exorbitant and unjust demand was intended to have commenced yesterday had not some parishes summoned meetings of the inhabitants to resist the imposition. Perhaps there is no class of persons who supply London with articles of the first necessity who ought to be more circumspect in their demands than the cow-keepers. There has already been a rise in the article of milk twice within these three years; and the present luxuriant pastures about London furnish but a very bad argument for the necessity of a further enhancement at present.

While we are upon the subject of milk, it may not be thought irrelevant to draw the public attention to the article of butter, which is kept up wholly by that baneful spirit of forestalling and the buying up of the dairies, instead of allowing their produce to come fairly to market, of which we have so often complained. Why not call parochial meetings, as has been done in many parts of the country, engaging not to buy butter beyond a certain rate? If the metropolis allows itself to be so imposed upon it deserves to bear its burthens.

(208.) THE cow-keepers declare that they are obliged to raise the price of milk, because they cannot lower the quality any further. They are ready to make oath, that one-third of all the mixture they sell is genuine milk, which therefore costs to the consumer no more than 1*s*. per quart. Butter at 1*s*. 6*d*. the pound offers a better profit, and the public must either pay the price they demand for their composition or drink their tea without milk and water.

(209.) FORESTALLING, ENGROSSING, AND REGRATING.—As the above offences are at all times, and more especially at the present moment, of a very serious nature, we shall lay before the public what Judge Blackstone says of them.

"The offence of forestalling the market is an offence against public trade. This, which (as well as the two following) is also an offence at common law, was described by Statute 5 and 6 Edward VI, ch. 14, to be the buying or contracting for any merchandise or victual coming in the way to market; or dissuading persons from bringing their goods or provisions there; any of which practices make the market dearer to the fair trader.

"Regrating was described by the same Statute to be the buying of corn, or other dead victual, in any market and selling it again in the same market or within four miles of the place. For this also enhances the price of provisions, as every successive seller must have a successive profit.

"Engrossing was also described to be the getting into one's possession or buying up large quantities of corn, or other dead victuals, with intent to sell them again. This must, of course, be injurious to the public, by putting it into the power of one or two rich men to raise the price of provisions at their own discretion. And so the total engrossing of any other commodity, with an intent to sell it at an unreasonable price, is an offence indictable and fineable at common law. And the general penalty for these three offences by the common law (for all the Statutes concerning them were repealed by the 12th Geo. III, ch. 74), is, as in other minute misdemeanours, discretionary fine and imprisonment. Among the Romans, these offences and other malpractices to raise the price of provisions were punished by a pecuniary mulct."

(210.) In consequence of some inflammatory handbills posted about the metropolis, inviting this day a mob on Kennington Common, the Life Guards were ordered out. The volunteer corps were also stationed in the environs. The police officers, in case of disturbance, attended at the Axe and Gate in Downing-street, and the following handbill was circulated:

"To the Public.
"Sunday, November 9, 1800.

"Whereas an inflammatory handbill has been distributed and posted up, inviting every journeyman, artizan, mechanic, and tradesman, every manufacturer, labourer, &c., to meet this day on Kennington Common under pretence of petitioning the King and Parliament; and whereas there is reason to apprehend that such meeting would, from its circumstances, endanger the public peace: Notice is hereby given, that the magistrates have taken measures to prevent any number of persons from assembling in consequence of such handbill; and all well-disposed persons are exhorted to abstain from going to such meeting, and to return peaceably to their houses, avoiding the hazard which they must incur by joining in any tumultuous proceedings."

(211.) The Society of Quakers have declared their sentiments in a manner which does them the greatest honour. They have addressed the public in an advertisement, declaring their abhorrence of adding to the high price of the articles of life by forestalling and regrating in the markets, and that they will discountenance any one of their Society who shall be guilty of such nefarious practices.

(212.) Various are the opinions that have been offered respecting the best means of keeping down the price of provisions in the metropolis. Perhaps it would be among the best remedies, to pass an Act of Parliament imposing a most severe fine on every builder who shall build upon another acre of meadow land within a certain distance of the metropolis.

(213.) Among the discussions upon the price of corn there has been advanced a proposition which cannot be too seriously reviewed—"that the dearness of it will lessen its consumption." The observation might be true, if its application was made to articles not of daily and absolute necessity; but it never ought to obtain the established reputation of an axiom. It is neither a benevolent nor wise policy that has made the assertion. Interested men could not have suggested a language more ingeniously calculated to protect their crimes and extortion.

The poor man must have bread. It is his first, his last subsistence. Let the price be ever so exorbitant, this food he must be supplied with or he starves. It is the only one thing needful in this world, without which if he is compelled to live but a single day he suffers in his physical constitution and his moral happiness. It is not that the labouring classes eat less bread when it is dear, but that they are constrained to relinquish all other requisites to their comfort to obtain this one. The butcher, the greengrocer, the cheesemonger, and the dealers in low wearing apparel may tell you that dearness lessens the consumption of their articles. These things the poor can and, unhappily, must forego for a time, but their common quantity of daily bread they must have, however high the price, or, if unable to obtain it, they will sicken in their health, spirits, and temper, and decay in their capacity for labour, as is exemplified in every garrison town where the allotment of this food is reduced below the demands of nature.

By the King.—A Proclamation.
George R.

(214.) Whereas an address has been presented to us by our two Houses of Parliament, requesting us to issue our royal proclamation, recommending to all such persons as have the means of procuring other articles of food, the greatest economy and frugality in the use of every species of grain. We, having taken the said address into consideration, and being persuaded that the prevention of all unnecessary consumption of corn will furnish one of the surest and most effectual means of alleviating the present pressure, and of providing for the necessary demands of the year, have, therefore, in pursuance of the said address, and out of our tender concern for the welfare of our people, thought fit (with the advice of our Privy Council) to issue this our royal proclamation, most earnestly exhorting and charging all those of our loving subjects who have the means of procuring other articles of food than corn, as they tender their own immediate interests, and feel for the wants of others, to practise the greatest economy and frugality in the use of every species of grain. And we do, for this purpose, more particularly exhort and charge all masters of families to reduce the consumption of bread in their respective families, by at least one-third of the quantity consumed in ordinary times, and in no case to suffer the same to exceed one quartern loaf for each person in each week; to abstain from the use of flour in pastry, and, moreover, carefully to restrict the use thereof in all other articles than bread. And do also, in like manner, exhort and charge all persons who keep horses, especially horses for pleasure, as far as their respective circumstances will admit, carefully to restrict the consumption of oats and other grain for the subsistence of the same. And we do hereby further charge and command every Minister, in his respective parish church or chapel, within the Kingdom of Great Britain, to read, or cause to be read, Our said proclamation, on the Lord's Day, for two successive weeks after receipt of the said proclamation.

Given at our Court at St. James's, the 3rd day of December, 1800, in the 41st year of Our reign.

God save the King.

(215.) THE number of coach and post horses in this Kingdom use as much corn as would keep about 1,000,000 persons, at a quartern loaf each person per week.

(216.) WE are extremely glad to find that the law will only permit one kind of bread in future. Nothing short of this compulsion could be effectual. The bread thus made is what is generally eaten in the country, and is equally nutricious, and in our opinion far more palatable than the common London bread.

(217.) CONSPIRACIES have been set on foot by journeymen of various trades, to enforce an augmentation of wages, which have been very properly resisted by the masters, and repressed by the magistrates. As the case of some of them is to be tried by appeal at the Quarter Sessions, we shall abstain at present from any particular reflections. In general, however, we do not conceive the high price of provisions to fall with that degree of severity upon any of those classes of men, which (compared with the lower mechanic and the agricultural labourer) can authorize even complaint in their mouths.

They do not certainly bear more than their share of the general pressure, and if every man who feels the burthens of these times is to revolt from his employment, and to discontinue his industry, society is disorganized at once. We trust, the journeymen, whose wages appear to be at least three times those of the laborious men who produce corn for them, will acknowledge their indiscretion, and return to their duty at once. Let them compare their lot with that of so many of their fellow-creatures, and then say whose wounds ought to be dressed first.

(218.) A COMMON practice prevails in the hay markets for gentlemen's servants, when they purchase hay, to make the seller add 5s. to the price for their trouble in buying. By these means hay is daily advanced in the markets, and on the roads about London.

(219.) IT is impossible to consider the universal frauds of trade without horror, or the sanction they have derived where it was least to be expected without indignation and disgust. But there is no part of them that requires correction more urgently than the practice of tradesmen corrupting the servants of their customers. The Coachmaster rewards the servant who brings his master's carriage for repairs. The Farmer overcharges his hay, in order to leave 5s. to the coachman who buys it. If you buy or sell a horse, the groom has a profit. In our houses it is the same, the upper servant is the pensioner of our butcher, baker, &c. What then? Have not these men a right to gain as much as they can? Does not the public good result from their private profit? We trust the commercial casuists will explain this to the nation a little more at large.

SCIENCE.

(220.) IN France, as in England, there have been disputes about the commencement of the 18th century. The Astronomer Lalande thus determines the question, which he says was equally agitated at the end of the last century, he having in his library a pamphlet published on the subject. "Many persons," says he, "imagine that because after having counted 17 they commence 18, that the century must be changed, but this is a mistake, for when 100 years are to be counted, we must pass from 99 and we arrive at 100, we have changed the 10 before we have finished the 100. Whatever calculation is to be made, we commence by 1 and finish by 100; nobody ever thought of commencing at 0 and finishing by 99." Thus he concludes that the present year 1800 incontestibly belongs to the 18th century.

(221.) YESTERDAY the Society of Arts, Manufactures, and Commerce, distributed before a numerous assemblage of persons of distinction of both sexes, at their house in the Adelphi, their annual rewards to the successful candidates for the year 1799. His Grace the Duke of Norfolk, as President, in delivering the gold medals paid Thomas Johnes, M.P., and the Rev. H. B. Dudley, particular compliments, the former for clothing a wild and barren waste in Wales, with plantations of forest trees; and the latter, for spiritedly augmenting, not his own hereditary estate, but the church demesne of St. Paul's Cathedral, by regaining as their lessee, a large portion of valuable land from the sea.

(222.) A SOCIETY, under the title of "The Royal Institution of Great Britain," and under the patronage of His Majesty, commenced its sittings for the first time, this day. Its professed object is to direct the public attention to the arts, by an establishment for diffusing the knowledge and facilitating the general introduction of useful mechanical inventions and improvements.

(223). THE Admiralty Board has given orders for the general introduction of the cow-pock into the navy.

(224.) THE state of the paper trade is truly distressing. The price of double demy is advanced lately 20s. a bundle, and single demy 10s., printing paper. We understand it arises from the great scarcity of rags, and the great price given for them. As this is a serious evil, it behoves Government to take the matter into consideration, and as they have loaded paper with such heavy duties, particularly printing paper, by remitting a part of the duty till the price of rags is reduced ; the paper-makers, knowing the state of the market, make the article much thinner, as the duty is laid on the weight instead of the bundle.

(225.) In consequence of the increasing price of paper, the booksellers and authors of works have stopped the press ; and by an agreement among the proprietors of paper-mills, the latter have consented not to buy any rags till all the stock they have in hand is worked up. Rags are now fallen 18*l.* per ton ; yet single demy for printing newspapers has risen 50*l.* per cent. within the last three months. It plainly appears there is a combination, either among the dealers in London or the paper-makers in the country, to enhance the price, otherwise paper would not rise in price, when the article of which it is made has fallen so considerably.

(226.) THE secret of extracting print from paper, and reducing volumes to rags, threatens cruelly the reputation of many a writer. It has been proposed in the Republic of Letters, that a Directory be elected, to whom this branch of the Executive of Parnassus shall be delegated. As soon as a book is published, these officers are to be solemnly assembled, in order to determine upon oath, whether it shall remain paper or be reduced to rags again. But as the flimsiest performances will return most readily to their original state, a drawback will be allowed to gentlemen poets and lady novel-writers. Hot-press and wire-drawn are subject to a small duty. But any author making affidavit that he verily believes no single person ever read the whole of his work, may receive its full value in clean paper, and begin another book as if nothing had happened.

By the new invention, books seems to run as great a risk of being reduced to rags as the authors of them.

(227.) YESTERDAY was presented to his Majesty at the levee, by the Marquis of Salisbury, a book printed on the first paper which has ever been made from straw alone, containing a succinct but general historical account of the substances which have been used to describe events, and to convey ideas, from the earliest date to the invention of paper, of an elegant transparent texture, which possesses all the qualities of the finest writing paper fabricated from rags.

The loose sheets indubitably demonstrate that paper may be made from straw alone in the highest state of perfection. It is regarded as a valuable discovery, and of great national importance ; and the ingenious inventor highly deserves the public esteem and support.

(228.) THE system of inoculating from the cow-pox is about to be introduced into most parts of Europe. Two physicians have lately sailed on board one of H.M. ships of war for Naples.

(229.) DR. MARSHAL has pursued his tour in the Mediterranean, inoculating the cow-pox with the success which has attended the discovery everywhere else. After being at Minorca, where the army and navy were equally eager to profit by it, the Doctor returned to Gibraltar Bay, where Lord Keith's fleet was, and where he was received with great kindness and attention. On board the fleet, as well as at Minorca, the cow-pox inoculation was practised with the usual safety and success. At Gibraltar the cow-pox has now become general. Dr. Walker still remains at Minorca, from whence he proceeds to Malta, where he will be met by Dr. Marshal, who then proceeds to Palermo, and, if circumstances permit, to Naples, spreading the benefits of the discovery.

(230.) MANY unfounded reports having been circulated, which have a tendency to prejudice the mind of the public against the inoculation of the cow pox ; we, the undersigned physicians and surgeons, think it our duty to declare our opinion, that those persons who have had the cow pox, are perfectly secure from the infection of the small pox, provided this infection has not been previously communicated.

We also declare, that the inoculated cow pox is a much milder and safer disease than the inoculated small pox.

William Saunders, M.D.	John Abernethy.
J. C. Lettsom, M.D.	Henry Cline.
Alex. Crichton, M.D.	Astley Cooper.
Thomas Denman, M.D.	And many others.

(231.) A FRENCH philosopher has lately published some serious apprehensions which he entertains respecting the limited duration of the universe. The globe, he thinks, will cease to exist when the radical humour which fructifies it shall cease to be any longer productive. The period at which this is to happen is fixed by him in the year 168,123. This is a very *serious* circumstance of alarm ; particularly as the theorist has established his assertion by the most irrefragable proofs drawn from observations on shells and petrifactions.

(232.) IT is a most curious circumstance in the natural history of the present year, that, notwithstanding the long continuance of dry and warm weather, we have had fewer insects than in any year within memory. Wasps have scarcely been seen, and the common fly is not numerous. Bees, under the care of man, have thrived beyond all example ; but the wild bee has shared the fate of other insects. We have heard this accounted for by an observation, that in April we were visited from the north-east by miriads of very small insects, which devoured the eggs of our native tribes, along with other perceptible ravages which they committed in the field, and that they died themselves as the warmth encreased. We leave it to naturalists to ascertain the truth of this fact.

(233.) AN experiment was lately tried at Rouen upon a new invented Diving Machine, called Bateau-Poisson, or Fish-boat. This boat sunk of itself seven or eight times, and then rose of itself

The longest time it remained under water was eight minutes. The descent into the inside of this machine is, by an opening made in the form of a tunnel, which is about a demi-metre above the surface of the water. When those who conducted the experiment wished to descend altogether into the river, and disappear, they let down this opening, sunk entirely under the water, and lost all communication with the external air. The inventors of this ingenious machine are Americans, the principal of whom is called Fulton. Three of them went into the boat, and remained during the experiment. The prefect and a vast concourse of spectators were present.

(234.) THE method of accumulating force by an application of water on the hydrostatic principle, lately invented by Mr. Bramah, of Piccadilly, is perhaps a discovery of as much importance as any of which former ages have to boast. The utility of such an extraordinary contrivance can know no bounds; not only as it supersedes the necessity of combining the mechanic powers, but renders even their simple application unnecessary in almost every instance. It is well known to those conversant in mechanics on the old principle, that no given active power can be applied with effect after the friction of the apparatus becomes a balance to it; and, on this account, when the power and the weight bear a very distant proportion the machine becomes complicated, ponderous, and unapplicable beyond a certain very limited degree. In this new system the case is otherwise, for by pursuing one simple method, without any variation, but of proportion, the smallest active power can be made to balance and overcome, or give motion to, the greatest passive or resisting force within the limits of practice. Great variety of machines have already been made, the surprising effects of which, with a primum mobile very inconsiderable, have proved the great usefulness of the invention beyond dispute. One of the most remarkable is, a machine used by the Rt. Hon. Lord Penryhn, at his slate-rock, near Penmanmuer, in North Wales; by the help of this apparatus, which is extremely simple, various masses of slate have been forced from the rock and thrown down, with the power of one man only, each mass not weighing less than between three and five hundred tons. However prodigious this may seem its authenticity may be relied on, and there can now be little doubt but man may accomplish any object it becomes him to encounter, where force is necessary for the purpose,—rocks may be rent, trees easily forced up by the roots, timber, iron, &c., readily broken or bent into any shape, and every kind of operation for expressing oils, compressing cloths, paper, and other elastic substances, and for compact baling, &c., of all sorts of goods, performed in a manner greatly superior to any former contrivance for those purposes.

(235.) ON Thursday, the 24th instant (July), at a few minutes past eight o'clock in the evening, as a party were returning from the survey of a considerable public work, which is intended to extend through the county of Surrey, they discovered a balloon of the Montgolfier kind gradually descending; they traced it till it settled in an orchard, close to the farm-house of Mrs. Batts, at West Barns. It is elegantly ornamented with purple, yellow, and white stripes, and a bandeau of blue silk round the bottom, on which is inscribed "Haldiman, Clapham Common." It has received very little damage, and is deposited at West Barns House till claimed by its owner.

(236.) WATCHES set in rings have become very common. The face of them is about the size of a sixpence, and many of them are very pretty; but they are rather too clumsy as the ornament of a ring.

(237.) THE animal flower seems a close link between the sensitive plant and the oyster. Since the discovery of the animal flower, the female botanists have redoubled their application in their favourite study of the "Loves of the Plants."

Some persons have thought that the animal flower, which hides itself at the approach of a stranger, was only a bold metaphor for the flour of some of our monopolizers and regraters.

(238.) FROM the first day of March last there has been a difference of twelve days between the old and new styles, instead of eleven, as formerly, owing to the regulations of the Act for altering the style, passed in 1752; according to which, the year 1800 was only to be accounted a common year, and not a leap year, as it otherwise would have been. In consequence of this alteration, old Lady-day will be April 6, old Midsummer July 6, &c., and continue so for 100 years.

METROPOLITAN IMPROVEMENTS AND OTHER LOCAL MATTERS.

(239.) IT is rather surprising that the watchmen of religion in the newspapers should have omitted so flagrant a breach of public decorum as the skaiters in the Park on Sunday, where accommodations are provided for them as regular and convenient as at any public place of amusement in the metropolis, and this, too, in the precincts of a royal palace!

(240.) THE immense sums that are raised every year in this country for charitable purposes ought to guard us against the sight and approaches of so many disgusting and mutilated objects as beg for charity about the streets. We have often had occasion to notice this inconvenience, and it is disgraceful to the police that so many vagrants should be permitted abroad.

(241.) JAN. 17th. At 10 P.M., the whole nave of Chelmsford chuch fell in with a great crash; fortunately no person was passing by at the time. It had been erected in 1424.

(242.) The storm on the night of Jan. 24th blew down the remains of King John's Castle, at Old Ford, near Bow. This ancient pile was built in 1203, and was the residence of King John.

(243.) DURING the performance at Covent Garden Theatre last Tuesday night, Mr. Fawcett came forward and addressed the audience, requesting to know if a Mr. Grey, of Thames-street, was in the house, and if he was, that he would come round to the stage door. It seems the premises of this gentleman were in imminent danger from the fire near the Custom House. A similar application was made by Mr. Powell, at Drury Lane, where it appeared the gentleman was with a party. At both the houses the company were rather agitated on the occasion, but an explanation having been made, the performance went on without any further interruption.

(244.) FIRE IN THAMES-STREET.—The alarming fire which broke out in the new-built warehouses of Mr. Lingham, nearly opposite the Custom House, on Tuesday night, destroyed a quantity of goods to the amount of upwards of 250,000*l*., consisting of sugars, coffee, cotton, brandy, and rum, which was not the property of Mr. Lingham, his premises having been let to merchants in general, for the reception of their goods. Such was the violence of the flames, that several times they extended to the warehouses opposite to them, which joined the Custom House. Nothing could have saved these buildings but the exertions of the firemen. Had they been involved in the conflagration, nothing could have prevented the Custom House and all the valuable stores therein deposited from sharing the same fate. The vane of the Custom House was repeatedly on fire. So imminent was the danger that the Commissioners who attended and witnessed the awful spectacle ordered all the important papers belonging to the Customs to be thrown indiscriminately into sacks and taken away, and it will occasion three months' labour to arrange them anew. The lower part of Mr. Lingham's warehouses were on fire the greatest part of yesterday, and it was a matter of curiosity to observe the large stream of liquors and melted sugars which forced itself from under the ruins. A large hole was made in the middle of the street for the liquid to run in, and several firemen were occupied for some hours in lifting it into pails, with which they filled many hogsheads. Some casks of liquor in the lower part of the premises were saved. Two or three small houses at the back of the warehouses were burnt down but no lives have been lost.

(245.) A PLAN upon a very magnificent and extensive scale is now drawing out for the rebuilding of both our Houses of Parliament, which is expected to be begun upon as soon as the present session closes. The buildings to be pulled down will include the Speaker's House in Old Palace-yard, and extend as far as the public house at the corner of Abingdon-street. The business in Parliament will, in the interim, be carried on in a temporary building, to be erected in Westminster Hall.

(246) THE condition of the hackney coach horses of the metropolis demonstrates that the hire is not adapted to the price of provender. If the fares were not too high when provender was but half the price it now bears they must, consequently, be much too low at present; and, inasmuch as public convenience is promoted by this establishment, and as common justice demands that where the service derived from it is restricted from finding its own value, that the power with whom the restriction rests shall at all times adapt it to circumstances under which it is rendered, so does it behove the legislature or the police to proportion the hire to the prices of the market.

(247.) A NEW dock-yard is about to be formed on the Isle of Grain, near the salt-pans; there is great depth of water, and the situation is convenient. Sheerness yard is, in this case, to be reserved for the victualing and ordnance departments.

(248.) AFTER all the wonderful discoveries which were made in the stagnant water of St. James's-square, and all the statues and shrubberies which were promised, it is surprising to find that square in all its former nakedness and deformity.

(249.) ON Saturday evening the building in the centre of that well-known place of public resort in St. George's-fields, called the Apollo Gardens, was levelled in ruins. It was about six o'clock that the inhabitants observed the whole pile rocked by the wind. In a few minutes the principal beam gave way, and then the walls and the roof fell in with a clattering noise, occasioned by the slated covering and the windows.

(250.) A VERY handsome pump has been erected in the front of the Royal Exchange, over the well lately discovered in Cornhill. The case is of iron, and forms a lofty and very handsome obelisk. It is elegantly painted and decorated with emblematic figures, among which is the plan of a house of correction, which was built on the ground adjoining the pump in 1282, by Henry Wallis, Esq., the Lord Mayor of London. One side of the pump bears this inscription: "This well was discovered, much enlarged, and this pump erected in the year 1799, by the contributions of the Bank of England, the East India Company, the neighbouring fire offices, together with the bankers and traders of the Ward of Cornhill." On the reverse these words appear: "On this spot a well was first made, and a house of correction built, by Henry Wallis, Mayor of London, in 1282."

(251.) IT would be a great public service if the legislature would lay a severe penalty on the money lenders who daily advertise their loans under fictitious names. There is a fellow now figuring away in every newspaper in town, with offers of accommodation for thousands, who is known to have never been worth a groat, and to have formerly lived with one of the most notorious Jew swindlers that ever pillaged the town.

(252.) THE Duke of Bedford has taken possession of Lord Gage's house, while Bedford House is rebuilt. The foundations of the new buildings round Bloomsbury are now about to be laid. They are to comprize a new square and crescent.

(253.) THE Duke of Bedford having disposed of the materials of Bedford House, a sale of the furniture, pictures, &c., by Mr. Christie, commenced this day, when the most crowded assemblage were gratified with a last view of this design of Inigo Jones.

The week after were sold the double rows of lime trees in the garden, valued one at 90*l.*, the other at 80*l.*, which are now taken down, and the site of a new square, of nearly the dimensions of Lincoln's-inn-fields, and to be called Russell-square, has been laid out.

(254.) A HERALDRY COLLEGE is to be established in Ireland, and the Earl of Roscommon is to be appointed Earl Marshal.

(255) THE Committee at Guildhall have agreed to allow the present and all future mayors, an addition of 1,500*l.* to support their dignity.

(256.) ON Saturday last, J. Russell, Esq., Citizen and Joiner, paid into the Chamber of London 400*l.* and 20 marks, to be excused serving the office of Sheriff for the year ensuing,—this is the third gentleman who has fined for the said office.

(257.) MR. YATES, master of a canal barge at Colebrook Dale, lately came all the way, 400 miles from thence, with his barge to London, he touched at Worcester and Gloucester, and was eleven days on his passage.

(258.) THE Duke of York intends disposing of his house in Piccadilly, and upon the ground is to be formed a grand new street containing 60 houses running in a line from Saville-row to Piccadilly.

(259.) GOVERNMENT have completed their purchases of the land on Millbank, Westminster, from Grosvenor House to the Timber-yard, for the purpose of erecting a Penitentiary House for the punishment of convicts.

(260.) A NEW Government House is about to be built at Fort William in Bengal, upon the old site.

(261.) A LARGE barge has been stationed near London-bridge for several days, for the purpose of taking soundings for the foundation of a new bridge, to be built of iron, after that magnificent one over the Weir, near Sunderland. The new bridge is to be upon a grand plan of three arches; the centre to admit ships to pass with striking their top and top-gallant masts. The first elevation, it is supposed, will be taken from Canon-street, that the ascent may be gradual and easy for carriages. The building of this bridge will be a very expensive undertaking, but it will be amply compensated for by the great advantages of enlarging the navigation for shipping to Blackfriars-bridge. The expense of the repairs of London-bridge, amount to several thousand pounds annually, and the present obstruction to boats passing and repassing as they can at Blackfriars and Westminster, must be an inconvenience. If the plan is carried into execution, it ought to be upon a grand scale, that it may be viewed as a national ornament.

(262.) IT is to be hoped that the Committee of General Purposes in the City, will order Blackfriars-bridge to be watered during the Summer. As the public pay an expense towards it by a Sunday toll, they ought to be accommodated. At present the bridge is neither watered nor swept, and is a most intolerable nuisance.

(263.) WE hear now of gentlemen going to shoot with their Attornies at their side, as we have seen Bow-street Officers superintend the ball and the card-table. The law and the police are, no doubt, admirable things, but it is quite a novelty that we can neither play nor kill our game without their assistance.

(264.) THE claim of the surgeons to be upon an equal rank with physicians is certainly novel. We shall not be suspected of meaning anything disrespectful upon this most useful body of men, when we remind our readers of a ridiculous circumstance which happened in the last war between Sweden and Russia. The former Court applied for liberty to engage some hundreds of English surgeons from the hospitals; and the terms were so advantageous, that these gentlemen accepted them with eagerness and competition. No sooner, however, were they on board the Swedish ships of war, that they were required to *shave the crews*, the surgeons of that barbarous kingdom being still one common profession with the barbers, of which we have some traces lingering among ourselves. Upon refusal, they underwent the discipline of the cat-and-nine-tails. Very serious complaints were preferred in consequence, and it was only in consequence of the most satisfactory explanation and apologies, that the national resentment was appeased.

(265.) THE first stone of the new Wet Dock, at the Isle of Dogs, was laid by the Right Hon. William Pitt, attended by a numerous concourse of noblemen and gentlemen.

(266.) To CHURCH WARDENS, &c.—As the long continuance of dry weather may possibly engender fever or other disease, particularly in the more confined parts of the metropolis, it is earnestly recommended to those who have the direction of the fire-engines in every parish, to order them to be used early every morning, about three times or twice in the week, in thoroughly washing the courts, streets, and footways.

(267.) IN order to freshen the streets after so long a drought, and so much sultry weather, the Lord Mayor has applied to the managers of the New River and London Bridge Water Works, requesting them to order the plugs and fire-cocks to be opened every morning and evening.

(268.) A SPACIOUS dock yard, and also an ordnance yard, are about to be erected in the Isle of Sheppey, under the direction of General Bentham.

(269.) It is mentioned that Cumberland House is likely to be taken for the use of the Union Club. The introduction of so many Irish families into London will, we fear, contribute to encrease still more the general luxury of the metropolis.

(270.) At Paris, every inhabitant is obliged by the police to water the spaces of the street before his own premises. Upon neglect, it is done by the police, who levy the payment with a small fine. We are not very often inclined to copy anything from the Republic, but we think in this instance we might imitate with advantage.

(271.) Water has been so scarce at Edinburgh, from the failure of the springs, that the magistrates have found it necessary to put some restrictions on the public wells, which are to be shut every day for several hours. Private families are to be served with water only twice a-week through the usual pipes; and they are properly ordered to keep their cisterns in a good state, that no waste of water may take place while this scarcity shall continue.

(272.) London Bridge.—This subject is taken up by the House of Commons, under the general head of "Improvement of the Port of London." The City Committee of Bridge-house Estates have conferred several times with the Select Committee of the House of Commons, and the following is the plan said to be finally agreed upon:—
1. London-bridge shall be rebuilt on such a construction as to permit a free passage, at all times of the tide, for ships of certain tonnage between London-bridge and Blackfriars.
2. That the bridge shall consist of three iron arches with stone piers, the centre not less than 65 feet high in the clear above high-water mark.
3. The river to be embanked, on a regular plan from the Tower to Blackfriars-bridge, and wharfs and warehouses erected.
4. That the new bridge shall be immediately above St. Saviour's Church, Southwark, and upon a direct line leading to the front of the Royal Exchange.

(273.) Two new spacious squares are now forming on the Duke of Bedford's Bloomsbury Estate, one of which is to be called Russell-square, and the other Tavistock-square. These are to be connected by three spacious streets, running north and south, and opening into Bloomsbury-square and Russell-street. At the north end of these improvements, and adjoining to the New-road, a very handsome dressed nursery ground and plantations are already inclosed and laid out; and northward of these, a road of 160 feet wide, in a direct line, is to be formed through the joint estates of the Duke of Bedford and Lord Southampton, from these buildings to the junction of the two London roads to Hampstead, saving the circuitous and unpleasant routes either of Tottenham Court-road or Gray's Inn-lane.

(274.) The charge of posting on the road should be put under the cognizance of magistrates, as continual disputes take place between the traveller and the post-master. From London custom has produced a demand of paying two miles extra, if a chaise only goes upon the stones, besides something extra per mile for the first stage. In many places in the same line of roads the charge varies. From Brighton they charge 1s. 6d. per mile, otherwise you cannot stir; 1s. 3d. per mile after. But those who return to London, if they take a post-chaise from Epsom, are charged 1s. 4d. per mile, and the post-masters have made an agreement not to take less. Nothing requires a greater regulation than the grievance now complained of.

(275.) In the year 1593, Queen Elizabeth issued a proclamation to prevent the increase of buildings in the metropolis, arising from the unaccountable humour of that age in foreseeing dangers that have never happened, nor are ever likely to happen, from an increase of the suburbs of the city of London. The common objection, says Anderson, in his "History of Commerce," that the head (London) was become too large for the body (England), first began to be made about this time. In this proclamation her Majesty declares, "that foreseeing the manifold mischiefs which daily grow more and more unto the city of London, by access of people to inhabit the same, not only by reason that such multitudes would hardly be governed by ordinary justice, but would not be provided with food and other necessaries for man's relief upon reasonable prices; and finally, that such numbers of people inhabiting small rooms whereof many be very poor, and such as must live by begging or worse means; and being heaped up together with many families of children in one house or small tenement, it must follow, if any plague or universal sickness come amongst them, it would spread through the whole city, and into all parts of the realm. For remedy whereof, she commands all manner of persons to desist from any new buildings within three miles of any of the gates of London, and only one family to inhabit one house.

(276.) That intolerable nuisance, Bartholomew Fair, so injurious to the morals and tranquility of the metropolis, was yesterday (3rd Sept.) proclaimed with its usual solemnities.

(277.) St. Bartholomew's Day.—We all of us know what a dreadful nuisance this fair now is; but this was not so much the case with our ancestors. The following article on this subject is extracted from an ancient and authentic record.
"On the eventide of the day the Aldermen met the Lord Mayor at Guildhall Chapel, and, after prayers, they took their horses and rode to Newgate, drank a cool tankard, and then rode to Cloth Fair, and opened it. They returned to the Lord Mayor's house through Aldersgate.
"On the fair day the Aldermen and Sheriffs dined with his lordship in their scarlet gowns, and afterwards rode to see the wrestling, distributing prizes according to merit, and then again returned to the Mayor's house.
"On the second day, his lordship and several Aldermen again attended to view the tilting, the shooting with the cross-bow, and throwing

the lance at targets; in all which exercises the London young men were very expert, and could at that time have challenged all Europe.

"The third day, the apron fair, was dedicated to the young women, some of the boldest of whom ran races in close jackets. Those who were diffident and industrious had small stands, where they sold laces and mittens of their own weaving and knitting, during their leisure hours in the preceding year. They had also worked neckerchiefs, ruffs, and frills. The company always encouraged the neatest workwoman; and on this day the Lady Mayoress and the ladies visited the fair, encouraging and rewarding the young women. It was looked upon as a high honour to sell their works to her ladyship.

"The last day was for the apprentices and boys, who were indulged in every kind of juvenile fun and amusement until eight in the evening, when the whole was stopped and the ground cleared."

(278.) THE Isle of Dogs, now converting to the first commercial purposes, derived its name from being the depôt of the *spaniels* and *greyhounds* of Edward III., as lying contiguous to his sports of woodcock shooting, and coursing the red deer at Waltham, and other royal forests in Essex; for the more convenient enjoyment of which, he generally resided in the sporting season at Greenwich.

(279.) THE proposed regulation respecting the watermen, obliging them to wear their numbers about them, is generally approved; as there is no class of individuals who require more to have a check placed on their conduct than the watermen.

(280.) WE should be very happy to see the attention of the police and of parish officers turned to the mendicants of the metropolis. Those who expose their sores, real or fictitious, are a disgusting and a dangerous nuisance; and every fellow with a long beard ought to be compelled to be shaved upon the spot. Many a sturdy scoundrel of thirty, by letting his beard grow, and discolouring it, imposes himself upon passengers as suffering the infirmities of age. We are not aware of any inconvenience in the parish officers committing them till they consent to be shaved.

(281.) THERE should be an adequate addition to those useful vehicles the hackney coaches, since it so frequently happens that the least temporary attraction to one end of the town subjects the other to considerable inconveniences. This has been the case during the last fortnight, as frequently not a coach could be had on any of the stands west of Temple-bar, so many being occupied in driving to Pope's Lottery Office, facing the Bank of England. But what a rattling through the streets will be heard towards that Office when the public come to reflect that Monday morning next entitles the first drawn ticket to 5000l.; that of the Thursday after to 1000l.; that of the Monday following to 20,000l.; and that of Thursday after to 10,000l.!

A VOYAGE IN A HOY.

(282.) A TRIP TO MARGATE.—We left Billingsgate on board the "British Queen," wind N.E., about half after one o'clock on Monday last. Our party amounted to 160, the principal of whom were ladies. Expectation of much pleasure during their excursion, and other causes, produced the most perfect harmony for several hours, and many excellent songs were sung with much spirit. We had not been on board above an hour before dinner commenced in the cabin, when all the female part of the company appeared to enjoy their provisions with a good appetite. They next expatiated on the inconveniences attendant on the voyage, as if they were only ideal. The seamen on board encouraged their hopes. "We shall be down in seven hours and a half; perhaps it may be nine; at any rate twelve," was the general opinion. This, however, was not the opinion of the captain, and the result was as he expected. The wind at five o'clock was due east, and we were then only at Northfleet; at seven we got off Gravesend, having made tack about an hour, and lost ground every tack. We then cast anchor until the next tide, having the mortification of remaining five hours on that station, till high water commenced at twelve o'clock. The steward providing the ladies with hot water, and the gentlemen being very attentive in waiting, tea was drank on deck by every judicious person on board; for those who preferred the cabin soon experienced the ill effects of it; and then "the joy of a sailor's life" appeared no more. We soon understood the situation of those below by the effect on the deck. After we weighed anchor a strong gale sprung up: it was then that sickness was the order of the day. The berths in the cabin were full in a moment, and every place occupied under hatch. From their being crowded, convulsions succeeded sickness, and the scene of horror was heightened by the whistling of the wind and washing of the decks; all above board were inundated, and all below lying over each other, huddled together by the rolling of the ship. Every passenger on board was sick, even the ship's steward. The morning appeared with a watery sun; a sure indication of wet weather. At six o'clock we were off Yantlet in the Nore, the atmosphere pouring down a torrent of rain.

A council was held among the ladies (the gale still continuing), when it was resolved to petition the captain to put back to Gravesend; and on their knees they requested the gentlemen to back their entreaties. A scene of more general misery never appeared on a pleasurable excursion. A 20l. note was tendered by one lady to the captain, who, being a good-natured fellow, said if the majority of the company wished to return he would comply. This being the case, we tacked about, at seven o'clock; the wind being still N.N.E., at eleven we got back to Gravesend, where thirty-five ladies went ashore and several gentlemen. There we left them to procure post-coaches to Rochester, from whence they proposed taking any casual conveyance to Margate. At one o'clock we set sail, to traverse the same course we had left; the wind having veered round to the west, we scudded along rapidly, and in half-an-hour Gravesend was out of sight. The favourable gale continuing, we continued on one tack till ten o'clock at night, when a dead calm succeeded, being then off the Sisters, about nine miles from Margate. The lights of the piers and at the Duke's Head Inn were clearly perceptible. A light shower, attended by lightning, which was extremely vivid, was succeeded by a gale of wind, and at a quarter after twelve we reached Margate Pier; and then every one endeavoured to secure a bed, after being thirty-six hours on our passage. The town, however, being full, no beds at that hour could be procured, we were therefore necessitated to remain on board for another night. We passed it in the manner of the preceding one, lying on the deck as close to each other, for the sake of warmth, as possible: however great our inclination might be for sleep, the cold prevented its taking place. When daylight appeared we walked round the cliffs and on the pier until the innkeepers arose at six o'clock, when we breakfasted, and concurred in one general opinion on the *pleasures* of a Margate hoy.

The parties who left us at Gravesend got into Margate at twelve o'clock, fatigued almost to death with the journey, and put to the expense of five guineas for a chaise, the distance from Gravesend to Margate being fifty miles.

Margate was never known to be so full; beds are 3s. a night, garrets are cheap at half-a-guinea per week. The ordinary is 2s. 6d. a head; last year it was 2s., and beds 1s. 6d. The extravagant charges will do no good to the place.

This morning left us the "New Rose in June" (the old one has been broken up). The passengers amounting to 120, returning to London.

THEATRES AND EXHIBITIONS.

(283.) THERE is one circumstance which so glaringly evinces the superiority of the present times to those of Charles II in respect of moral delicacy, that we are astonished it should have escaped any man of reading. We allude to the drama, always a criterion of the public manners. There is not a comedy of the last century that would be tolerated in its original state by our present audience for an hour. Whatever our secret sins may be, it is undeniable that public licentiousness is universally checked.

(284.) AMONGST the arrivals in London is the truly celebrated and astonishing Mr. O'Brien, (the Irish giant) from his country residence at Epping Place, where he had retired for twelve or thirteen years past. We are informed that he means to continue for a few weeks to gratify the curiosity of the world, and is to be seen next door to the Cannon Coffeehouse, Cockspur-street, nearly opposite Spring-gardens.

(285.) THE Milton Gallery, consisting of a series of pictures from the poetical works of Milton, painted by N. Fuseli, R.A., and Professor of Painting, will be opened to-morrow with additional pictures, at the Old Royal Academy Rooms, No. 118, Pall Mall.

(286.) A GREATER assemblage of musical conoscenti was never perhaps experienced in Britain than what will be seen this evening at Covent Garden Theatre. Haydn's oratorio of the Creation is to be brought forward for its first performance in this kingdom. The accounts from Vienna of this most sublime work are such as Fame may be said to be truly proud of. It is indisputably the *chef-d'œuvre* of Haydn's composition, and has proved such a magnet of attraction at Vienna as its theatre, though immensely large, never before witnessed.

(287.) No sooner did Mr. O'Brien, the celebrated Irish giant, announce his return to town in the public papers, than his apartments, which are very elegant, No. 33, opposite to the Admiralty, were crowded with people of rank and fashion.

(288.) IN the harlequinade at Sadler's Wells are some very curious pieces of mechanism, particularly a tailor's box changing into a basket of cabbages, and a cabbage changing again to a bundle of rags; a drum to a temple of harmony, a box of quack pills to a basket of ducks, and one of the pills to a single duck, which is a most extraordinary piece of mechanism; a coffin to a sedan, and numerous other changes, equally evincing ingenuity and producing delights. The serious ballet excites strong applause, and for dress, decoration, arrangement, and costume has rarely been equalled. Davis sings some excellent comic songs, particularly the "King's Picture," in answer to "Abraham Newland." The opera dancers display themselves to the best advantage. Richer's tambourine dance on the rope is the first rope-dancing ever exhibited in this country. The entertainments are to be repeated every night this week.

(289.) The dancing of St. Pierre and the opera girls at Sadler's Wells, Richer's tight rope, the comicality of Dubois and Grimaldi, Davis's songs, &c., kept the hands and risible muscles of the holiday folks last night in perpetual employ. The harlequinade was received wonderfully; but the *chef-d'œuvre* of the evening was the new spectacle of Blackenberg, in which the spirit of Havier rises from the bosom of the River Elbe by moonlight, arrayed in all the effulgence of celestial appearance, while the guilty subject of the piece is precipitated for his crimes into a sulphureous and vapourous chasm which opens in the earth. The degree of applause exceeded description, and the house was uncommonly full.

(290.) LAST Monday night there was a choral concert at Oxford, at which Madame Mara assisted; she was on her way to Bath.

(291.) IT is said that between 3 and 400 seamen are to walk in procession to the Opera House on Wednesday evening next.

(292.) THE balls and routs being over, there can be no doubt of Ranelagh, for the remainder of the season, being the genteel resort of all the fashion in town.

(293.) THE gentlemen of the Admiralty, Navy, Victualling, and Transport Boards have unanimously agreed to attend at the Opera House, on Wednesday evening next, as a tribute due to the gallant seamen, defenders of our King and country.

(294.) ON the subject of mental relaxation and amusement, were it a point of discussion what scene possesses, at this season of the year, a decisive pre-eminence of attraction and public patronage, it would be sufficient only to appeal to that most splendid and respectable throng of company which graced Vauxhall on Thursday evening. Upon a moderate calculation, there could not be less than five thousand of the *beau monde*, seen traversing this delightful spot, illuminated with all the brilliance of variegated lustre, and captivating the ear with many a fascinating strain of music. Fancy can better paint, than description can do justice to, a scene of such enchantment. Such, in truth, has been the fame on Thursday night's gala among the higher circles, that their Graces the Duchesses of Devonshire and Gordon, with several others of the principal nobility, have requested that it shall be repeated on Monday evening, and for which great preparations, we understand, are making, that it may be presented with much additional splendour.

(295.) THE effect produced by the introduction of two squadron of horse on the stage, the horsemen habited in gold and silver armour, may in some manner be conceived, but not described. Those, therefore, who never witnessed a scene so noble, and at the same time ludicrous, have only to attend the performance of the last new pantomime of Quixotte and Sancho, or Harlequin Warrior, produced for the first time on Monday last, at the Amphitheatre, Westminster-bridge, and we can venture to promise them a treat of the most luxuriant and pleasing nature, independent of the unrivalled horsemanship of the surprising Crossman, Handy, &c., who finish their engagement with Astley after this and the two following evenings.

(296.) THE pretty little Mrs. Simpson, who succeeded Mrs. Siddons as the heroine of the Bath stage, a station she held with repute many years, died lately in a baggage-waggon, following her husband, a common soldier, who, a few years ago, when she married him, was an eminent Baker at Southampton.

(297.) REPORT says the new grand equestrian spectacle of the Magic Flute, which is so much the subject of public admiration, cost the managers near 2000*l*., indeed the scenery, dresses, and decorations are the most splendid ever brought out at any theatre, and the appearance of the knights clad in armour, and mounted on real chargers on the stage, has a most striking and beautiful appearance.

(298.) MRS. SIDDONS made her *entrée* on the Margate stage on Friday evening, in the character of *Lady Randolph*.

(299.) INCLEDON and MUNDEN set off after the play on Friday night to perform *Young Meadows* and *Justice Woodcock*, at Birmingham, on Saturday.

(300.) QUICK the Comedian, made his first appearance at the Margate Theatre, on Tuesday. He acted two of his most favourite characters, *Lovegold* and *Cadwallader*.

(301.) AN ox weighing 2996 lbs.; in length, from the nose to the tail, exclusive of the brush, 17 feet 3 inches; in height 6 feet $2\frac{1}{4}$ inches, and 9 feet $3\frac{1}{2}$ inches round the girth, is now exhibiting in America; it was bred in New Jersey, and is considerably larger than the Darlington ox last year exhibited in this metropolis.

(302.) THE following most surprising instance of maternal affection, affords a gratification to the curious beyond anything ever seen in this Kingdom :— Two kangaroos (a male and female) are now exhibited in the same room with the male elephant at Mr. Pidcock's Grand Menagerie, over Exeter Change; and incredible to relate, the female brought forth a young one on the 20th of September last (which it had concealed in a cavity or pouch provided by nature, under its belly, until Tuesday the 14th inst.), when it came out for the first time to feed, but returned again into the pouch. The young creature, beautiful beyond description, frequently appears with its head and shoulders exposed to view, eats hay and other food, then retreats at pleasure. Nature, beyond doubt, has provided teats within the pouch, affording milk sufficient to support the young animal until able to provide for itself; although the above relation may appear doubtful, the writer, who was an eye-witness, pledges himself for its authenticity.

SPORTS AND FEATS.

(303.) THE Hon. Mr. Caulfield, an Ensign in the Guards, is the best skaiter on the Serpentine river. With one foot, without allowing the other to touch the ice, he makes nine half circles. The crowd was twelve deep, forming a ring round the Marquis of Lorn, Lord Villiers, Mr. Caulfield, &c., skating together on Sunday; and so deeply did the ice bend in with the weight of the spectators, that the skaiters seemed on rising ground in the middle.

In consequence of the numerous skaiters and others drowned in the Serpentine river, the Humane Society, by permission of the King, have erected a receiving house for the recovery of persons drowned, and have taken measures to apprize the skaiters of the dangerous parts of the ice.

(304.) THURSDAY last, a man belonging to the Victualling Office at Chatham, undertook for a bet of 20*l.* to roll a butt of water from the Victualling Office to Gravesend, in seven hours, which he performed in six hours and twenty-three minutes, distance eight miles, in which are three long and steep hills.

(305.) AN ingenious Parisian has taught cats to sing, as appears by the following advertisement, which has been published at Paris:—"On the 5th Germinal will be performed a Miaulic Concert, in which twenty-six cats will execute the air of Ran tamplan tire lire, and of the Epoux assortis. The concert will conclude with a grand chorus by all the twenty-six cats, in perfect concord and excellent time." How far the appearance of a mouse would put the *Miaulists* out of tune, is somewhat doubtful.

(306.) A SHORT time since eight members of the Society of Cumberland Youths made an attempt to ring 15,136 changes of Oxford triple-bobs on Edmonton Church bells. It requires upwards of ten hours time to perform this task, at twenty-five changes a minute. They had entered the ninth hour, when an unlucky accident befel Mr. Gross, the composer of the peal; making an attempt to slacken his knee-buckle, his leg entangled in the coil of the rope, by which he was elevated to a considerable height, and thence falling down on his head, he broke his collar-bone.

Had it not been for this accident, no doubt the feat would have been accomplished, and the performers crowned with perpetual honour, as nothing to be compared with such an achievement of strength and skill can be found in the records of the campanilogers art.

(307.) THE first Consul would have hardly boasted of his dispatch in travelling from Paris to Dijon, 140 miles in 25 hours, had he known that an English gentleman, Mr. Thornhill, of Stilton, rode 214 miles in 14 hours only.

(308.) THE famous parrot of Colonel O'Kelly is now become so perfect a prattler, that he promptly answers any question that is put to him. 1000 guineas have been offered for him and refused.

(309.) ON Wednesday evening last, being the anniversary of His Majesty's birth, the students of Eton College, according to ancient custom, supped at Surly Hall. Their boats bearing elegant and appropriate silken banners, left Mr. Zachary Talbot's Wharf at six o'clock, manned by many of the nobility, and having on board the band of the Staffordshire Militia. On their landing at Boveney Church, they were received by the upper gentlemen, 300 of whom had followed them up the banks of the Thames on horseback. Mr. Grover of the Royal Buckinghamshire Cavalry, ordered the greatest part of his field to be mowed for their accommodation, and it is but justice to add, that his behaviour on this occasion merited the praises which the Etonians (in private conversation) bestowed upon him. After the repast was ended the gentlemen crossed over to the other side of the river, and honoured the company at Mr. Ward's, by giving them three cheers. Fireworks, &c., concluded the entertainment.

(310.) A LATE match at Newmarket was won, say the records of sporting, by *half a nostril*. After this it will be considered a qualification in a race-horse that he should have *a long nose.*

(311.) A YOUNG MAN of good character and figure, proposes a lottery in *The Bordeaux Journal*. The conditions are—all the widows and maidens who have not attained the age of 32, are invited to take of him a ticket at the price of 25 francs. There are to be 4,000 of these tickets. Only one number is to be drawn from the wheel, and the fortunate holder is to gain the young man for a husband, and to partake with him the 100,000 francs produced by the lottery.

(312.) A MATCH for 500 guineas was determined on Wednesday, between Captain Blake, who resides in Haslemere, and Mr. Tyson, who lives four miles from it, on the way to Chichester. Mr. Tyson, at three o'clock in the morning of the preceding Saturday, started with a phaeton and pair of hired horses from Haslemere, and in three hours and a-half drove to Hyde Park, a distance of fifty miles. Captain Blake was to drive a curricle, and on Wednesday he drove the given distance in three hours and eleven minutes, beating his antagonist by nineteen minutes.

(313.) ON Thursday last, on Sunbury-common, Mr. Goldham undertook, for a bet of 100 guineas, that his galloway should go nine miles in three different paces and leap over a five-barred gate in one hour. Notwithstanding he was forty-two minutes walking the first three miles, he trotted the next three in ten, and galloped the last three in seven minutes, and won his match by fifty-five seconds. It was four to one against him after the walking.

(314) ON Thursday last, a most ludicrous circumstance occurred at Bristol. A man undertook to walk through the city backwards with a weight of five pound and a half affixed to his nose by three yards of string; this he actually did to the no small amusement of an immense crowd, for the sum of five shillings.

(315.) CRICKET.—On Thursday last was played a grand match of cricket, in Lord's Ground, Marylebone, between eleven gentlemen of Westminster School against eleven gentlemen of Eton College, for 500 guineas, which was won by the latter by one innings and 128 runs. Five to four in their favour at starting.

(316.) DOGGET'S Coat and Badge were yesterday rowed for by six young watermen just out of their apprenticeship. They started at London Bridge about 5 o'clock, and proceeded to the Old Swan Stairs, Chelsea. Much skill was displayed on the occasion, and victory declared in favour of John Burgoing, a very powerful young man, standing six feet high. A dispute, however, has arisen, as some think it unfairly decided;

and it was reported that they would again start for the prizes. Burgoing returned as far as Blackfriar's Bridge with a drum and fife, and was carried a-shore triumphantly.

(317.) Two gentlemen, a few days ago, undertook for a supper and twenty guineas, to row from Westminster Bridge to Richmond Bridge against a gentleman who was to walk the same distance. The wager was won by the latter by thirty minutes; the rowers performed it in two hours and ten minutes.

(318.) A FEW days ago, a shoemaker, in the neighbourhood of East Smithfield, for the trifling wager of two quarts of beer, undertook to cleanse a grocer's shop of the flies. He took three pieces of paper spread with treacle, one he placed on his head and one on each hand, then walking to-and-fro in the shop, he contrived a humming sound like that of a large fly, and in the space of three minutes the man's head was entirely enveloped in a cloud of flies. In this manner he walked as far as the Tower Stairs, where he lodged his booty in the bar of a small gin shop, to the no little astonishment of a great concourse of people.

(319.) A GENTLEMAN at Ipswich last week betted fifty guineas that he would walk from that place to Sudbury and back again (a distance of forty-four miles), in twelve hours, which he lost. He then proposed to ride his horse the same distance for double the sum in four hours. The bet was accepted, and he accomplished it with apparent ease.

(320.) A MARE of Mr. Dyson's, of Park lane, has been engaged for a bet of 200 guineas, to trot 17 miles in 56 minutes, which she performed lately in 53.

(321.) The Pontefract pedestrian, 66 years old, some days since, walked 66 miles in 22 hours; he was allowed 24 hours.

(322.) A MARE, belonging to Mr. Robson, of Little Britain, was matched last week to trot 17 miles in 56 minutes, with Mr. Marsden, who betted Mr. Robson 400 guineas to 100 she did not do it; Mr. Marsden thinking it impossible any horse, mare, or gelding could do it. She performed the match with great ease in 3 minutes and 10 seconds within the time given. She also had an engagement with Mr. Dyson, of Parklane, who betted Mr. Robson 2000 guineas to 100 she did not trot 19 miles in one hour; but on her last performance, Mr. Dyson being called on to cover, chose to forfeit the money down rather than make the stakes good.

(323.) A FEW days since a Frenchman gained a bet of 50 guineas by eating, at a house in Piccadilly, 22 dozen, or 264 of the largest oysters, raw from the shell, which he swallowed within an hour, together with two bottles of sherry and 3 lb., of white bread!

CURIOUS INCIDENTS AND FACETIÆ.

(324.) HAUT TON.—About a fortnight ago a subscriber to the opera was induced to lend his silver ticket to the wife of a celebrated butcher near Trinity-lane, in the City, of the name of J——s, whose size does infinite honour to the roast beef of Old England. The lady having engaged her sister to go with her applied to the husband for a coach, as the opera required that sort of dress which it was impossible to walk through the streets in. "Oh!" says Mr. J——s, "it is a fine clear night, and Jack has nothing to do, he shall therefore drive you, and your feathers and finery, in our chaise cart." Off, therefore, they went, in this elegant vehicle, and honest Jack, like an experienced Jehu, landed them safely at the end of Pall Mall. With equal skill and ability Jack contrived, towards the close of the evening's entertainment, to get his carriage into the line next the Opera-house, and kept his station with the greatest care, till at last he came directly opposite the door. On this the next son of the whip, belonging to a lady of quality, hallowed out—"Hey-day! you butcher, what the devil do you do here? move off, directly." "What do you mean?" says Jack, "Who do you come for?" "I come for my lady, duchess," says whip. "Well," says Jack, "and I come for my lady too." "Who is your lady," says whip? "Lady J——s," says Jack. The word immediately passed, and was continued that "Lady J——s's carriage stopped the way," till the butcher's wife and sister were conveniently seated in their fashionable vehicle, and honest Jack bore them off in triumph (feathers and all in excellent order), in spite of the efforts of the Jehus of duchesses, countesses, viscountesses, or all the list of fashionables at the West end of the town.

(325.) THE following circumstance is said to have happened last week in the vicinity of Charing Cross:—Two ladies of considerable distinction stopped in a carriage at a jewellers; one of them only got out; the coach stood across the causeway. Some gentlemen wanted to cross to the other side, and desired the coachman to move on a little; the fellow was surly, and refused; the gentleman remonstrated, but in vain. During the altercation the lady came to the door of the shop, and foolishly ordered the coachman not to stir from his place. One of the gentlemen then, without hesitation, opened the coach door, and with boots and spurs on, went through the carriage; he was followed by his companions, to the extreme discomposure of the lady within, as well as the lady without. To complete the jest, a party of sailors coming up, observed, that if this was a thoroughfare, they had as much right to go through it as the "gemmen," and they accordingly went through the coach. The lady had some difficulty to get into her carriage, as a mob was soon collected to enjoy the scene.

(326.) AN orator of the sister kingdom observed, in a recent speech in favour of legislative union, that the beneficial effects of that measure would convert their *barren mountains* into *fertile valleys!*

(327.) It was wittily asked, upon a certain promotion,—How many little actions are equal to one great one? The Tunbridge poetasters may ask one another a question of the same nature,—How many rhymers are equal to one poet?

(328.) The Joe Miller story of an Irishman who, when travelling, always breakfasted *over night*, to save time, is really no joke with our people of fashion, who are very happy to take a substantial *luncheon* before they go to *a public breakfast!*

(329.) It must now be confessed that the late dearth was, according to the Irish phrase, *a very plentiful scarcity!* and it is to be feared, without measures of great vigour, that the corporation of forestallers and speculators will render the present *plenty* a very *scarce abundance.*

(330.) When Mr. Horne Tooke was justifying to the Commissioners his return of income under 60*l.* a-year, one of those gentlemen, dissatisfied with the explanation, hastily said, "Mr. Tooke, I do not understand you." "Very possibly," replied the sarcastic citizen, "but as you have not *half* the *understanding* of other men, you should have *double* the *patience.*

(331.) At Ashton Church, in Lancashire, a short time ago, a woman was persuaded, that if she went to church *naked* her intended husband would not be burthened with her debts; and she actually went as a bride like mother Eve; but to the honour of the clergyman, he refused the damsel the honours of wedlock.

(332.) Mrs. Egerton, formerly well known on the stage, has *re-married* her former husband, whom she had left about thirty years ago.

(333.) It is said that eggs are forestalled in order to raise the price of pelting the forestallers in the pillory.

(334.) A gentleman observing the Town Crier of Bristol standing in the market-place unemployed, asked him why he did not *cry* as usual? "Good sir," replied the man, "*I cannot cry to-day, for my wife is dead!*"

(335.) The cowkeepers are really very hard upon John Bull, whom they want to treat like an errant *calf.*

(336.) The blue cover of one of the periodical publications advertises for the following combination of talents:—"Wanted, a person who understands the different branches of husbandry and dairy (a partner), who can lodge in the business the sum of three or five hundred pounds, a strictly religious character—if a *Calvanist,* most agreeable. If he hath abilities for a *preacher,* the better!!!"

(337.) In the last "Gazette" there is a very proper memorandum, superseding Lieutenant — Robinson, of the 66th Foot, *being a boy at school!*

(338.) It has been said of a certain Lord and his Lady, that the only time they ever agreed in their lives was when they parted by consent.

(339.) A German author, we are told, has published thirteen folios upon the subject of marriage. Harlequin, in the Italian Theatre, mentioned this book one hundred years ago, observing that the first volume contained a dissertation upon its possible delights, and the twelve last upon its certain disappointments.

(340.) A ridiculous report was spread on Friday, that a gentleman had been sent off by Government to inquire into *the state of the public mind in France.* Such a task, for one man, would have required very inquisitive talents. It is no secret that forty thousand failed when sent to Holland upon a similar errand.

(341.) A bellman at Stayleybridge last week announced a singular loss: "Stolen or strayed, a hearse with two horses, and a corpse in it."

(342.) At a village near Shaftesbury resides a respectable matron, aged 90, who is mother, grandmother, great and great-great grandmother to upwards of 300 children, most of whom reside in one mansion, within four miles of the house in which her own children were born, where they milk upwards of 1000 cows. They all dined with the old lady at Christmas.

(343.) By a singular sympathy, scarcely was it agreed to introduce 100 Irish *Members* into the House of *Commons,* when it was proposed to plant all the *commons* in England with *potatoes!*

(344.) Sunday Amusements.—An able calculator estimates the number of persons belonging to the metropolis, who spend the Sunday in the adjacent villages, inns, tea-houses, &c., at two hundred thousand. These, he calculates, will spend each half-a-crown, amounting in the whole to twenty-five thousand pounds. This sum, he thinks, cannot be thought as exaggerated, when it is considered that he has taken the numbers so low as 200,000, and the sum spent by each at half-a-crown.

Twenty-five thousand pounds multiplied by the number of Sundays in the year, give, as the annual consumption of that *day of rest,* the immense sum of one million three hundred thousand pounds.

Of these 200,000 persons, he calculates the *returning situations* as follows:—

Sober ..	50,000
In high glee	90,000
Drunkish ..	30,000
Staggering tipsy ..	10,000
Muzzy ..	15,000
Dead drunk ..	5,000
	200,000

(345.) Alarm to the Ladies.—A few days ago we stated that a tax of two guineas per annum was to be laid on every one wearing a wig, and that this measure was suggested in revenge on those who have left off the use of hair powder. Our readers perhaps thought this a jest; but we gravely and positively assure them it is a fact; and as the tax must, from its nature, extend to all those who wear *false hair*, the intelligence is most alarming to the fair sex. Not only wigs, but braids, ringlets, and every lock not of nature's growth, which may be necessary to hide nature's niggardliness, must be subject to the duty. The *crops* and *bald crowns* will of course increase in number, and we shall not be surprised to see *Welch wigs*, or *night caps*, all the rage in the fashionable world.

(346.) A CURIOUS cause of war. In the year 1005, some soldiers of the Commonwealth of Modena ran away with a bucket from a public well, belonging to the State of Bologna. This implement might be worth a shilling, but it produced a quarrel, which was worked up into a long and bloody war. Henry, the King of Sardinia, for the Emperor Henry the Second, assisted the Modenese to keep possession of the bucket, and in one of the battles he was made prisoner. His father, the Emperor, offered a chain of gold that would encircle Bologna, which is seven miles in compass, for his son's ransom, but in vain. After twenty-two years' imprisonment, and his father being dead, he pined away and died. His monument is still extant in the church of the Dominicans. This fatal bucket is still exhibited in the tower of the Cathedral of Modena, inclosed in an iron cage. Tasso has very humourously described it in his Della Secchia.

SINGULAR ADVERTISEMENT.

(347.) THE following curious advertisement is to be found in a Hamburgh paper of the 15th ult. The lady, who is the advertiser, is Wilhelmina Henrietta Antonia, of Altona. It has been so often repeated since that period, that there can be little doubt of the sincerity of her wishes to find a proper companion. "As I have not yet found a man," says Miss Antonia, "whom I can love, I have contracted a general desire to please, either by politeness, by following the fashions, or by a spirit of malice, which, however, never degenerates into genuine coquetishness, an invincible love for liberty, and a certain taste for idleness and ease, which renders every kind of authority insupportable to me, have prevented me hitherto from marrying. I have not yet found any man so superior as to command me, so amiable as to enslave me, so void of character as to be my slave, so discreet and so faithful as to be my friend. I have a mind too elevated, a heart too timid, and an imagination too ardent, for me to be the subject of a long continued delusion. I neither wish to command or to obey any man. I wish for a friend with whom I may pass my life, and divide my fortune, united by the purest, the truest, and the most virtuous sentiments, without constraint, without reserve, without false delicacy, and without vanity, music, interesting reading, the society of some well-informed and highly educated man, would fill up our lives.

"If therefore, there is to be found a woman between the age of 26 and 36, of a good constitution and moral character, well brought up, who together with a pure and sensible heart, a reasonable and unaffected mind, and a correct taste, possesses politeness, feminine qualities, prudence, and that sincerity which the common intercourse of society requires, I should be happy to offer her my friendship and my house. I should wish that she should neither be ugly nor absolutely poor.

"If the particulars which I have enumerated are found to answer, I hope she will with a noble frankness acquaint me, through the medium of the *Affiches des Empires*, with her good qualities, and even with her failings, and that she will consent to partake with me the pleasures and the pains of life; she will find in my house an income of 4000 marks annually, a commodious and extensive apartment, with a fine view over a large garden to the Elbe, entirely at her own disposal. My carriage and my servants shall be entirely at her command. She shall eat by herself when she pleases. We shall make trial of each other's disposition for three years. All I stipulate is, that she shall be neither a French woman, a Jewess, nor a lady of quality.'

THE COURT AND HAUT TON.

(348.) WEYMOUTH, AUG. 2.—His Majesty bathed for the first time yesterday morning.

The Princess Amelia also bathed in the warm bath.

(349.) AN event which happened in the evening, added very much to the anxiety that had been felt from what had occurred in the morning. Their Majesties having announced their intention of going to the Theatre at Drury-lane, the house was extremely crowded. The Princesses first came into their box, as usual, the Queen next, and then the King.

The audience had risen to receive and greet the royal family by clapping of hands, and other testimonies of affection, when at the instant His Majesty entered, and was advancing to bow to the audience, an assassin, who had placed himself about the middle of the second front row of the pit, raised his arm and fired a pistol, which was levelled towards the box. The flash and the report caused an instant alarm through the house, but after an awful suspense of a few moments, the audience perceiving His Majesty unhurt, a burst of most enthusiastic joy succeeded, with loud exclamations of "Seize the Villain!" "Shut all the doors!" The curtain was by this time drawn up, and the stage was crowded by persons of all descriptions from behind the scenes. A gentleman who stood next the assassin immediately collared him, and after some struggling he was conveyed over into the orchestra, where the pistol was wrenched from him, and delivered to one of the performers on the stage, who held it up to public view. There was a general cry of "Shew the Villain!" who by this time was conveyed into the music room, and given in charge of the Bow-street Officers. The cry still continuing to see him, Mr. Kelly came forward to assure the audience that he was safe in custody. The band then struck up "God save the King," in which they were cordially joined, in full chorus, by every person in the Theatre, the ladies waving their handkerchiefs and huzzaing. Never was loyalty more affectionately displayed, and never was it called forth towards a Sovereign who more justly deserved the love of his people. His Majesty, who at the first moment of alarm, had displayed that serenity and firmness of character which belong to a virtuous mind, was now evidently affected by the passing scene, and seemed for a moment rather dejected. The Duke and Duchess of York, who were in their private box below, hastened to the king, who was eagerly surrounded by his family. A more affectionate and interesting circumstance cannot be imagined.

After the Duke of York had conversed for a few moments with the King, His Royal Highness and Mr. Sheridan went into the music room, where the traitor was secured. Being interrogated, he said his name was Hatfield, and it appears he formerly belonged to the 15th Light Dragoons, and served under the Duke of York in Flanders, where he was made prisoner. He is much scarred in the forehead, of low stature, and was dressed in a common surtout, with a soldier's jacket underneath.

In the music room he appeared extremely collected, and confessed that he had put two slugs into the pistol. He said he was weary of life. Sir William Addington then came in, and at his request no further interrogations were made, and the man was conveyed to the prison in Coldbath Fields, where, in the course of the evening, the Prince of Wales, and the Dukes of York, Clarence, and Cumberland went to see him.

As soon as the event came to the knowledge of the ministers, a Privy Council was summoned, and at ten o'clock the traitor was carried to the Secretary of State's Office, where the Cabinet Ministers and principal Law Officers were assembled, and he continued under examination when this paper was put to press.

We have omitted no pains to investigate all the circumstances of this extraordinary and dreadful transaction; and we believe they have been faithfully and accurately detailed, as far as it is prudent to publish them. Were it possible to divest the mind so quickly of all the horrors inspired by this atrocious parricide, or to feel any other sentiment than of devout gratitude for the public deliverance in the King's escape, we should advert to the satisfaction His Majesty must receive in the general undisguised, and natural testimony of zeal, tenderness, and affection which was displayed upon this unhappy occasion by his people.

(350.) For some time past it is well known that the Prince of Wales has occasionally been very seriously indisposed. This has induced his Royal Highness to make an application to the King for leave to go to Lisbon or Madeira, for the recovery of his health. As this permission could not be granted without the consent of Parliament, His Majesty referred the subject to his ministers, who, upon due consideration of all circumstances, have recommended the Prince not to make such an application, as they could not give their consent to it. His Royal Highness has perceived the propriety of the recommendation, and is satisfied with remaining at home. His intention, in the event of going abroad, was to have taken the title of Duke of Cornwall.

(351.) We are happy to be able to inform our readers that the health of the Prince of Wales; though by no means in that state we could wish it, is not judged to require a journey to the south of Europe; nor has the inclination of His Royal Highness to try the air of Lisbon or Madeira proceeded farther than a very natural expression of it in conversation. The Prince is fully aware of the possible danger and inconvenience to the empire from his absence, from the casualties of his voyage, or his residence in another country.

(352.) The Countess of Leicester's ball, on Monday night, was given in compliment to her son, Lord Charles Townshend, to the young noblemen educated with his lordship at Eton School, and to the younger branches of the female nobility. The company consisted of near 200 persons, among whom was His Royal Highness the Prince of Wales. Country dances, with reels, and strathspeys, were led down till twelve o'clock, when three supper-rooms were thrown open. After supper the company repaired again to the ball-room, where they kept dancing till three in the morning.

(353.) Our fashionable dames still continue to endeavour to outvie each other in the expense, style, or peculiarity of their entertainments. One lady founds her title to fame in the crowd she can squeeze together in so many square feet of drawing-room; another has the glory of filling half a column in a quack newspaper more than her rival; and a third mounts to celebrity upon the first peas and the dearest strawberries. The last ball always causes many aches and pangs to the fair giver of its predecessor; and a great lady who has been at home every Friday during the season, is actually confined to her bed-chamber since the Duchess of Devonshire's gala effaced all the flippant magnificence of a ready-furnished house and a confectioner.

So passes the glory of the world, and here would have been extinguished the thirst of glory and the spirit of competition if it had not occurred to a lady of great celebrity in the fashionable world to be at home at breakfast, at dinner, at a ball in the evening, and at supper in the morning. If, therefore, Mrs. Fitzherbert has not been able to run a race with her fair rivals in the beaten course, she has certainly won it by the eccentricity of her entertainment, and the length of it.

About 400 persons visited her charming villa, among whom were most of the ladies of fashion in town. In the gardens three marquees were erected for the accommodation of the company, who met about two o'clock, and dined at seven. The entertainment did not conclude till past five o'clock yesterday morning.

(354.) Of all the balls lately given we have not heard of any in the style of that of the Archduchess Palatine. It was as follows:—

During the last Carnival she had invited the nobility of Buda, in Hungary, to a ball. At the time appointed they made their appearance, but not any preparations seemed to have been made, and their expectations were raised to the highest pitch. Some time after the company had assembled, a young girl appeared with a basket, containing tickets for property pawned by a number of the poor inhabitants of Ofen, which the duchess had taken up, and for which she had paid the sum of thirty thousand florins. The amiable princess declared that she had thought proper to apply the sum intended for the festivity to a nobler purpose, and convinced that the nobility of Breda entertained similar sentiments, she wished that they might share her pleasure.

(355.) SEVERAL of the gala-giving ladies are busily employed in devising a method how to receive company and to pay visits on the same night.

(356.) A FEW days ago, Edward le Pryce O'Brien was naturalized, and baptized by the Rev. J. Weeks, Vicar of St. George's Hanover-square, on his coming to the title of baronet. He is a young gentleman of genteel address; and we understand that a lady of fashion and fortune has settled an annuity on him, to enable him to support the dignity of title.

(357.) SEVERAL servants have lately been discharged from houses of fashion for refusing to pay to Bow-street officers and the puffs in the newspapers, along with the cards and candles. We are seldom disposed to blame any act of economy, but upon this occasion we think the footmen are to be pitied. Townsend is said to recollect so many old acquaintances amongst them that it seems very hard he will not make his visits for nothing.

(358.) THE fineness of the day yesterday attracted a good deal of company to Hyde Park and Kensington Gardens, and a few bucks sported "The Hack Bucephalus of Rotten Row." Our fashionable belles, by dressing à la victime, seem to indicate a strong desire to be led to the altar.

(359.) THE Carnival at Berlin has this year been very brilliant. At the last redoute the Queen appeared in the costume of the Indians of Owyhee, with a cloak of feathers, adorned however with diamonds and rubies. Prince Augustus, of England, appeared at the ball in the dress of a monk, but he was most terribly perplexed, particularly by a fair nun, who asked him in Latin for absolution, His Royal Highness having forgot his knowledge of that language.

(360.) AT a masquerade lately given at Hamburgh, a mask entered the rooms late in the evening in a paper dress, garnished all over with real maccaroons. The mask was received as a hare among a kennel of hounds, hunted the room over, and in less than five minutes all his sweetmeats, even to his paste cap, were devoured. It soon appeared that the maccaroons had been made with a mixture of jalap, and the scene which ensued may be more easily conceived than described.

(361.) FASHIONABLE *gambling* has been very prevalent at *Brighton!* A young heir to a large north country property, being received into what is called *good company* only for one evening, found the demand upon him the next morning, for his supper, 2500 guineas!

(362.) MARGATE is now thin of visitors. The *city* quality are returned "to reason and their shops." The supplies for the campaign were exhausted, and just enough was left to convey the troops to winter quarters.

(363.) SIR HYDE PARKER, who is coming home from the West Indies, has gained the largest fortune of any individual during the war. His share of prize-money has netted, for the last two years, ten thousand pounds currency per month.

(364.) LORD NELSON is much followed at Vienna, whenever he stirs abroad; and the fashions of that city are adopting his name. The "Nelson ribband" and the "Nelson cap" are all the rage. Some of the Paris papers report that his lordship is much indisposed.

(365.) LORD NELSON was last week chosen High Steward of Ipswich.

(366.) COVENT GARDEN THEATRE.—LORD NELSON, of the Nile, visited this theatre last night, with Lady Nelson, Sir William and Lady Hamilton, and his lordship's father, the Rev. Mr. Nelson, to see the pleasant "Comedy of Life," and the musical entertainment of the "Mouth of the Nile." Every part of the house overflowed at the beginning of the comedy; and when he appeared, "Rule Britannia!" was sung by the performers, amid the enthusiastic acclamations of the audience.

The comedy was never performed with more *éclat*, and the admirable spirit of Lewis, with the whimsical humour of Munden, who gave the popular ballad which he had before sung, in allusion to the victories of our gallant navy, and who was frequently interrupted by the plaudits of the house; but when he delivered the following lines:

"May peace be the end of the strife we maintain
For our king and our freedom, and our right to the main.
We're content to shake hands; if they wont, why —what then?
We must send out brave Nelson to thresh'em again."

the exultation of the audience at the sight of the hero himself could alone be gratified by a repetition of the compliment in the justice of which every heart participated. His lordship proved by his conduct that the gratitude of his countrymen made a deep impression on his bosom; and when he bowed to the audience the action was accompanied by a modesty, which enhanced the value of his glorious achievements.

Lord Nelson, with his party, occupied the two boxes next to that on the stage, opposite to the King's side, and the theatre has seldom displayed a greater assemblage of beauty and fashion.

(367.) PETER PINDAR threatens the public with another of his low, illiberal works, called "A cut at his Cobler,"—it is to be hoped it will be his last.

(368.) A RENCONTRE took place on Monday in the shop of Mr. Wright, the bookseller, between the celebrated Peter Pindar and Mr. Giffard, author of the "Baviad." In reply to the many sarcasms thrown out by Peter Pindar against the author of the "Baviad," and other poems, Mr. Giffard lately published a severe satire against Peter. This literary combat on Monday produced blows. Dr. Walcot went into the shop of Mr. Wright, where Mr. Giffard was seated reading a newspaper; he asked him if his name was not Giffard? He replied in the affirmative. Upon which the Doctor aimed a blow at his brother poet with a cane, which Mr. Giffard dexterously warded off, wrested the cane from Peter, and in an instant broke the head of his assailant with his own stick. Some gentlemen who were present interfered, and Peter was thrust into the street, where a mob collected, to whom he made his appeal. He had lost his hat in the affray, which was thrown out to him; but the poet of the "Baviad" kept possession of the cane as a trophy of his triumph. Peter threatens a prosecution.

(369.) PINDAR and GIFFARD.—WE have hitherto contented ourselves with the mere mention of the fact of the late fracas at Mr. Wright's, in Piccadilly, between Peter Pindar, and the "Baviad" Mr. Giffard; but as the parties have each published their own story of the transaction, the one in his own name, the other by his aide-de-camp, Mr. Wright, it may not be unamusing to our readers to recapitulate the different statements of the transaction:—

Peter Pindar.—" Determined to punish a R— that dared to propagate a report the most atrocious, the most opprobious, and the most unfounded, I repaired to Mr. Wright's shop in Piccadilly, to *catch him*, as I understood that he paid frequent visits to his worthy friend and publisher. On opening the shop door I saw several people, and among the rest, as I thought, Gyffard. I immediately asked him if his name was Gyffard? Upon his reply in the affirmative, without any further ceremony, I began to cane him. Wright and his customers and his shopmen immediately surrounded me, and wrested the cane from my hand. I then had recourse to the fist, and really was doing ample and easy justice to my cause, when I found my hands all on a sudden confined behind me, particularly by a tall Frenchman. Upon this Gyffard had time to run round, and with his own stick—a large one too, struck me several blows on the head. I was then hustled out of the shop, and the door was locked against me. I entreated them to let me in, but in vain. Upon the tall Frenchman's coming out of the shop, I told him that he was one of the fellows that held my hands. I have been informed that his name was Peltier. Gyffard has given out as a matter of triumph that he possesses my cane, and that he means to preserve it as a trophy. Let me recommend an inscription for it:—'The Cane of Justice, with which I, William Gyffard, late cobler, of Ashburton, have been soundly drubbed for my infamy.' —I am, Sir, &c., J. WALCOT."

Mr. Wright.—" Whoever is acquainted with the miscreant calling himself 'Peter Pindar,' needs not be informed, that his disregard and hatred of truth are habitual. He will not, therefore, be surprised to learn, that the account this Peter has published in a morning paper, is a shameless tissue of falsehoods from beginning to end.

"I was not in the shop when it happened; but I am *authorised*, by the only two witnesses of it, to lay before the public the following statement:—

"Mr. Giffard was sitting by the window with a newspaper in his hand, when Peter Pindar came into the shop, and saying, 'Is not your name Giffard?' without waiting for an answer, raised a stick he had brought for the purpose, and levelled a blow at his head with all his force. Mr. Giffard fortunately caught the stick in his left hand, and, quitting his chair, wrested it instantly from the cowardly assassin, and gave him two severe blows with it; one of which made a dreadful impression on Peter's skull. Mr. Giffard had raised the stick to strike him a third time, but seeing one of the gentlemen present about to collar the wretch, he desisted, and coolly said, 'Turn him out of the shop.' This was *literally* and *truly all* that passed.

"After Peter was turned into the street, the spectacle of his bleeding head attracted a mob of hackney coachmen, watermen, paviours, &c., to whom he told his lamentable case, and then, with a troop of boys at his heels, proceeded to a surgeon's in St. James's-street to have his wounds examined, after which he slunk home.

"*Piccadilly, Aug. 22.* J. WRIGHT."

(370) NORWICH (June 21.) GUILD-DAY.—For a long series of years, the day on which the Chief Magistrate of the city is sworn into office, has been celebrated with a degree of splendour and festivity that may challenge competition with the most opulent and extensive city or town in the kingdom; and our ancestors, in setting us this example, seem to have been impressed with the policy and the utility of such occasional displays of munificence and hospitality, as tending, on the one hand, to draw closer the various ranks of polished society, and, on the other, to afford employment to the industrious and ingenious.

(371.) IT is said to be finally determined that there should be no public dinner on Lord Mayor's Day at Guildhall.

(372.) WE take the earliest opportunity to explain a paragraph in our paper of yesterday, which is important to so many hundreds:—

The Lord Mayor's dinner will be held as usual at Guildhall. It is at *Bath* that it is to be omitted.

(373.) YESTERDAY afternoon the lord mayor, several aldermen, the two sheriffs, with the city officers, went in state to Westminster Hall, in the city barge, with the courts of assistants of the Clothworkers' and Stationers' Companies, in their barges, up the Thames, and landed at Westminster. About three his lordship and the whole cavalcade came into the Exchequer Court, where they were received by Baron Maziers. The lord mayor, being paramount of the fee, stood covered. The recorder made his long harangue in praise of the late sheriffs, and then proceeded to expatiate on the high characters of the present gentlemen. The baron shortly replied, that His Majesty could not have any objection to the choice of his faithful citizens of London.

John Perring, Esq., clothworker, and Thomas Cadell, stationer, were then sworn into office. Thomas Perring, Esq., the head under-sheriff, was also sworn. Warrants of attorney were recorded, and then came the mirthful part of the ceremony, about which so many fables have been propagated; the truth being that the sheriffs have not the most distant share in the business.

Usher of the Court.—"Senior alderman below the chair, come forth, and perform suit and service for a certain manor and tenement called the Moor, in com. Chester." Alderman Newman accordingly mounted the table, when the usher presented him with a bill hook, himself holding a bundle, by the two ends, of white rods, with both hands; these the alderman cut in the middle with the hook.

Remembrancer.—"How many are there?" Usher.—"Twelve." Answer.—"A very good number."

Then a hatchet was delivered to the alderman, and another bundle of sticks was cut in like manner; but the alderman missed his aim, and cut his finger.

Usher (again).—"Senior alderman come forth, and perform suit and service for a certain tenement called the Forge, without side Temple Bar, in com. Middlesex."

A bag was ready upon the table, and the usher assisted the alderman in counting out six large horse-shoes, and fifty-four very long horse-nails. Remembrancer.—"How many are there?" Usher.—"Six shoes and fifty-four nails." Answer.—"A very good number." And accordingly they were registered.

The ceremony being ended, the lord mayor, Aldermen Boydell, Le Mesurier, Skinner, Curtis, Watson, Newman, Staines, Eamer, Shaw, and Leighton, the sheriffs, recorder, common sergeant, and the city officers returned to Stationer's Hall, where, with a great number of gentlemen of respectability, they partook of an elegant entertainment, provided at the expense of Mr. Sheriff Cadell.

Combe, Mayor.

(374.) IN a meeting or assembly of the mayor, aldermen, and liverymen of the several companies of the city of London, in common hall assembled, at the Guildhall of the said city, on Thursday, the 9th day of October, 1800:

Resolved, that the lord mayor, aldermen, and livery of London, in common hall assembled, have immemorially exercised the right and privilege of presenting petitions to the King upon the throne, and such right hath not been disputed or denied, except under the corrupt and infamous administration of those persons who were the authors and conductors of the cruel and unnatural war against our brethren in America.

Resolved, that when a petition is presented to the King upon the throne, the petitioners have the satisfaction of knowing their complaints are heard by His Majesty, by having their petition read to him in their presence, and receiving an answer thereto; but when presented at the levee they receive no answer, nor do they know that their petition is ever read by His Majesty, it being immediately delivered to the lord in waiting.

Resolved, that the only reason assigned for not receiving their petitions in the accustomed manner on the throne, is contained in a letter from Lord Hertford, dated the April 11th, 1775, addressed to John Wilkes, Esq., lord mayor of the city of London, wherein he states, "That the King has directed him to give notice, that for the future His Majesty will not receive on the throne any address, remonstrance, and petition, but from the body corporate of this city."

Resolved unanimously, that it appears to this common hall that two addresses from the court of lieutenancy have since been received by His Majesty on the throne, the one on the 16th day of December, 1795, and the other on the 30th day of May, 1800, although the said court of lieutenancy be not the body corporate of this city; they are therefore of opinion, that it would be highly derogatory to the lord mayor, aldermen, and livery of London to present their address in any other manner, and whoever advised His Majesty to persist in refusing to his faithful subjects free access, in these times of peculiar difficulty and distress, is equally unworthy of His Majesty's confidence and an enemy of the rights and privileges of the citizens of London.

Resolved unanimously, that the sheriffs, attended by Mr. Remembrancer, do wait on His Majesty with the foregoing resolutions.

Resolved unanimously, that the thanks of this common hall be given to the sheriffs, for their prompt and diligent attention to the resolutions of the last common hall.

Resolved unanimously, that the thanks of this common hall be given to the Right Hon. the lord mayor, for his impartial conduct this day.

Resolved, that the resolutions of this common hall, together with the petition agreed to at the last common hall, be signed by the town clerk, and published in the morning and evening papers.

Which petition is as follows:

Most gracious Sovereign.

We, your Majesty's most dutiful and loyal subjects, the lord mayor, aldermen, and livery of the city of London, in common hall assembled, penetrated with compassion for the sufferings of our fellow-creatures, by the present exhorbitant price of every article of life, beg most humbly to lay their unhappy situation before Your Majesty.

We deeply regret the strong necessity of addressing your Majesty on this occasion, but we feel ourselves impelled by the long and severe sufferings of Your Majesty's poorer subjects, who, through extreme want, have been irritated to madness and despair; while the middle classes of society are scarcely able to maintain their families with their wonted comforts and respectability.

The poor, hopeless of relief, and rendered furious by the incessant cries of their half-famished children, join the tumultuous crowd of their suffering brethren, and, in the tone of angry despondence, demand food at a reasonable rate. Think not, most gracious Sire, that we are disposed to justify acts of tumult or disorder, but while we lament the excesses by which the public tranquillity has been disturbed, and the rights of private property violated, we cannot forbear deploring the sufferings of our fellow creatures.

Exhausted by solicitude and toil, faint and emaciated through want of food, thousands of unhappy families exist under the torturing expectation of falling victims to merciless famine and extreme distress.

We, therefore, most humbly implore Your Majesty to convene parliament, to consider of such measures as they in their wisdom may think most salutary and effectual towards remedying those grievances, which your people suffer, and to remove those causes which may in future produce the destructive evils which the poorer classes of Your Majesty's subjects cannot sustain. And we will ever pray.

(375.) On Saturday the usual festivities were kept up with great conviviality at the Mansion House. It was the day of the retreat of the old lord mayor from the fatigues of office, and of the assumption of its duties by the new prætor. The honest knight, who is now at the head of the city of London, loves his pipe, and was with much pleasantness indulged with one. In yielding up his place and honours to him, the late chief magistrate had the good nature to share in the humour of his successor; they were observed after dinner both of them lighting their pipes at one candle, like the Duke of Buckingham's two Kings of Brentford smelling at one nosegay.

Lord Mayor's Day.

Yesterday the usual ceremonies took place on the swearing in of the new lord mayor. At half-past eleven, the late and present lord mayors, accompanied by several aldermen, took water at Queenhithe, from whence they proceeded to Westminster. On their return they landed at Blackfriars, and the procession went forward to Guildhall. The fineness of the day drew together a vast concourse of people, but everything was conducted with great decorum. When the procession reached the top of Ludgate-hill, the mob took the horses from the carriage of the late lord mayor, and also from that of Lord Nelson, and drew them to Guildhall, amidst repeated huzzas of "Lord Nelson." All the way he passed along Cheapside, he was greeted by the ladies from the windows with their handkerchiefs, and the loudest acclamations. The mob prevailed upon his lordship to put his hand out of the carriage that they might kiss it.

At six o'clock the Company sat down to a very elegant dinner, which was extremely well conducted.

After the usual toasts had been drank, the company were gratified by the presentation to Lord Nelson, of a very elegant sword, voted to his lordship by the corporation, after the battle of Aboukir, which was delivered to him by Mr. Chamberlain Clark, who read to his lordship the resolutions which passed on that occasion. His lordship returned for answer, "that he received with satisfaction that mark of their approbation of his conduct, and he hoped with that sword shortly to make one in reducing our insolent and implacable foe within her proper limits, without which Great Britain could never hope to obtain an honourable, safe, and permanent peace."

Several toasts were introduced in the course of the evening, among which were the present and the late Lord Mayor, Lord Nelson, Lord Spencer, and the Court of Aldermen. Several appropriate songs were sung by Dignum, Sale, and Neild.

The company were very numerous, but the Cabinet Ministers were prevented from attending on account of the reading of His Majesty's speech to the Members of Parliament.

Among the company that were placed round the lord mayor, were Lord Spencer, Lord Nelson, Lord Rolle, Sir William Hamilton, The Hon. O. Ellsworth, Admiral Mann, the Hessian, Portuguese, Sardinian, and Bavarian Ministers, His Highness Mirza, and the Persian Prince, and Judges Hotham and Graham.

The evening concluded as usual with a ball.

Another account.

(376.) The old and new lord mayor, &c., proceeded in the accustomed state to Westminster, were Sir W. Staines was sworn into office for the ensuing year. On returning from Blackfriars-bridge, the populace took the horses from the carriage of the old lord mayor, Alderman Combe, and drew him to Guildhall, and did the same by Lord Nelson, who (having obtained the King's permission to appear in public before he was introduced at Court) was one of the numerous company that dined with the lord mayor, when he received the sword voted by the city of London.

(377.) Mr. Taylor the Apothecary, who married Mr. Pitt's niece, is appointed Deputy Comptroller of the Customs, worth about 2000l. a-year. The place is a sinecure.

A Quack Doctor, who advertises no cure no pay, is very angry that a Kentish Apothecary should get 2000l. a-year *sine-cure*.

FASHIONS.

Female Fashions for January.
Full Dresses.

(378.) 1.—White muslin round dress, with long train, trimmed all round with brown satin ribband, ornamented with chenille; white crape corset, trimmed in the same manner; velvet hat, with blue feather affixed on the left side, and falling over the front; silver bear or white muff. 2. White muslin dress the same as above; Sicilian corset, made of coquelicot velvet, and trimmed with chenille; the Arabian sleeve, made of muslin and lace, and tied at the bottom with a bow of ribband; black velvet cap, trimmed with coquelicot ribband, and a coquelicot feather.

Head Dresses.

1. White satin turban, covered with stripes of crape, ostrich feather in front. 2. White satin turban, long end and tassel, ornamented with beads and feathers. 3. Black velvet bonnet, ornamented with two black feather bandeaux, bow in front, short lace veil. 4. Bonnet made of slate coloured willow, trimmed with pink ribband, rose, bow, and feather. 5. Spangled velvet turban, ornamented with gold sprig in front. 6. Bonnet *à la Pallas*, made of spangled velvet, white feathers.

General Observations.

The prevalent colours are poppy, rose, scarlet, coquelicot, and pink. Gold and silver ornaments are very general. Black and coloured velvets continue to be worn in every article of dress.

LONDON FASHIONS FOR FEBRUARY.

(379.) THE following are the prevailing and most fashionable dresses now worn:—

Morning Dress.

Robe of white sarsnet, trimmed with elastic coquelicot velvet,, deep black lace veil hanging as low as the knee, open before and drawn round the bonnet. Etruscan bonnet of black velvet, with coquelicot flower. In the hand *an indispensable* worn instead of a pocket.

Full Dresses.

White muslin dress, over the body a corset *à la militaire*, made of blue velvet, trimmed with brown fur and gold, and fastened in front with gold cord and tassels; the sleeves made of lace and white satin ribbon. Bonnet *à la militaire*, made of blue velvet, and trimmed with brown fur and gold, coque feather. Robe *en Etrusque* of pink muslin, trimmed with white satin ribbon and brown cord; the body plain and cut very low before with a full front of white satin, which draws up round the bosom, and is trimmed with lace; sleeves of white satin, full on each side and drawn up in the middle; the corners of the train fastened back. *Chapeau à la Grecque* of brown velvet, spangled with silver stars, silver cord and tassel, pink feather.

Head Dresses.

1. Turban of blue velvet, embroidered and spangled with silver, ostrich feathers hanging over towards the front. 2. Poppy or coquelicot velvet cap, trimmed with two puffings of white ribband, bow at the top and behind. 3. Le Brun's York hat in white and gold, ornamented with gold trimmings, and gold loop and tassel, white feathers hanging over in front. 4. Cap of lace and muslin, trimmed with puffings of white satin ribband, with puffings under the chin. 5. Cap of lace and muslin, ornamented on one side with white roses, and on the other with a large bow and rose, necklace of topazes, mixed with pearls. 6. Hat of slate-coloured willow, turned up in front with bunch of flowers. 7. Turban of white satin, ornamented with silver, puffings of white satin ribband under the chin, white ostrich feathers, necklace and ear-rings of topazes, pearls, &c. 8. Cap of muslin and silver, diamond crescent, silver cord and tassels, *esprit* plume, topaze drop, and diamond or gold necklace. 9. Black velvet bonnet trimmed with poppy.

General Observations.

Silver and gold muslins are much worn in dresses. The colours are poppy, tea-green, purple, slate and white. The hair is worn full and long on the forehead, and none appears behind. The hair and head-dress is made to assume the Grecian, or long shape, as much as possible; pelisses are universal. Necklaces and other jewellery are much worn.

LONDON FASHIONS FOR MARCH.

Morning Dress.

(380.) 1. THE *Georgian* half dress of white muslin, made high in the neck with a collar and trimmed with lace, the binding of elastic coloured velvet. The cloak or shawl of pink satin, covered or not covered with white crape, and trimmed with black lace. 2. The *Aerial* dress, made of white muslin, the body plain, and trimmed round the bosom with lace, the sleeves of lace and muslin; the drapery goes over the left shoulder, and fastens in different parts with gold or silver sliders, or diamonds, gold or silver trimmings round the bottom. Indispensable, gold chain, necklace, &c. Turban of white crape, fastened in front to correspond with the dress, white ostrich feather fixed behind and falling over the front.

Full Dress.

1. Silk pelice, trimmed with broad black lace. Hat of purple chip or willow, with bow behind, and white roses on the left side; silver bear muff. 2. Russian robe of velvet, trimmed all round with silver; the bottom of the train likewise trimmed with silver. Amanthis cap of white spangled crape, with wreath of flowers, and an end on the left side.

General Observations.

Silver and gold flowers and ornaments of all kinds are universally worn. Crape or velvet netting, plain, spangled, beaded, and bugled, are much introduced into caps and bonnets, with flowers to match. To match the spangled nets a very beautiful flower, the lily of the valley, with corresponding wreaths, has been made. Gold and silver spotted tiffanies are much used in turbans. The prevailing colours are brown, purple, blue, and tea or olive green. The feathers generally worn are the argus pheasant, the Indian macau, the argilla, the flat and porcupine ostrich, and the Seringapatam plume.

PARISIAN FASHIONS.

Black velvet is now the only colour for capotes. Satin, more worn than velvet, is almost always white. The bows of ribbon have the extremities cut in points.

Morning Fashions.

A close mob tied under the chin, with a straight lappet striped with coloured ribbon, and a round cap made of a coloured handkerchief edged with lace, are among the subaltern fashionables the usual morning head dress. The height of the sleeves admit of wonderful variety, some plait them lengthways, others wear them with twisted columns, puffed or in diamonds, exclusive of the various designs in the embroidery and trimming. The chemise handkerchiefs and lawn aprons are ornamented with a narrow trimming. The sashes have the ends flying, and the trains of the robes are about half-a-foot on the ground. Wadded spencers, tippets, and no muffs, are the order of the day.

Male Fashions.

The capes of the coats have no turn back, and silk or worsted buttons are generally worn instead of metal ones.

FASHIONS FOR APRIL.
Morning Dress.

(381.) Round dress of blue or other coloured muslin, drawn round the bosom, half sleeves of blue muslin, with full white muslin sleeves under them, confined to the size of the arm at bottom. Scarf of white muslin. Straw bonnet turned up in front, and ornamented with flowers, strings across the crown to tie under the chin; this kind of straw and Leghorn so turned up before, and with a button and loop, is likely to be the prevailing and favourite spring shape. Round dress of thick white muslin, drawn close round the bosom. Short silk pelice, edged with elastic velvet. Long white or black veil.

Full Dress.

Dress of white muslin with a long train, short robe of pink muslin over it, bordered all round with leaves of very dark brown satin and silver. The hair dressed loosely, and ornamented with a wreath of roses and ostrich feathers. Body and drapery of pink muslin or crape, with a long train of white muslin, drawn for dancing through the pink drapery, sleeves of black lace. Petticoat of white sarsnet. A bandeau through the hair, with ostrich feathers.

Head Dresses.

1. Hat of black velvet and silver, ornamented with red and white roses. 2. Cap à *la capricieuse* of muslin and blond lace, wreath of roses. 3. Cap of white silk gimp and ribbon, bow and rose, in front silk tassel, and rose behind. 4. Bonnet of white satin, wreath of purple and silver, ostrich feathers. 5. Mob cap of worked muslin and narrow lace, open at top to admit the hair. 6. Turban of white crape, furnished with a very long end on the left side, and ornamented with gold, green spray in front. 7. Spanish hat of white satin and beads, two ostrich feathers fixed behind to fall over the front. 8. Close cap of white muslin, with double quillings of lace and white bows. 9. Bonnet of white satin, trimmed with elastic blue velvet, white ostrich feathers.

General Observations.

Chips and Leghorns in the Spanish shape, turned up before with a button and loop, are the prevailing favourites. The flat crown, or Henry the Eight's shape, has also been introduced. Very tasteful bonnets are made of penny satin ribband, wove in various coloured checks. Feathers and flowers continue to be much worn. Lilac, brown, tea-green, and purple are the prevailing colours.

FASHIONS FOR MAY.
Head Dresses.

(382.) An undress cap of white crape, trimmed with white ribbon and yellow roses. A turban of white crape, ornamented with three bands of bugles and a wreath of red roses from the front across the crown. The Venetian bonnet, made of straw and trimmed with wreaths of straw or various flowers, the strings fastened with a bow behind, and tied loose on the bosom. The Neapolitan bonnet, made of Leghorn, trimmed with straw flowers; strings of the same colour as the bonnet, fastened to the crown and tied loosely on the bosom. A bonnet of straw, with an open edge, trimmed with white riband and with wreaths of flowers. A cap made of black crape or gauze, trimmed with a blue wreath and bows. Bonnet *a l'Atalante*, made of point lace trimmed with a wreath of red roses. A straw hat, with horizontal rim, turned up in front, and a red rose. A cap of point lace trimmed with white ribbon and with lilies of the valley. The vestal cap, made of a lace veil, formed and fastened with a wreath of flowers. A morning cap of muslin, with a single lace border. An undress bonnet of white chip and satin, trimmed with green ribbon, and with a bunch of flowers in front. A dress hat of white satin, looped up on one side, white ostrich feathers. A lace cap, ornamented with a blue wreath of flowers. A dress hat of raised striped sarsenet, with white ostrich feathers. A bonnet made with crape net in brown or any other colour, lined with satin of other suitable colour, bow of ribbon in front. A bonnet, the cawl of which is made of chequed penny-satin riband, in purple and brown or other colours, the front of satin of the same colour, bow in front. Cap of lilac crape, with three silver bands, silver tassel fastened to the bag behind.

General Observations.

The prevailing colours are lilac, pea-green, and yellow. Sewed Leghorn and chips, of the new gipsey shape, are worn generally. The Oatland Village hat, that made of straw, twist, and Leghorn; and the Carleton hat, of new beautiful open straw, have just been adopted. Flowers of hyacinths and lilacs are the most worn.

FASHIONS FOR JUNE.
Walking Dress.

(383.) Coloured chip hat, tied under the chin, and ornamented with flowers in front; dress of white muslin, made and worn very low in the neck and bosom, and fastened down the front with bows of riband, the sleeves loose.

Full Dress.

Bandeau of silver or diamonds, with a bunch of red roses and white ostrich feathers; dress of white muslin, trimmed and spangled with silver, one side is drawn through the belt and finished at the end with a tassel.

Morning Dresses.

1. Hair dressed and ornamented with a wreath of roses; dress of white muslin, trimmed with printed coloured muslin; corset of the same coloured muslin; full necklace, earrings, &c.

2. Bandeau of crape or spangled muslin, with ostrich feathers; round dress of variegated silk, looped up in front with a silver slide, short white sleeves with full silk epaulets; the dress crossed loosely over the bosom and fastened on the left side with bows and ends.

Head Dresses.

Bandeau of small white flowers and bows of riband, white ostrich feathers. Cap of white lace, ornamented with a wreath of roses. Bonnet of silk and chip, turned up in front, and tied under the chin. Cap made of white crape, trimmed with bows of pink ribband. Turban of white crape drawn full at the top of the crown and ornamented with a wreath of flowers. Dress cap of yellow crape, trimmed at the front with white lace, white ostrich feathers. Dress bonnet of white satin, trimmed with silver, silver cord and tassels fastened on the top of the crown to fall behind, white ostrich feathers. Bonnet of black satin, turned up in front and trimmed with green riband, May flowers in front. Cap of net crape, made to the form of the head, and ornamented with bows of riband.

General Observations.

The colours are lilac, yellow, and pea-green. The feathers are the ostrich, the bird of paradise, the cocque, and the esprit plume. The waist shortens. Ruffs are still worn. The hair continues close and short behind, and the neck bare. The large sewed gipsey chips, pressed chips, chips of all kinds, and superfine Leghorns, in the poke, and in all shapes, are in general wear. Several new bonnets have been introduced, particularly the Windsor bonnet, made of plated riband and satin; and the hair bonnet in various colours; the new shapes all made to cover the ear. Flowers are adopted in profusion, chiefly the lily of the valley, wheat ears, and mignionet. A new elastic puff trimmed, figured sarsenets, checked ribands, and a new velvet, called Prince's cord, are much used in bonnets and cloaks.

Fashions for July.
Evening Dress.

(384.) Bonnet of yellow crape, finished with a bow of white riband at top, trimmed and tied on one side with white riband, bunch of flowers in front. The dress of white worked muslin edged with white gimp.

Full Dress.

Black muslin robe over pink sarsenet, trimmed with black satin riband and lace, the sleeve fastened on the shoulder with a topaz, and to the arm with gold chains composed of small balls linked together. Bracelets ornamented with antique gems. The head-dress of black lace lined with pink, bows of pink crape edged with black elastic velvet, pink feather.

Walking Dresses.

1. Pelice of nankeen-coloured muslin, open at the sides and front, and trimmed with black lace. The bonnet of white muslin trimmed with nankeen-coloured riband. 2. Wrapper of cambric muslin reaching only to the waist, with long loose sleeves, trimmed with white lace. Bonnet of crape and lilac riband.

General Observations.

An elegant new hat has been fabricated, made of frivolity and cambric muslin, in the cottage shape. An elegant straw bonnet has also been introduced, called *the Nootka* or *thatched bonnet*, worn with a fancy straw wreath.

The Leghorn and fine chips are still universally adopted, chiefly in the cottage shape. The prevailing colours are purple, lilac, nankeen, and pea green. Flowers are general.

Colour checked silk handkerchiefs are now worn, tied loosely on the bosom; hat bouquets of blue field flowers, mixed with scarlet poppies, are also fashionable. White silk open wove gloves are universally adopted. The gauzy net mitten is worn in the evening.

Fashions for August.
Walking Dresses.

(385.) 1. Round hat of green and white chip, wreath of red roses, white veil; round dress of white muslin; scarf of green muslin, one end thrown carelessly over the right shoulder, the other over the left arm. 2. Habit of bottle green or dark brown, buttoned loose over the bosom, with a white waistcoat, edged with pink or other colour. Round beaver hat and feather. 3. Dress of white muslin, the body made to button in front, with the collar to button occasionally, full and long sleeves, made of alternate stripes of lace and muslin, and confined with bands of muslin. Hat of white chip and yellow crape, ornamented with flowers.

Head Dresses.

1. Turban of white crape ornamented with beads and white feathers in front, bows on the top of the crown and behind. 2. Cap of single crape, transparent, tied up in a bunch on the top of the crown, ornamented with a wreath of flowers. 3. Turban of worked muslin, made to form a half handkerchief behind, trimmed with lace, lilac flower in front. 4. A bonnet, the front of white chip, edged with pink, full crown of pink crape, bows and flower. 5. Turban of striped muslin, ornamented with two rows of beads round the front, white ostrich feather. 6. A bonnet with white chip front and green silk crown, ornamented with flowers and bows. 7. Bonnet with white chip front and yellow crape crown, ornamented with crape wreath and yellow flower in front. 8. Bonnet of brown satin, covered with black lace, bows and trimmings of the same. 9. Bonnet of cambric muslin, trimmed with lilac ribbon, lilac spray in front.

General Observations.

Straws, chips, and Leghorns are still much worn, particularly in the gipsey shape.

The ornaments are flowers, chiefly the poppy and convolvulus. The fashionable colours are Leghorn, rose, pea-green, and lilac. In cloaks, those of white muslin and of patent lace, of the usual shapes, are the prevailing varieties.

Fashions for September.
Full Length Walking Dresses.

(386.) 1. ROUND dress of white muslin; black lace cloak, made to hang full on the shoulders, and trimmed on the outside edge and on the ends with broad lace. Bonnet of yellow silk, ornamented with a wreath of roses, and tied under the chin with yellow ribbon. 2. Dress of white muslin, made to wrap over with one lappel, which is tied in with the girdle, and which hangs down before in a long end, finished with a tassel; square silk shawl; small round chipped bonnet, wreathed with oak leaves.

Head Dresses.

1. Cap of lace and muslin, ornamented with crape flowers, with bow and tassel on the left side. 2. Cap of muslin, with a broad lace border, the cap made open behind to shew the hair, and trimmed with lace, bows of white ribbon behind and before. 3. Cap of brown satin, trimmed with lace, ornamented with a red rose and white ribbon in front. 4. Bonnet made of white chip and pink silk, green flower in front. 5. Cap of lace muslin, with a wreath of marone flowers, the hair exposed behind. 6. Hat of black chip, turned up in front, trimmed with green ribbon and feather. 7. Hat with white chip front and full crown of green silk; green feathers and white ribbons. 8. Bonnet of Leghorn, tied under the chin with coloured ribbon. 9. Cap of muslin and lace, wreathed with laurel, trimmed with green ribbons.

General Observations.

In bonnets, the *Swinley Slouch* and the *Weymouth Shade* and *Slouch* are the newest and most favourite shapes, in chip, straw, and Leghorn. Flowers continue to be universally worn, and the Weymouth trimming, which consists of a very small flower wreath, is generally adopted. The prevailing colours are the *geranium*, the marone, pea-green, and crimson.

Fashions for October.
Full Length Dresses.

(387.) 1. ROUND dress of plain or figured cambric muslin, sleeves full, the top part of them in alternate stripes of lace and muslin, the bottom bound to the size of the arm. Hat of white chip, tied with coquelicot ribbon, coquelicot flowers in front. 2. Circassian dress, and robe of plain or spotted cambric muslin; the dress made quite round, with two pieces which are fastened to the shoulders behind, and which fall quite loose to the bottom of the dress in front; the sleeves full, and bound to the size of the arm in the middle. Plain round turban.

Head Dresses.

1. A cap of white cambric, spotted with pearls, and ornamented with coquelicot ribbon and flowers; a deep lace border. 2. A cap of black lace, with a deep veil. 3. A cap of black lace, made open behind to admit the hair, and ornamented with coquelicot; a lace border. 4. A plain round turban of white crape, with a small green spray in front. 5. A cap of black muslin or lace, trimmed with coquelicot, and a coquelicot feather in front. 6. A cap or bandeau of white crape, one side is made rather full, and fastened to the ribbon which forms it, the other side hangs nearly loose, and finishes in a point on the shoulder; a small blue wreath on the left side. 7. A hat made of yellow silk. 8. A straw hat trimmed with a wreath of roses.

Paris Fashions.

The most fashionable head dresses are made of crape, and the favourite colours are green, violet, or rose colour. Wigs *à la Grecque* are still general. Tuniques of black crape are coming into wear.

General Observations.

Scarlet, crimson, poppy, and yellow are the favourite colours. The Weymouth trimming, consisting of small wreaths, coque feathers in all colours, and poppy and amber beads are the prevailing ornaments. A new velvet, called velvet cord, in all cords, has been introduced with approbation.

Fashions for November.
Full Dresses.

(388.) ROUND dress of white muslin, over which is worn a petticoat of the same, open behind, and trimmed all round with red ribbon; the body is a plain corset, trimmed the same as the train; the sleeves full and trimmed with lace; the cap of white crape, trimmed with red; one red feather. A short robe of black and scarlet printed muslin; the train and sleeves of white muslin; the bottom of the train trimmed with the same as the robe. Cap of white crape over yellow silk; white flower in front, and bow behind.

Head Dresses.

Hat of white raised velvet, turned up in front, and ornamented with white ostrich feathers; cap of white lace, ornamented with gold beads; a down feather in front; cap of white crape, trimmed with lace; bows of lilac, and black ribbon behind, and on the left side. Turban of white raised velvet, trimmed with coquelicot ribbon; roses in front. Bonnet of black raised velvet, trimmed with black ribbon; black feather in front. Hat of velvet, trimmed with elastic blue velvet; blue feather in front, and a bow behind. Circassian turban of white crape or satin, trimmed with gold trimming, white ostrich feather in front. Cap of white crape over pink silk, ornamented with ribbon; a deep lace border cap of pink crape, trimmed with black lace and pink ribbon; red roses in front.

General Observations.

The prevailing colours are scarlet, crimson, purple, brown, and puce. A small spotted velvet, and the shaded cord, in the preceding colours, are generally worn in bonnets. A new bonnet in the Swinley shape, made of clouded chenille and silk, and a new figured Barcelona handkerchief, with ribbons to match, are likely to become general favourites. Several new feathers and flowers have recently been introduced, and these, with gold and silver trimmings, are much worn. Jewellery ornaments are disused. Pelices, as usual, promise to be general throughout the winter.

Fashions for December.
Head Dresses.

(389.) CAP of white lace, ornamented with bows of ribbon; feather of brown, or any colour, in front. Round cap of white lace, confined with ribbon, and ornamented with bows of ribbon. Turban of white muslin, ornamented with a small velvet wreath. Close bonnet of purple, or other coloured velvet, with a coquelicot flower. A Scots bonnet made of velvet, silver trimming round the front, silver cord and tassel fastened to the top of the crown, with white ostrich feathers in front. The Nelson cap, made of coquelicot velvet, trimmed with silver, two ostrich feathers in front.

Full Dresses.

Round dress made of white muslin, drawn round the bosom, and trimmed with lace; loose robe of silk, trimmed with elastic velvet; cap of silk corresponding with the robe, trimmed also with nacarett elastic velvet, and ornamented with white ostrich feathers. Dress of muslin, fastened on the left side with bows of ribbon; sleeves full, and confined in the middle; the Sheridan cloak, made of blue velvet, tied close round the neck, and falling open on one side from the top of the shoulder, the sides trimmed with elastic velvet, and the bosom with deep black lace; a cap of gauze, or velvet, ornamented with bugles and white lace, blue ostrich feathers in front.

Walking Dresses.

Plain round dress of white muslin, velvet cloak formed to the shape of the back, tied round the waist, and trimmed all round with black lace; bonnet of velvet, ornamented with yellow, small yellow feathers on the left side. Dress of thick white muslin; short round cloak of black velvet, cut as a half circle, trimmed with deep lace, or with fur; bonnet of black velvet, with pink or coquelicot feathers.

Observations.

The fashionable colours are scarlet, purple, puce, and mazarine blue. The fancy articles generally adopted are beads of various colours, as amber, scarlet, pink, and rose; plain and figured terry velvets. Feathers of all kinds, flowers, gold and silver trimmings. Figured Barcelona handkerchiefs. Black bear muffs for morning dress, and scarlet and white goat's beard for full dress. Weymouth tippets, instead of long tippets. Very short fans, and lace round the bottom of dresses.

(390.) THE following is stated to have been an expedient which Bonaparte successfully resorted to, in order to effect a change of the late immodest *half-naked* fashion of the Parisian belles. A numerous assembly of both sexes having been invited to the Luxembourg by Madame Bonaparte, the First Consul entered the drawing-room, where they were all present, and, after paying his respects to the company, ordered the servants to make a good fire. He affected even to repeat his orders two or three times, till one of them took the liberty to observe, that the grate would hold no more. "Very well, very well," replied Bonaparte (rather in an elevated tone of voice), "I was anxious to have a good fire; for it is excessively cold, and besides, *these ladies are almost naked.*"

(391.) THE Parisian ladies (say the French papers) have lately resumed the wearing of silk dresses. They have not been forced to it by the inclemency of the weather, but by an appearance of decorum. Bonaparte had more than once declared his dislike of the scanty dresses worn in public assemblies, and the females have at length been induced to clothe themselves, with the sole view of gratifying the delicacy, and appearing amiable in the eyes of the First Consul.

(392.) THE Grand Consul is thought to have aimed a blow at our trade, by making the Parisian ladies wear silks in lieu of English muslins. The Parisian ladies, however, according to all accounts, wear so little dress of any kind, that the loss to commerce cannot be very great.

(393.) IT is curious to observe the pains daily taken in some of the prints to introduce amongst us all the French fashions and foppery that can be imported. We have French milliners who essay every mode and shade between dress and nakedness upon their own limbs. We do not know what success these efforts may be attended with in half a dozen great houses; but we will venture to say, the present French fashions have but little chance of being adopted at Court.

(394.) A GRAVE old lawyer observed on Saturday at the Opera, that in a little time there would not be a *femme couverte* in the nation.

(395.) THE two swindlers who were brought to the bar of Bow-street on Saturday, were dressed in the extreme of fashion: their wadded sleeves, puckered shoulders, pigeon breasts, trunk breeches, and jack boots, received the further addition of an enormous shirt collar, which completely buried more than half the head of the owner; the hair was quite the *ton*; but a man not acquainted with the reigning mode would have said, it was certainly meant for a *scare-crow*. If the appearance of such fellows at the bar of a court of justice does not make every man of real fashion revolt at the preposterous stile of dress which very generally prevails, we know not what will.

(396.) THE effects of scarcity have not been more severely felt by the lowest classes of society, than by the loveliest part of the highest; who are dreadfully complaining at present of the effects of the late dreadful scarcity of cloathing.

(397.) THE fashionable artists who invented for our females the mode of going without pockets, are the victims of their own ingenuity. The wearing no pockets has naturally led to that of *having no money about one*, and has added much more to the *credit* of the wearer than to that of the inventor.

(398.) THE poor mantua-makers are much to be pitied during the present scarcity of petticoats; their employment has fallen off dreadfully, and it is thought in the course of next month it will be reduced to an absolute sinecure.

(399.) AMIDST the fashionable circle at Kensington Gardens yesterday, was noticed the zebra chip hat in various shapes, as being the only novel hat introduced; also the leghorn oatland hat, with straw plumes, was much worn.

(400.) A GENTLEMAN lately returned from the Continent, and not acquainted with all the new modes and fashions that have crept in since his absence, was greatly surprised at receiving a card from a lady, informing him she was "at home" upon such an evening. After much difficulty and hesitation what answer to return to so novel a communication, he wrote back, "By Jove, it's a wonder!"

(401.) WE can assure the public that there were neither black satins nor black elastic velvets at the Duchess of Devonshire's breakfast.

(402.) RESPECTING the constant critiques and satires upon the dress of our fair countrywomen, we shall only observe, that so much was never yet said and written about so little.

(403.) NOTWITHSTANDING the late dreadful scarcity of female dress, it is extraordinary that we have heard of no forestallers of petticoats, regraters of neckerchiefs, or engrossers of *corsets* and *chémises*. The whole trade, to do it justice, has been fair and open, and every commodity exposed, (not by sample, as in our grandmother's time), but in bulk in the market.

(404.) IT is calculated, that from the present fashion of muslin dresses, eighteen ladies have caught fire, and 18,000 caught cold.

(405.) THE present fashion of low carriages, as it has been said, was invented for the low people who have lately set them up; but to get in a carriage at all is the highest thing in the world for some of them to think of.

(406.) WE hear a great deal of nonsense about a *Peeping Tom* at the watering places. Few women go so naked into the water as they walk upon the shore.

(407.) WHILE the inferiors in offices are too apt to complain of their superiors, by saying they themselves do all the work at small salaries, while their superiors sit quietly at home, and receive the great emoluments of the place; the Under-petticoats, on the contrary, complain that they have nothing to do, that they are entirely discarded and turned out of place, while their superiors strut alone about the town, and take all the trouble off their hands!

(408.) SEVERAL beautiful women, who used to pick up a livelihood by sitting to painters and statuaries, are thrown out of their bread by the cruel transparency of the fashion. A painter who with his brush and pallet takes up his stand at a window in Bond-street, now wants no models, alive or in stone.

(409.) THE Queen Elizabeth's ruff begins to be introduced among the people of fashion. It requires a pretty face to suit this ornament. Some wrinkled countenances look for all the world like John the Baptist's head in a charger!

(410.) FASHIONS.—*Dialogue between a Lady and a Man milliner at Paris.*—"Citizen, I am just come to town; pray have the goodness to inform me how I must appear, to be in the fashion?"—"Madame, it is done in a moment; in two minutes I shall equip you in the first style. Have the goodness to take off that bonnet." —"Well." "Off that petticoat."—"There it is." "Away with these pockets."—"There they go." "Throw off that handkerchief."—"'Tis done." "Away with that corset and sleeves."—"Will that do?" "Yes; Madame, you are now in the fashion. 'Tis an easy matter, you see. To be *dressed* in the fashion you have only to *undress!*"

(411.) PARIS FASHIONS.—THE hair is no longer worn loosely, but twisted, and the combs in gold continue still in fashion. Several of the dashing *beaux* and *belles* have attempted, but in vain, to restore the use of powder. All the cloaks of the first women of distinction are adorned with ribbons, disposed in the manner of shell work, and arranged in triple rows. The embellishments are generally red and fanciful, with the appearance of a ranunculus. White ostrich plumes are in considerable repute. The ribbons appropriated to common purposes are white, or of a red poppy colour. India muslins are worn in a zig-zag fashion, white, with an amaranth ground; and shawls of a square shape, in silk, preserve their former influence.

THE FINE ARTS.

(412.) WE trust that as soon as circumstances will permit, a proper mansion will be built for the Parliament of the United Kingdom. Surely, when money is spent so prodigally on other occasions, it is a miserable thing to economise in an object that interests the national honour and dignity. It is pitiful to see the representatives of this empire huddled together in such a place as St. Stephen's Chapel, with the improvements that can be made on it. Whenever a proper attendance takes place, they must squeeze up in corners, pigging to their heads and points. Not to mention that the appearance of such a hall is contemptible, and must disappoint every stranger, there is a want of accommodation for members.

We hope, therefore, that Mr. Wyatt will soon have an opportunity of erecting a building worthy of the British Parliament, and the architecture of the nation. Our public buildings in this country are in general very mean. Those buildings which ought to be executed on such a scale as to afford encouragement to genius, and to prove monuments of the arts, possess neither elegance nor convenience. In a country that aims at all sorts of glory, this branch, which depends so much upon public patronage, has been too much neglected in modern times. The public buildings of the ancients continue to be the admiration of men of taste, because they formed the object of attention and pride to the government. Here they are a sort of temporary barracks, and the men in place care nothing farther, provided they last *their* time.

(413.) To-morrow Hogarth's celebrated Southwark Fair will be publicly exhibited at the European Museum, St. James's-square. The holiday folks from every part of the metropolis, and its vicinity, will, of course, embrace the opportunity of viewing that humorous and extraordinary performance.

(414.) At a general assembly, held at the Royal Academy on Monday last (February 10), Messrs. M. A. Shee and John Flaxman were elected Academicians in the room of John Bacon, Esq., deceased, and James Barry.

(415.) ROYAL ACADEMY.—The anniversary dinner of the Royal Academicians and Associates was attended last Saturday by a numerous and certainly one of the most distinguished companies for rank and talents, which the country can boast.

Among the visitors and amateurs were His Royal Highness the Prince of Wales, the Chancellor, the Archbishop of York, the Lord Chamberlain, the Duke of Norfolk, Earls Spencer, Camden, Besborough, the Bishop of Rochester, several of the foreign Ambassadors, Sir Joseph Banks, Sir G. Beaumont, Sir H. Inglefield, Messrs. Long, Windham, Knight, Townley, Locke, Malone, Desefans, Kemble, &c.

More attention than on any former occasion appears to have been bestowed on the dinner, which was better than usual. The number that sat down to dinner exceeded one hundred and fifty. The wine was excellent, and the glees were sung with considerable spirit and effect.

The motto for this year's exhibition is taken from *Ovid*, and like that for the last season, affords no very favourable specimen of Mr. Bennett Langston's taste in selection, and judicious application to the subject. We are not so absurd and fastidious as to object to it, because it is common and in every schoolboy's mouth, for our best-known proverbs, and our most generally received sentences, are perhaps those which are the wisest. But is it not rather extraordinary that the vast range of ancient literature could not have supplied its academic professor with a more appropriate quotation? There is nothing in it that does not relate as intimately to all the kindred arts as to that one to which it serves as an index. There is not, we conceive, any necessity for a motto; but since the Academy are determined to have one, let them choose that which is peculiarly characteristic of their institution? Let them shake off the rust of antiquity, and consult the works of the English, French, or Italian classics, for a sentence illustrative of their establishment, and they will not be obliged to have recourse to a motto like that for their last year's exhibition, in praise of ancient excellence, or the one now prefixed to their catalogue:—

"Ingenuas didicisse fideliter artes,
"Emollit mores nec finit esse feros."

which is too lax in its signification.

The present exhibition is allowed to possess fewer objectionable pieces, but it has also fewer works of distinguished merit than that of the two preceding years. With the exception of ten or fifteen compositions, its principal *trait* is a kind of polished and "*amiable mediocrity.*" We do not discover many faults, the display is smooth and pleasing; but there is not much to fascinate the attention, to excite delight or wonder, to interest the heart or captivate the imagination. There is throughout great correctness and a considerable degree of taste; but we meet with very few instances of original genius in the historical or dramatic department, in the sublime and terrific, or in the mean and humorous.

It cannot be expected that, in our cursory account of the Exhibition, we should enter into an analysis of the respective merits of the pieces produced by the different artists and amateurs. We shall merely give a summary sketch of the principal articles, ranking under the names of the exhibitors, and reserving to ourselves the power of making more minute criticisms on future occasions.

The works of the President, Mr. West, are, as they have repeatedly been, multifarious and disproportionate in merit. His scriptural pieces are admirably correct in design, but the colouring is in many instances defective. In his mythological sketches he has been much happier.

The larger and one of the finest pictures which the Exhibition displays, is the Rolla of Mr. Lawrence. Independently of the boldness of the design, the animation of the canvas, the vigorous correctness of the figures, it bears a striking resemblance of the manner and features of the first tragedian of the present day in this country.

Among the painters from the Holy Writ, the President has found formidable competitors in Wm. Hamilton and Zoffani. Their respective talents may be thus estimated:—West has correctness of design, Hamilton has strength of expression, and Zoffani possesses character. In the landscapes there is a striking competition between the productions of Sir Francis Bourgeois and Mr. Dance, formerly a Royal Academician but now an honorary member, it would be difficult to ascertain the exact difference between pieces of such extraordinary merit; but if we are to hazard an opinion, it would seem that Sir Francis has displayed more vigour in his general system, and more glow in his colouring, than his competitor, while the latter has been more minutely correct in the arrangement and more luminous in his background.

Amid the promise of great talents, the productions of Mr. W. Turner hold the very first rank. In them all there is system, execution, and embellishment, not generally cultivated, but so admirably finished as to excite the admiration of the oldest professors.

Smirke has contributed several pieces from his favourite subject of Don Quixotte, which are not inferior to his best sketches from the same source.

Sir Wm. Beechey, Hoppner, Shee, and Copley, support that eminent reputation among portrait painters to which they are so justly entitled.

Northcote has furnished proofs of the correctness of his judgment and the strength of his colouring, and Westall continues to maintain his superiority in smoothness of execution and happiness of effect.

Opie deserves particular notice. His improvement is evident at the first glance, and strikes the mind with a full conviction of the talents of the painter.

Sir George Beaumont's faculties have never been more happily displayed than in his landscapes for this Exhibition. There is in every distinct part of the whole picture a sufficient consistency to form a whole.

De Wilde continues to support the reputation which he has so justly acquired, and his representation of Cicely Homespun is consonant to every just knowledge of human nature. We must not omit noticing the names of Daniell, Russell, Wheatley, Fuseli, Paul Sandby, Stubbs, Bigg, Girtin, Reinagle, Cosway, Mrs. Cosway, Arnold, Owen, Rooker, Garvey, and Kirkley.

In the pieces Naval, Sculptural, and Architectural, there is much of laudable competition. Upon the whole, it must prove a subject of great satisfaction to the enlightened part of the public to find that, though the works of our English artists have not exceeded every moderate expectation, they have, however, been free from those faults which are incurred by precipitancy, neglect, and inability.

(416.) ROYAL ACADEMY DINNER.—SATURDAY last the President and Members of the Royal Academy dined at the Milton Gallery. This mark of respect for the talents and genius of Mr. Fuseli was paid in consequence of an unanimous resolution of the Academy, and certainly does honour to their friendly liberality and taste. The company was more numerous than was expected, various patrons and amateurs of the fine arts joining in this public testimony of respect for the truly and classical illustrations of our divine poet. At half-past five Mr. West, the President, took the chair, and, after an elegant dinner, several toasts appropriate to the business of the day were drank; his Majesty's health, in particular, was received with an uncommon fervour of applause, and congratulation: "Prosperity of the Arts," "The Milton Gallery," &c., &c., were likewise loudly applauded. The company were enlivened by songs from Messrs. Bannister, Maddocks, &c., and the evening was spent with the utmost cheerfulness and conviviality. On drinking Mr. Fuseli's health, he returned the company thanks in a modest and neat speech. Mr. Alderman Boydell, whose health was likewise drank, made a speech to the company highly expressive of his zeal for the interest of the arts. The Duke of Bedford's health was drank with three times three, on account of his Grace having made the Academy a present of the celebrated Cartoons lately in Bedford House.

(417.) MRS. COSWAY has nearly finished a series of pictures, illustrating the contrasted enjoyments and miseries of winter.

Northcote has lately finished a capital picture, which at least possesses novelty in the subject. Three English cavalry officers had gone to Rome in the course of this War, and were introduced to the Pope: his Holiness took the helmet of one of them, and blessed it with great fervour, wishing success to the cause in which they were engaged. This scene the painter has delineated with masterly skill.

(418.) KEMBLE is sitting for his picture to Shee. This is the *one hundred and thirteenth* portrait which has been painted of that actor.

(419.) A MORNING paper observes that Mr. Kemble is sitting to an artist for his 113th portrait. This is not so wonderful, when it is recollected that Mr. Kemble has acted almost as many characters as Bonaparte.

(420.) MR. BARRY, the late Professor of Painting to the Royal Academy, author of the celebrated work in the Adelphi, and who was deprived of his professorship by some of the members of the Academy, has lately engraved a slip of copper, which is to be joined to two other engravings with the following characters, viz., Magellan, Las Casas, and Isabella of Spain (a character worthy of imitation), who pledged her jewels to assist Columbus in his discoveries. The Dedication is as follows:—"As a testimony of veneration for the integrity and transcendant abilities which for more than twenty years have been, though unsuccessfully, yet vigorously, uniformly, and gracefully exerted in the public service, this little slip of copper, which, as the key-stone of an arch, binds together these groups, and the virtues they commemorate, is inscribed with the honourable and glorious name of
CHARLES JAMES FOX,
By his humble Servant,
JAMES BARRY."

(421.) ON the Anniversary of the Institution of the Royal Academy, B. West, Esq., was unanimously re-elected President; H. Tresham, T. Daniell, T. Banks, J. Russell, M. A. Shee, J. Flaxman, J. Nollekens, and T. Wheatley, Esqrs., Council; T. Banks, W. Hamilton, F. Bartolozzi, J. Nollekens, R. Smirke, H. Fuseli, J. Flaxman, M. A. Shee, and J. Opie, Esqrs., Vistors; G. Dance, and W. Tyler, Esqrs., Auditors; and J. Richards, R. A., Secretary; Messrs. D. Riviere, and W. Lockner, received premiums for the best drawing of Academy figures, and in architecture.

(422.) LORD NELSON'S statue, in marble, is to be placed in Guildhall. Mrs. Damer has undertaken the sculpture of it; and Lord Nelson now attends one hour every day on the fair artist.

(423.) WANSTEAD HOUSE, the seat of Sir James Long, and the noblest piece of architecture amongst the mansions of the great, is undergoing a complete repair. It is one of the very great ornaments of this kingdom, and one of the most overlooked.

(424.) IT will be a curious circumstance in the annals of the eighteenth century, that in the close of that era, two branches of the polite arts exhibited such an almost impossible rapidity of execution,—Mr. Porter accomplishing the immense historical picture of Seringapatam in the short space of nine weeks, and Mr. Southey composing his fine epic poem of Joan of Arc during the small interval of six.

LOTTERIES.

(425.) It is obvious even to common observation, that at least two-thirds of the community have no other probable prospect of bettering their condition and rising to independence, than through the means of a lottery prize. Whether the lottery be English or Irish the security is the same; whether the drawing commences in July or March the chance is the same; but prudence of adventure in regard to economy materially differs. The consideration therefore is—which of the two lotteries, the Irish or the English, presents the most productive chance at the least risk? This point is manifest; and the preference is decisively in favour of the Irish scheme, since the immense sum of 20,000*l.* (and numerous other capital prizes) is attainable for eight guineas! and even 1250*l.* to be won for so very trifling a stake as 11*s.* 6*d.* chances which no English lottery, or any other speculation, is capable of affording. Observe then, the drawing at this lottery begins on Monday, the 21st of July, and finishes within twenty-five days. Moreover, from the seventh day, every third morning being entitled to a capital prize; determination, then, should be immediate, and more particularly as the rapid demand for Irish tickets, must obviously produce a considerable rise.

(426.) The boarding-school ladies in and about London are determined not to be behind-hand with the one at Greenwich, where Miss Knight, and a young lady who resided with her, were so fortunate in the last lottery to gain the 10,000*l.* prize, by purchasing their tickets and shares at No. 16, Cornhill. The great scheme at the present lottery is so truly tempting that all ranks and descriptions of persons, old and young, rich and poor, are scraping up sufficient to become adventurers. This accounts for the very extraordinary demand there has been for tickets and shares; and though the price has risen to sixteen guineas, it is expected they will be seventeen or eighteen before Monday fortnight, the day on which the drawing begins.

(427.) The price of tickets was 100*l.* on Wednesday evening, and the same yesterday, as there is a 20,000*l.* prize still in the wheel, and only two days to draw.

(428.) Yesterday the English lottery for the present year was contracted for. The biddings were as follow:

	£	s.	d.
Bish, Cooper, Bannister, Richardson, and Beardmore	16	10	6
Cope and Co.	16	4	3
Shewell, Towgood, Ellis, and Granville	15	19	0

A Mr. La Favre, wanted to give in a price but Mr. Pitt told him, unless he could give some respectable names to guarantee the payment, he could not take the bidding, which not being complied with he withdrew. After the bargain was concluded, Mr. Pitt wished the purchasers joy, and well he might. 100 tickets were, however, sold in the course of the afternoon at 17*l.* a ticket.

VARIETIES.

(429.) A most humane and laudable scheme for contributing to the relief of the poor, has been set on foot by some young ladies of Belfast. They devote part of their time to making up several useful and ornamental articles of dress, &c., which are exposed for sale in a shop opened for the purpose, and the produce is employed in purchasing coals, &c., for poor housekeepers. This scheme has been attended with the most beneficial effects; last week they were enabled to distribute ten tons of coals amongst a number of poor families.

(430.) The insolence and fraud of hackney-coachmen, form the subject of frequent complaints. It were much to be desired that the amateurs of driving, instead of wasting their talents in idly traversing the streets upon the coach-box, would enter into an association to serve the public on reasonable terms. Thus might they not only acquire dexterity in the art they are so desirous to attain, but they would, by a new competition in the calling, compel the old practitioners to be honest and civil. We humbly submit this suggestion to the consideration of the noblemen and gentlemen coach-drivers, who now so unprofitably waste their skill!

(431.) The present combination among the tailors has induced several masters to employ females, and it is thought that a new opening will thus be made for many thousand industrious women. We shall be very glad if the introduction of the sex into this branch of business should have the effect of constraining these men to return to their work. The combination is of the most dangerous consequence to the State, as it is extending itself through every branch of trade.

(432.) Horses and Oxen.—Within the last twenty years, 1280 bills of inclosure have passed Parliament, and by many of these, land, now amongst the best in the kingdom, has been reclaimed. During the seventy-eight years preceding, there were only 851 inclosure bills, being of late years an increase in the proportion of forty-seven to eleven. This increase of cultivation has greatly exceeded any possible increase of population, and yet, instead of a surplus stock of grain, our exportation thereof has not only ceased but we are rendered dependant on fortuitous and impoverishing supplies from abroad. Surely the cause of this extraordinary effect deserves investigation. Lord Somerville ascribes it, in a considerable degree, to the vast number of useless horses idly kept. He observes, that the breed of heavy cart horses began to prevail in 1754, and about the same year the exportation of corn began to slacken. The number of horses employed in husbandry in England and Wales, is stated at 1,978,000; horses for pleasure, 237,000:—total, 2,215,000; a sum, however, greatly exceeding the number accounted for to the revenue. Mr. Pitt estimates the number of cart horses in Great Britain at 500,000, of which Lord Somerville conceives 300,000 to be absolutely superfluous; and each of these, his Lordship contends, consumes one peck of corn per day for nine months, or 63 bushels per year: that, in Scotland, a man with a wife and four children require, on an average, about four pecks, or forty pounds of good oats per week, being 208 pecks, or fifty-two bushels per annum. A labouring horse, on an average, receives a peck and a quarter per day for eight months, or within that term, 280 pecks; so that the consumption of one horse is equal to that of seven or eight human beings for the same period. In those parts, however, where oats do not form the ordinary food of man, the account stands thus: the averaged weight of oats is nine pounds per peck, and of wheat fifteen pounds; hence sixty-three bushels of oats, the annual consumption of a horse on the average, are equal to thirty-six bushels of wheat, capable of making upwards of 500 quartern loaves, and allowing one and a quarter per week to each of 10,000,000 of inhabitants, (the general estimate is less than a quartern loaf on the average of all the kingdom, infants, and adults), the 300,000 superfluous cart horses consume as much annually as would support 2,100,000 persons, being a loss of more than ten weeks' consumption of the whole kingdom, and at the present average price of wheat throughout England, namely, 16s. per bushel amounts to the enormous sum of *eighty-six millions four hundred thousand pounds sterling* per annum. Admitting the impost to be equal in six weeks, there would remain for export, one month's consumption or one-twelfth part of the whole produce.

The substitution of oxen for horses in agricultural labour, in all such cases as local circumstances would warrant the change, would, in the opinion of our most scientific farmers, obviate all our present difficulties.

Lord Somerville observes, that on a statement of comparative expense between 65 horses and 107 oxen, used by His Majesty in agricultural labour in 1797, there was a balance of 513*l*. 15*s*. 6*d*. in favour of the oxen; or on the same comparative average statement of each animal singly, the horse at 20*l*. 9*s*. per annum, the ox at 7*l*. 8*s* 6*d*. per annum, there appears a balance in favour of the ox of 13*l*. 6*d*.; not to mention the difference in favour of the oxen in the prime cost; the casualties and ailments to which horses are more peculiarly liable; the little attendance required by the ox; and the consideration, that if an accident happens to the horse, he is worth no more than his skin; whereas, in this case, the ox, in any tolerable working order, is ever worth half his former value.

(433.) RATES OF PORTERAGE.—THE following are the charges allowed by Act of Parliament for conveying parcels from the inn:

For any distance, not exceeding a quarter of a mile 3*d*., half a mile 4*d*., one mile 6*d*., one mile and a half 8*d*., two miles 10*d*., and 3*d*. for every additional half mile.

Any person, or porter, demanding more than the above rates for any parcel, not exceeding 56lbs. weight, to forfeit 20*s*., or not less than 5*s*.

Any inn or warehouse-keeper neglecting to send a ticket with every parcel, containing the name or description of the inn or warehouse, from whence the same is sent, with the Christian and surname of the porter who is to deliver the same, and the carriage and the porterage marked thereon forfeits 40*s*., or not less than 5*s*., and the porter not leaving the ticket with the parcel, or altering, or willfully obliterating any thing written thereon, forfeits 40*s*., and if he demands more than written on the ticket 20*s*.

Every parcel arriving by coach, to be delivered within six hours after such arrival (if not after four in the evening, or before seven in the morning), then within six hours after seven in the morning; or by waggon, within twenty-four hours after such arrival, or innkeeper to forfeit 20*s*., and not less than 10*s*.

Parcels *directed to be called for*, to be delivered on payment of carriage, and 2*d*. warehouse-room for the first, and 1*d*. for each week after, or forfeit 20*s*., and not less than 10*s*.

Every porter misbehaving, forfeits 20*s*., and not less than 10*s*.

These offences are cognizable before any justice of the district.

(434.) A ROYAL patent has been obtained for making an alteration in playing cards, on an entire new plan, to be named *Brilliant, new invented Knights' Cards*, 1800, which are intended to have a perfect distinction in the suits, in general to reverse the pips as much as can be and to make a difference in the packs, that they may always be known from each other. As this plan unites elegance with convenience, and apt accommodation, there can be no doubt of its proving acceptable to the public and beneficial to the patentee.

(435.) YESTERDAY, at a court of common council, Mr. James Dixon, of Tower Ward, moved the thanks of the court to Sir Edward Hamilton, knight, and to the officers, seamen, and marines of His Majesty's ship, "Surprize," for their gallant conduct in attacking, cutting out, and recapturing His Majesty's late ship "Hermione;" and that the freedom of the city be presented to Sir Edward in a gold box of 50 guineas value, as a testimony of their regard; which was unanimously agreed to.

(436.) IT seems to be the fate of our gallant Sir Sidney Smith to receive rewards and honours from every country but his own! It has long perplexed the public mind to discover what promotion, title, or pension is to follow the panegyrics of Ministers, and the thanks of Parliament! We shall receive great pleasure whenever it is in our power to satisfy this commendable curiosity.

(437.) MARMONTEL, the celebrated author, died at a very advanced age. It was observed of him, that when the Christian religion was established in France, he attacked it by some very impious works; and when it was overthrown, he became its zealous defender.

(438.) WE are told that a benevolent confectioner, of Bond-street, has for several weeks past given to fifty poor persons, once a week, a quart of soup and meat to each person. Such an example is worthy of imitation.

(439.) The Duke of Northumberland, in a letter to a gentleman at Dublin, states the expense of the life boat presented to the town of North Shields at 160*l*., and that it has already saved nearly 1000 seamen and passengers, besides several ships and their cargoes.

(440.) WHIT TUESDAY.—(*Holiday at all the Public Offices.*)
The prisoner Hadfield is kept on milk diet and light puddings. During the last week he attempted to throw one of Mr. Kirby's men over the staircase.

(441.) MR. HORNE TOOKE is said to have had an annuity of 1000*l*. secured for him by a select subscription, so that when he next meets the Commissioners of Income he will have a more satisfactory mode of solving their questions than he had last year.

(442.) FROM a Barbadoes "Mercury" we have copied the following articles:
For sale.—A Negro woman, who is a washer, and her son, a youth 17 years. Enquire at this office.
For sale.—A young, healthy, boot and shoe-maker, a complete master of his trade. Apply at this office.
For sale.—A young, healthy, Barbadian woman, who is a complete washer and ironer, and is calculated to do any house business in a family. She has four children, who will be sold with her, three girls, and a boy; the eldest girl is about ten years of age, and has been taught to work at her needle; the second is seven, and the boy four; the youngest girl is an infant, five months old!

(443.) NEVER was a more impolitic scheme proposed than that suggested by Mr. Sheridan, of obliging men who engage in any measure likely to be of great public utility, to be limited to a profit of five per cent. If such a proposition could be rendered general in its operation, there would be an end to the spirit of trade, and this country would no longer be able to value itself on its commercial prosperity.

(444.) THE following are the salaries of some of the King's household:—
Lord Chamberlain, wages 100*l*. a year, and board wages 1100*l*.
Vice-Chamberlain, wages 600*l*. a year, and board wages 559*l*. 8*s*. 4*d*.
Assistant Master of the Ceremonies, 6*s*. 8*d*. a day.
Assistant Gentleman Usher, 66*l*. 13*s*. 4*d*. a year.
Grooms of the Privy Chamber, at 73*l*. each.
Pages of the Presence Chamber, at 25*l*. each.
Pages of the Back Stair, at 80*l*. each.
Principal Barber, 170*l*.
Serjeant at Arms, attending the Lord Chancellor, 3*s*. a day.
Serjeant at Arms, attending the House of Commons, 100*l*. a year.
Surveyor of the Pictures (Benjamin West), 200*l*.
Principal Portrait Painter (William Lawrence), 50*l*.
Herb Strewer, 24*l*.
Confessor of the Household, 36*l*. 10*s*.
Clerk of the King's Closet (Bishop of Worcester), 6*l*. 18*s*.
Composers attached to the Chapel Royal (Dr. Arnold and T. Atwood), 73*l*. each.
Gentleman of the Pantry, 200*l*.
Clerk of the Spicery (an F.R.S.), 200*l*.
Clerk of the Wood-yard, 170*l*.
Deliverer of Greens, 85*l*.
Children of the Kitchen, at 90*l*. each.
Master Scourer, 80*l*.
Turnbroches, 25*l*. each.
Butter and Egg Office Keeper, 60*l*.

(444*.) GOVERNMENT has lately increased the pay of the Junior Clerks of the Admiralty, and has deducted from those gentlemen at the head of the office. The salary of the Principal Secretary is fixed, in future, at 4000*l*. a year in time of war, and 3000*l*. during a peace.

(445.) MR. HAMILTON, of Richmond, has sold seven pictures from his collection to Mr. Treward, of Norfolk-street, for 6000 guineas.

(446.) THOMAS PAINE seems to have fallen into as complete contempt at Paris as he once enjoyed in England.

(447.) POLITICAL indisposition seems to be very general among Ministers. At the time of Mr. Pitt's illness in Downing-street, Lord Castlereagh fell sympathetically ill at Dublin. This complaint is supposed to arise from *indigestion* of their plans.

(448.) THE eloquence of Mr. Christie never shone more conspicuous than in the sale of a late property at Gatton. He said, the estate possessed a fortunate contingency, which commanded "the smiles of princes, and kept ministers in submission." Every person who heard Mr. Christie seemed to wish the contingency might fall upon his own head.

(449.) THE silver coin of this country is so reduced in value, that sixpences, on an average, are not worth more than two pence halfpenny; the shillings eight pence half penny; the half-crowns two shillings and two pence; and the crowns four shillings and eight pence.

(450.) THE Commissioners for Hackney Coaches and Chairs are empowered, by Act of George III, to license 1000 hackney coachman.

(450*.) THE number of coaches which are yearly overturned, by being overloaded at the top with more outside passengers than they can carry with safety, prove the inefficiency of Acts of Parliament, if they are not enforced. We now scarcely ever hear of a fine levied on a coach-master, although a person cannot travel five miles out of town but he sees the laws infringed upon, in numberless instances, to the danger of many valuable lives.

(451.) WE cannot conceive anything more childish than filling the Gazette every day of its publication with a number of senseless threatening letters, sent to different people throughout the country. The letters are inserted, word for word, and are more calculated to furnish materials to the discontent of the populace, than to obtain a discovery of the authors. We doubt whether any discovery has been made by all the rewards offered for the last three months in so many instances; while to circulate such stuff in the Gazette, may suggest mischief where it was not previously conceived.

Review.

(452.) Observations on the Manners, &c., of the English, from Madame Roland's Trip to England, just published.

Country Life.

The houses of the villagers (says our author) built either of brick or wood, announce neatness and comfort; the smallest garden appears cultivated with assiduity by its peaceable possessor; here the agreeable is always blended with the useful, and seems to form but one with it: there is not a plant that is unaccompanied with a flower; every cabbage has its rose-tree, and all is laid out in this taste. The roads kept in good order, are lined with hedges neatly clipped and trimmed, and, in many places, have been made for the convenience of people on foot. It is evident that man, whatever he may be, is reckoned something, and that a handful of rich does not constitute the nation.

Town Life.

There are neither guards nor muskets at the entrance of the public places, nor in the inside, and there is not any bustle and confusion as is seen in ours; the audience call out *encore* as we cry *bis*, and they frequently make the actors sing over again the songs that please. As people in London dine very late, commonly at four o'clock, (and at six among the great,) the public places hardly begin till between six and seven at soonest, and are not over till late in the night; we came out of the Haymarket Theatre at eleven o'clock, and left the afterpiece just begun. A person must take care of his pockets and look about him in the evening, when he happens to be in the streets. In London there are a great many robbers, they assemble together to a certain number, and even stop carriages; they never assassinate, unless in case of an obstinate resistance, as happened three days ago, near the Opera House, to a musician, about midnight; he attempted to defend himself against several, and he was killed; if, however, a passenger can escape from their clutches by calling stoutly for the *watchmen*, they are frightened, and he thus gets rid of them.

The *watchmen* are men, sometimes old soldiers, set to guard the streets of London, there are so many assigned to each parish; they walk about with a rattle, a lanthorn, and a long white pole, and call the hours as they strike; they have places of rendezvous, and small watch-boxes in several parts. Persons in easy circumstances, who leave town in the summer, carry with them their plate and what they have most valuable, or send it to their bankers; on their return they expect to find their house robbed; frequently travellers take the precaution to carry what is called the *robber's purse*, that which is meant to be given them in case of being attacked. A great talk has been made about taking methods to put a stop to these frequent robberies; but some opposition has always been started. It is here nearly as it was in Lacedemonia, to the vigilance of every individual is left the care of avoiding these daily little losses; besides, it would be apprehended that every well-armed guard, every means of police or of rigour at first established for the safety of the citizens, would shortly become an instrument of oppression and tyranny. In this point of view, it is, perhaps, the extreme of wisdom not to persist in annihilating the abuse. In the town there are quarters well known, where the thieves assemble and hold their consultations. However, they are hung, without mercy, when they are caught in the fact, or the crime is evidently proved; the mere deposition of a person robbed would not be sufficient, for here neither the liberty nor the life of man is sported with; it is necessary to prove, the judges examine the proofs, and the law alone pronounces the penalty. Scarcely a month passes without an execution of thieves taking place, by ten or twelve at a time, more or less.*

Sunday.

Here Sunday is rigidly observed, the shops, the public places are shut, and games of all sorts are prohibited; in the morning people go to church, in the evening they take a walk; it must not be imagined, however, that the crowd is as great at the one as at the other; the inhabitants walk still more than they pray.

Men, Women, and Children.

The race is vigorous; the children are charming, with their fairness, their open bosom, their head bare, ornamented with fine hair in natural curls, falling carelessly on their neck, which powder has never soiled. The women, who are well educated, have a maiden and affecting look; their fair but rather pale complexion, a soft and melancholy expression, inspire an interest very different from the sensations excited by our smart figures and sprightly air; these entice, the others soften: a man would be tempted to amuse himself with the one and to love the other. The women above the middle class, who walk in St. James's Park, are very few in number. they are distinguished by footmen, and by their gowns being longer and always trailing. In general, the women in England employ themselves a great deal about their children, and lead a very domestic life. The two sexes here live much more asunder than in France. The men form among themselves what are called clubs; there are some of lords, some of porters, some of men of science, and some of lawyers; the Royal Society have their club, and so on. When the men have dispatched their private business. they repair to the club, there they read the public papers; first they converse on politics, this is the subject of most general interest, the affairs of the State being also those of every one; they then talk over

---

* Small mistakes, in point of fact, are incident to all strangers. Executions, however, were more frequent at the time our authoress was in London than since the colonization of Botany Bay. None but very hardened or daring offenders suffer the punishment of death.

matters which more particularly concern the persons who compose the club. The women, therefore, remain most commonly alone; they visit each other, play little, take a walk, and are not diverted from the management of their family; the house and the children are in their department; to these they confine themselves. The boys are sent to the public schools and to the university, the girls scarcely quit their mother, and are brought out very late into company. Till the age of fifteen or eighteen they continue with their hair out of powder, falling in natural ringlets, and covered with a plain hat. They wear flat-heeled shoes, and generally a white dress; they pay no visits, and do not make their appearance on ceremonious occasions. It is during these years of retreat that they are formed under the eye of a mother, entirely devoted to the care of instructing them in things within their sphere, and in such agreeable accomplishments as may be added. The women being of a sedate turn, they read a good deal; they are not in want of information, and yet make no display of it; for they are not spoiled by the vain encomiums of a crowd of idlers, and everything fosters in them serious and prudent inclinations. Freedom and cleanliness are the two laws of their early age; the children are washed every day from head to foot, they are suffered to do whatever they please that does not hurt others; they are before their parents what they are in reality; they do not feel themselves restricted by their presence, and their parents on that account know them the better; hence, also, results that the children have a certain something, free, easy, and bold in their actions and in their countenance, which is imprinted for ever, and is happily blended with the pride of a republican and the independence of a man. The children of the great are not much urged toward the sciences, but pains are taken to instruct them in the laws of their country, to understand their language correctly, to inspire them with the social virtues, to make them men, patriots, and even heroes. The people are in general enlightened; there are schools well kept where the mother tongue and French are taught and notions given of the most important things; even the women know their language very well by principle, and speak and write it correctly.

The energy of this people is very singularly manifested in some circumstances; if a thief happens to be caught in the fact, a mob collects around him and seizes hold of him; he who has most warmth or facility of expression, or is better acquainted with the particulars, steps forward and states what has just happened; the votes are successively taken, and the majority of these determine the treatment that the malefactor is to be made to suffer; in general he is roughly handled, he is placed under a pump and copiously drenched with water, or ducked in a pond, and afterwards pelted with mud, everyone is eager to give his blow, and sometimes he is left either dead or very nearly so. What a diversified spectacle is the manners of a city, containing so much wealth, so much luxury, where reign laws so wise, passions so warm, so many sources of crimes and of virtues!

Ranelagh.

We concluded this day by going to Ranelagh; we went there before nine o'clock, in order to be able to examine the gardens; the company does not crowd thither till between eleven o'clock and midnight; every one retires about three. The gardens of Ranelagh, although agreeable, are insignificant, and do not constitute the essential part of this charming place, the principal building of which is a rotunda of an elegant form, and ornamented in the best manner. The music animates in a singular degree the concourse of a considerable number of persons; it is entirely in the Italian style, although the words of the air are English. The women go there dressed; they in general take each other by the arm, and walk in this manner several together, without any gentleman. Everything there breathes the air of liberty, the *ton* of decorum, and of the greatest tranquillity; no noise, no crowd, no confusion; it is the same in all the places of public assemblies, even among the populace, and in the markets. The people everywhere display a prudent character; they take their enjoyments quietly, and with voluptuousness; warmth, energy and passions, are manifested only in elections, or against acts of injustice.

Kew Palace and Gardens.

It was at Kew, a country-seat belonging to the King, that we stopt with the greatest satisfaction. The buildings are nothings; simple and neat they are like the common houses of individuals in easy circumstances, and do not deserve to be visited. The gardens spacious, and kept in admirable order, in the English style, are the most interesting that I have ever seen; the most skilful art cannot be better disguised; everything breathes nature and freedom; everything is grand, noble, and graceful. The lawns extend on all sides their soft and elastic carpets; vigorous trees shoot up and cover them, here and there, without affecting their beauty. The walks, seldom in a straight line, perfectly insulate the visitor from all that surround them; in every one of these he thinks he is in a place favoured by the gods, and unknown to the rest of the world; they are formed, on all sides, of a great variety of trees, to the depth of five or six feet on the lines described by the alley; the least lofty of them are the nearest the border, which is terminated by shrubs intermixed with flowers; the fir and the acacia, the oak and the lime, the holly and the tulip tree, the ash and the cypress, interweave their branches; while the plane-tree and the pine rear their heads to the most remote row; the little shrub trefoil, and the dogwood, flower by the side of the rose tree, and look down on the herbaceous plants which terminate the border, always a little more elevated than the middle of the alley; the latter is rounded in the middle with drains on each side for carrying off the waters under the borders; it is made with gravel rolled and crowned, so that the path is smooth and firm, and fit for walking on in all weathers, without dust or dirt. These beautiful walks, which cross each other in a hundred different ways, lead to those side lawns where the sight extends, settles and seizes some charming vistas, which are embellished by canals of running water. How awkwardly and ridiculously have we imitated the English gardens, with our little divisions, our ruins, which have the appearance of children's baby-houses, our affectation of gloominess, that assemblage of contradictions and monuments, only fit to be laughed at! I have seen the celebrated Ermenonville, with its little *tour de Gabrielle*; its temple, where six persons could scarcely stand upright; its blackish waters; its prospects, which often present melancholy and interesting solitudes, without ever relieving the mind by smiling nature; and I wonder more than ever that in that place, of an immense extent, all the edifices which it has been intended to represent, have been built on so small a scale. Kew has its temples, but they do not shock improbability by their smallness; Kew has a pagoda, but it is 190 feet high; the pagoda has five or six stories, it is from the upper one that must be seen the magnificent plains of the environs; the eye discovers the whole horizon as far as the sight can extend, as far as Windsor, at the distance of ten or twelve leagues, on one side, and so forth: the spectator sees but one superb garden, watered by the Thames, where land never lies idle, and the smallest space of which is not lost. After having surveyed this fine picture, let him run through the details of it; he will not find there a miserable house, where the stubble and the dirt, dung and indigence, are heaped up and attest, as in the greater part of our villages, the state of the people, and the nature of the Government under which they groan.

(453.) THE last day of the sixteenth century gave birth and form to the first English East India Company. The members thereof (says Anderson, in his valuable History of Commerce) immediately raised the sum of 72,000*l.*, though not in one joint stock or capital, as in succeeding times, there having been no joint stock in this Company till the year 1613. In the year 1601, they sent out their first fleet for India, consisting of four ships, and one as victualler to the whole fleet. In the Island of Sumatra they laded pepper for some of their ships, but not meeting with enough, sailed for the Strait of Molacca, where they found sufficient by the capture of a Portuguese ship laden with calicoes, &c. After sailing to Bantam, and settling factors there they returned homeward, and arrived in the Downs in September, 1603, having made this first voyage very prosperously in two years and seven months.

(454.) A MAN of the name of Williams, and some others, when yesterday dragging for fish near Chiswick, discovered a shark of an uncommon size entangled in their net. By an exertion of dexterity, with the help of some other fishermen, they brought it ashore.

(455.) A BEAUTIFUL figure of a Bird of Paradise, delicately formed, was brought from Seringapatam by the Hon. Mr. Wellesley, lately arrived in the ship "Cornwallis," and was deposited at the East Indian House. It formed part of the superb throne belonging to the late Sultan of Mysore, and is valued at 60,000*l.* sterling! The jewels about this figure are of the first kind; its tail exhibits a profusion of rubies and emeralds, fancifully placed so as to represent real life, and is as little short of the reality as exquisite workmanship could make it; the neck is adorned with brilliants, and the whole tout-en-semble a perfect masterpiece; the tuft of the head is composed of a vast number of exceedingly fine emeralds, which give it a lively green tint, finely shadowed with similar jewels of a deeper hue; the eyes are brilliants, and the beak consists of a large topaz, to which is suspended a remarkable large onyx, with drops of pearls hanging to its breast, of immense value; the legs are gold, studded with jewels; the representation of natural plumage is so happily executed as to surpass any kind of description. We understand this superb figure is to be presented to the king.

(456.) THE Bird of Paradise, which the Hon. Major Wellesley has brought to England as a present from the Marquis to His Majesty, has been very much overrated in value. The article in this journal was copied from an evening paper. The Marquis of Wellesley purchased the bird at Seringapatam for 1600*l.*, but it appears, on the examination of the jewel merchants, to be intrinsically worth only 500*l.* It is, however, a great curiosity.

(457.) THE Bird of Paradise brought from India has not been presented to His Majesty, as stated in some of yesterday's papers. It is in the possession of Mr. Dundas, who is to deliver it to the Queen.

(458.) THE following is said to be the progress of the rise of the "Prince of Peace:"—A man of Godoig was, about twenty-five years ago, a private soldier in the Walloon Guards, and mounted guard one day in the gardens of the Escurial, near the Queen's window. Her Majesty thought him very handsome, and ordered him to be advanced to the rank of Lieutenant; after which he was desired to attend in her apartments, when he saw and conversed with Her Majesty. After some time this soldier one day told his benefactress that he had a brother, and requested that he might be admitted into the ranks of the regiment. The Queen immediately ordered that the brother should be made Lieutenant, and he a Portegé or Captain. Unfortunately for the Captain, he requested the honour of introducing his brother to the Queen, who found him handsomer than himself; from which time the Captain disappeared, and the Lieutenant, now "Prince of Peace," rose rapidly to his present situation. The old and haughty nobility of Spain are amazingly mortified and displeased by this sudden and great rise, to a rank superior to any of their order; and the more so, that the abilities of the man have not warranted so extraordinary a promotion.

(459.) A LETTER to the present Emperor of China is preparing to be sent from hence by the ships of this season, congratulating His Imperial Majesty on his ascending the throne of that empire.

THE LATE EMPEROR OF CHINA, KIEN LONG.

(460.) EXTRACT from the letter from the British factory at Canton, dated the 5th of July, 1799:—

The whole empire is in great distress on account of the death of the emperor, whose virtues had endeared him to all his subjects. He was a person of a very graceful appearance, of about five feet ten inches in height, and of a slender and elegant form; his nose was rather aquiline, and the whole of his countenance presented a perfect regularity of features, which by no means announced the great age he was said to have attained; his person was attracting, and his deportment accompanied by an affability which, without losseniug the dignity of the prince, evinced the amiable character of the man.

His dress consisted generally of a loose robe of yellow silk, a cap of black velvet, with a red ball on the top, and adorned with a peacock's feather, which is the peculiar distinction of Mandarins of the first class; he usually wore boots embroidered with gold, and a sash of blue silk girded his waist.

In regard to capital offences in China, the final determination rested in the breast of the Emperor, although it was very rare indeed that a criminal was sentenced to die; but if such a circumstance was to happen in the most remote corner of the empire, application must be made to the Emperor himself to annul, to mitigate, or enforce, the sentence; but humanity always appeared to be a prevailing virtue with this sovereign; hence executions were very seldom in China. Some persons, of at least seventy years of age, had never seen or known of a capital execution, though, for lesser crimes, punishment follows conviction without the delay of a moment. The declaration of the Emperor to the British Embassy, at his palace at Callachotressingsu, in the city of Jehol in 1793, pourtrayed his greatness in the extreme. He refused, in the first instance, to sign, and of course to enter into any engagement by a written treaty with the Crown of Great Britain, or any other nation, as such conduct, on his part, would be contrary to the ancient usage, and, indeed, an infringement of the ancient constitution of the Empire. At the same time he was pleased to signify his high respect for His Britannic Majesty and the British nation, and that he felt a strong disposition to grant them greater indulgences than any other European Power trading to his dominions; nor was he unwilling to make such a new arrangement of the duties payable by British ships arriving at Canton as appeared to be a leading object of negotiation; at the same time, however, he should be ever attentive to the real interests of his own subjects, an atom of which he would never sacrifice; and should, therefore, withdraw his favours from any foreign nation, whenever it might appear to be incompatible with the interests of his own, or that the English should, by their conduct in trade, forfeit their pretensions to any advantages which might be granted them in preference to other nations trading to China. These were the exact declarations of the emperor, which did not, in his opinion, require any written instrument or signature to induce him to realize and fulfil.

At the same time, to prove the high regard and esteem which the Emperor entertained for the King of Great Britain, His Imperial Majesty delivered from his own hand into that of the ambassador, the Earl of Macartney, a very valuable box, containing the miniature pictures of all the preceding emperors, to which is annexed a description, in verse, by each emperor, of himself, and the principal features of government, as well as a line of conduct recommended to their successors. The emperor, on presenting this gift to the British ambassador, spoke to the following purport, which conspicuously marks his dignified mind:—"Deliver this casket to the King, your master, with your own hand, and tell him, though the present may appear to be small, it is, in my estimation, the most valuable that I can give, or my empire can furnish, for it has been transmitted to me through a long line of my predecessors, and is the last token of affection which I had reserved to bequeath to my son and successor, as a tablet of the virtues of his ancestors, which he had only to peruse, as I should hope, to inspire him with the noble resolution to follow such bright examples and, as they had done, to make it the grand object of his life to exalt the honour of the Imperial Throne, and advance the happiness and prosperity of his people."

The emperor died in his 90th year, and the Grand Choulaa, who is the prime minister, and retained in office, still preserves the affections of the people.

(461.) PRICES of Corn for 1800.

Wheat.	Oats.	Barley.	Beans.
Highest, 16/10	6/4	Highest 9/4	9/6
Lowest 11/10	4/0	Lowest 5/8	7/7
Average 14/1	5/2	Average 7/6	8/7

(461*.) IN Smithfield Market, Beef sold, in June, for 4s. 6d. to 6s. 4d. per stone; Mutton and Pork, 5s. 4d. to 6s. 8d.—In Newgate and Leadenhall Markets, Beef, 9d. to 1s. 2d. per lb.; Mutton, 8d. to 10d.; Veal, 9d. to 1s.—In St. James' Market, Hay, 64s. to 122s. per load; Straw, 54s. to 68s.

(462.) PRICE of Stocks, 1st January, 1800.

Bank Stock, 155.
3 per Ct. Red., 61¼, ⅛, 62, 1⅞.
3 per C C. shut.
4 per Ct. C., 76¼, ⅛, ⅜.
5 per Ct. Navy, shut.
5 per Ct. Loyal, 90¾, ¼, ⅜.
L. A., 17¾.
Short Anns., 5 13-16.
Im. 3 per Ct., 59¼.
Im. A. 25 ys., 11 7 16¼.
Irish 5 per Ct., 85¼, ½.
Oma.
India Stock
Lottery Tickets, 15l. 19s.
Irish ditto
Bank for Acc.
India for Jan.
Con. for Open, 62¼, 63¼, 63.

T. BISH, Stock Broker, Old State Lottery Office, No. 4, Cornhill.

463.) SELECTION of the Acts of Parliament in the 4th Session of the 18th Parliament passed of Great Britain:—

For raising 20,500,000l. by annuities.
For authorising bakers to sell new bread to soldiers on their march.
For prohibiting the sale of bread not baked a certain time.
To continue and amend Act to prohibit the exportation and permit the importation of corn.
For altering the fairs of licenced hackney coachmen.
To permit horse hides to be used for boots, &c., and to prevent the damaging of raw hides and skins.
For better ascertaining and collecting the duties on income.
For the union of Great Britain and Ireland.
For raising money by lottery.
For granting 200,000l. for reduction of national debt.

To prohibit the exportation of rice.
To prevent the making of spirits in Scotland from grain.
To prohibit the use of wheat in making starch.
To allow the use of sugar in the brewing of beer.
To indemnify persons serving in volunteer corps respecting the duty on hair-powder certificates.
For the better observance of Good-Friday.

(464.) Greatest, Least, and Mean state of the Barometer, Thermometer, and Hygrometer, and the quantity of Rain, in the year 1800.

1800	Barometer.			Thermometer out.			Thermometer in.			Hygrometer.			Rain.
	Greatest	Least	Mean	G.	L.	M.	G.	L.	M.	G.	L.	M.	Inches.
January	30·18	29·14	29·61	51	23	40·7	50	35	46·8	77	55	65	2·66
February	30·40	29·42	29·98	50	31	37·8	51	40·5	44·9	80	52	61	0·19
March	30·34	29·47	29·98	56	27	40·8	55	39	46	72	50	58	0·82
April	30·18	29·88	29·79	60	43	53·2	58·5	50	54·7	76	44	57	3·11
May	30·87	28·98	30·08	74	47	57·9	67	52	59·1	63	43	57	1·17
June	30·47	29·83	30·18	70	46	57·9	66	59	58·4	68	37	52	1·07
July	30·56	30·10	30·32	78	54	65·4	71·5	60	65·5	75	35	48	None
August	30·51	29·67	30·16	88	52·5	65·5	74·5	56·5	66·9	71	53	52	1·58
September	30·87	29·26	29·88	74	44	60·5	69·5	58	63·7	72	54	59	2·92
October	30·56	29·15	29·87	64	38·5	51·8	62	48·5	55·7	76	59	63	1·89
November	30·49	28·90	29·80	58·5	33·5	45·8	59	45·5	51·2	76	60	67	4·09
December	30·29	28·91	29·78	52	33·5	43·6	55	41·5	48·1	86	…	74	1·81
Whole year	…	…	29·95	…	…	…	…	…	55	…	…	58	20·81

(465.) GENERAL REMARKS ON THE WEATHER IN 1800.—The distinguishing feature of this year is a hot and dry summer. Little more than an inch of rain fell in the former part of June, and from the 22nd of that month, there was a continued drought for fifty-eight days, to the 19th of August. In all this period the barometer was constantly above thirty inches. The coldest day of the year was the 1st of January, and the hottest the 11th of August. The latter months were mild, and the thermometer never so low as the freezing point.

(ANGLETERRE).—*Londres, 20 Septembre (3e jour Complémentaire.)*

(466.) CHABRAN, du corps de ballet de notre opera, et de celui du théâtre de Margate, a été arrêté Samedi dans ce dernier port, en vertu d'un *warrant* émané du Duc de Portland, qui interdit à tout étranger de rester en-deçà de dix milles des côtes d'Angleterre.

(ANGLETERRE).—*Londres, 14 Juillet (25 Messidor.)*

Voici l'etat des diverses sommes que l'Angleterre a fournies par voie de subsides à différens états, depuis le commencement de cette guerre, y compris les intérêts :—

	Liv.	s.	d.
A la Prusse, 1794	1,223,891	10	6
A la Sardaigne, en 1793, 1794, 1795, et 1796	500,000	0	0
A l'Empereur, en 1795, 1796, et 1797	6,920,000	0	0
Au Portugal, en 1797 et 1798..	367,218	0	0
A la Russie, en 1799	825,000	0	0
A l'Empereur, a l'Electeur de Bavière, etc. ..	500,000	0	0
A l'Empereur	1,066,666	13	4
A la Russie	545,494	0	0
A la Bavière	501,017	6	0
A l'Empereur, pour remplacer ses magasins pris à Stockach	150,000	0	0
Total ..	12,599,287	9	10

Londres, 21 Juillet (2 Thermidor.)

Hier on a exposé au pilory, à Cheapside, John William, évêque Anglais, convaincu d'avoir favorisé une fausse déclaration d'un individu qui s'etoit annoncé comme garçon pour épouser une jeune demoiselle d'une grande beauté et d'une fortune considérable, quoiqu'il fût marié.

Heureusement pour la demoiselle, le mariage n'a pas en lieu, quelques-uns de ses amis ayant decouvert la fraude. Une foule considérable, composée surtout de femmes, s'est assemblée a cette occasion : chacune d'elles s'empressoit de lui reprocher l'infamie de sa conduite. Les soins des officiers de police ont empêché que le trouble ne fût plus grand.

Après avoir subi l'exposition pendant le tems accoutumé, le coupable a été conduit à Newgate, où il doit rester enfermé pendant deux ans.

Londres, 18 Mars (27 Ventose.)

Le Docteur Jenner a inoculé dernièrement la vaccine à plus de 200 individus de tout âge, chez Lord Egremont à Petworth. L'operation a parfaitement re-ussi. Nous espérons que cet exemple trouvera beaucoup d'imitateurs, et nous apprenons même qu'il est suivi dans un grand nombre de paroisses de la campagne.

Journal des Débats, an 9 de la République.

FINIS.

PRINTED BY HARRISON AND SONS,
ST. MARTIN'S LANE, LONDON, W.C.

CPSIA information can be obtained at www.ICGtesting.com
Printed in the USA
BVOW051137100112

280228BV00003B/8/P

CW01271717

DISCOVER
PLANTS

Predominant artwork & imagery source:
Shutterstock.com

Copyright: North Parade Publishing Ltd.

4 North Parade,

Bath,

BA1 1LF, UK

First Published: 2019

All rights reserved. No part of this publication may be reprinted, stored in a retrieval system or transmitted, in any form or by any means, electronic, mechanical, photocopying, recording, or otherwise, without the prior permission of the copyright holder.

Printed in China.

CONTENTS

INTRODUCTION	05
PLANT CELLS	07
PLANT ANATOMY	09
LEAF STRUCTURE	11
PHOTOSYNTHESIS	13
FACTORS AFFECTING PHOTOSYNTHESIS	15
TRANSPIRATION	17
TRANSPORT	19
PLANT NUTRITION	21
PLANT GROWTH	23
GERMINATION	25
POLLINATION	27
REPRODUCTION	29
PLANT DEFENSE	31
PLANT DISEASES	33
CLASSIFICATION OF PLANTS	35
CROP PLANTS	37
RESOURCES FROM PLANTS	39
PLANT TISSUE CULTURE	41
GENETICALLY MODIFIED CROPS	43

INTRODUCTION

Plants are multicellular organisms that have the ability to manufacture their own food. They provide the foundation for the existence of other life forms on Earth. Plants are responsible for the oxygen and food that enables other organisms, incapable of producing their own food, to survive on the planet.

Evolution of Plants

There are over 400,000 species of plants on the planet and they exhibit amazing diversity. Apart from the Arctic and Antarctic landscapes of extreme freezing temperatures, plants have adapted to all other landscapes. The fertile, terrestrial environment that we live in is made possible because of plants.

Plants have evolved over hundreds of millions of years, increasing in complexity over time. It is believed that algal scum over water was the first plant form to develop about 1200 million years ago. At least 1000 million years ago, complex photosynthetic plants are believed to have evolved. Bryophytes and gymnosperms that do not bear seeds or fruits were the first plant species to flourish on Earth.

The Great Permian Extinction Event occurred roughly 250 million years ago and resulted in the extinction of several terrestrial and aquatic species. However, most plant species survived intact. Following this event, flowering plants or angiosperms slowly evolved and began to thrive in different environments.

Grasses are considered to be the latest major group of plants to evolve, about 40 million years ago. Grasses had the capability to survive in low carbon dioxide concentration and warm, dry conditions.

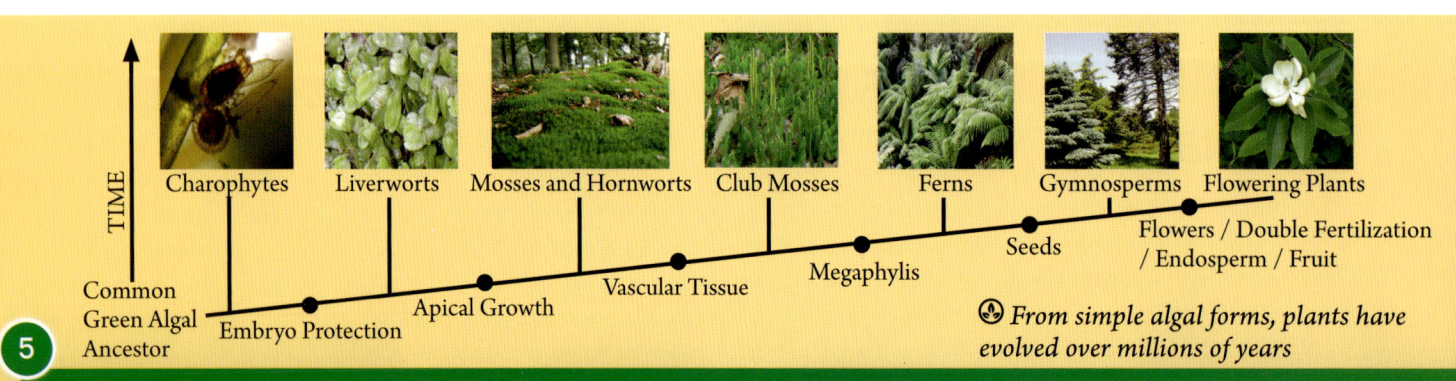

From simple algal forms, plants have evolved over millions of years

Plants as Producers

Plants are multicellular organisms possessing the ability to harvest sunlight and manufacture food in the form of sugars. The sugars supply energy for the plants to grow and reproduce. As an important food source for herbivores, they play a vital role in supporting complex food webs. Plants capable of producing vegetables, fruits and cereal grains have been selectively bred and domesticated for thousands of years for food.

Relationship with Other Organisms

Even though plants are capable of producing their own food, they depend on other organisms for pollination. Pollination is the process by which pollen from flowers is passed on to other flowers for reproduction. Plants achieve this through wind, water, insects, birds and animals.

⊕ *Plants that produce useful products are selected and cultivated*

Plants also associate with fungi in a mutualistic relationship. The fungi help the plants absorb water and minerals from the soil while the plants provide the fungi with the sugars manufactured through photosynthesis. Plants can also be parasites. Mistletoe takes nutrients from its host though it also possesses leaves capable of photosynthesis. Other species such as toothwort and broomrape are completely dependent on other plants for nutrients as they are incapable of photosynthesis.

⊕ *Insects, particularly bees, play an important role in pollination*

Fact File

The pitcher plant (Nepenthes) produces a sweet syrup that attracts insects, birds and small rodents.

⊕ *Broomrape is a plant species that is incapable of photosynthesis*

A small percentage of plants (about 630 species) are carnivorous. The most well-known example is the Venus flytrap, which traps insects. The insects are digested to provide nitrogen, phosphorus and other nutrients otherwise poorly available in the soil where it grows.

PLANT CELLS

Plants are multicellular and eukaryotic. They are made up of millions of cells possessing organelles and well-defined nuclei. Plant cells vary from animal cells in different ways, but the presence of cell walls is the most important feature providing rigidity and support to plants.

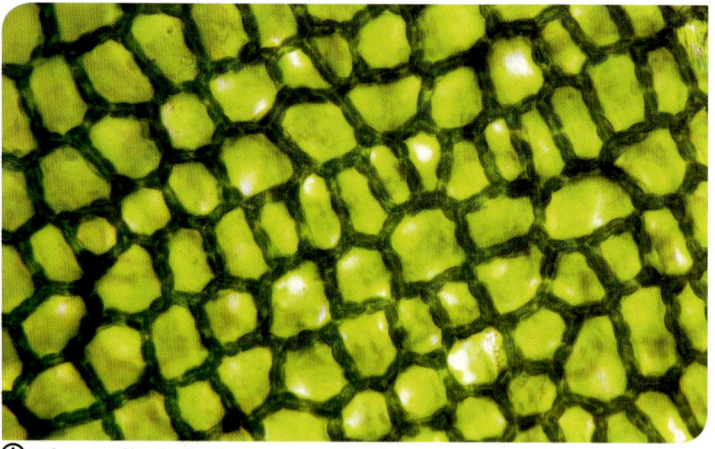

🌱 *Plant cells differ from animal cells in possessing thick cell walls*

Cell Organelles

Nucleus: Plant cells have a well-defined nucleus that stores the genetic material, DNA, and is responsible for coordinating all metabolic processes such as cell division and growth.

Cell Wall: Located outside the cell membrane, a cell wall provides the rigidity to the cell. It is made up of cellulose and lignin. Apart from providing a structural framework, a cell wall is also useful for limiting the amount of water entering into the cell to prevent it from bursting or damaging organelles. The cell wall is a feature that differentiates plant cells from animal cells.

Vacuole: A plant cell will have one or more large vacuoles that act as storage vesicles. Vacuoles are never found in animal cells. A vacuole is usually surrounded by a membrane and stores dissolved substances and water. A vacuole is useful for maintaining pressure inside the cell to balance the pressure exerted by the cell wall, thus giving the cell shape and support.

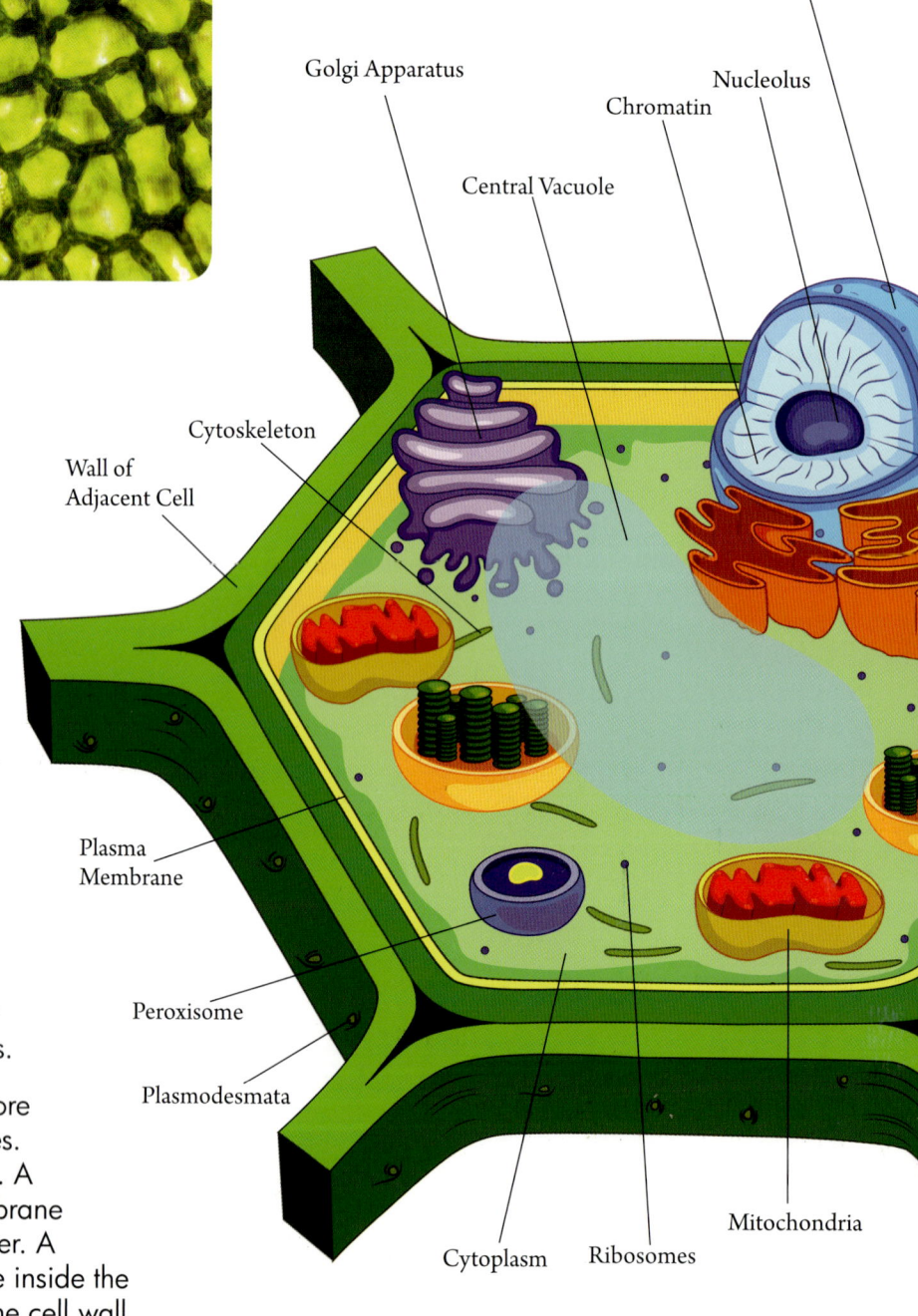

🌱 *A plant cell consists of different organelles, including prominent vacuoles*

Ribosomes: They may be found occurring freely or bound to the endoplasmic reticulum. The main role of ribosomes is protein synthesis.

Mitochondria: These organelles are responsible for generating energy by breaking down sugars. They are called the 'powerhouses of a cell'.

Endoplasmic reticulum: It is a network of interconnected sacs that serves as a connection between the nucleus and the cytoplasm. It manufactures, stores, and transports protein molecules.

Golgi apparatus: This organelle is vital for transporting chemical molecules such as proteins and lipids in and out of cells. It packages proteins into the right shapes before releasing them outside the cell.

Chloroplasts: They are organelles containing the green pigment 'chlorophyll', which is used to carry out photosynthesis. Apart from chloroplasts, some plants also possess 'chromoplasts' containing pigments that give plants different colors such as yellow, purple or orange.

Peroxisomes: They contain oxidative enzymes necessary for the break down of fatty acids into simple sugars.

Fact File

The crunchiness of pear fruit is due to the presence of sclerenchyma cells called 'sclereids'.

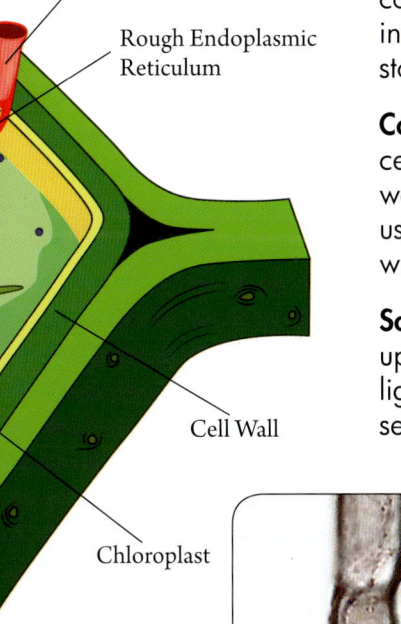

Types of Plant Cells

Plants are made up of three basic types of cells. They are:

Parenchyma: They are cube-shaped cells that are loosely-packed and contain chloroplasts. They take part in photosynthesis, respiration and storage of food.

Collenchyma: They are elongated cells with unevenly thickened cell walls. Collenchyma cells are mainly useful for support and providing wind resistance.

Sclerenchyma: These cells are made up of very thick walls usually of lignin and the main purpose they serve is support and strength.

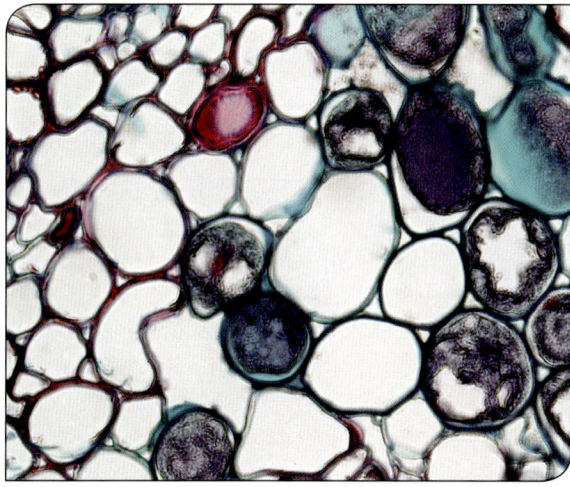

Parenchyma cells

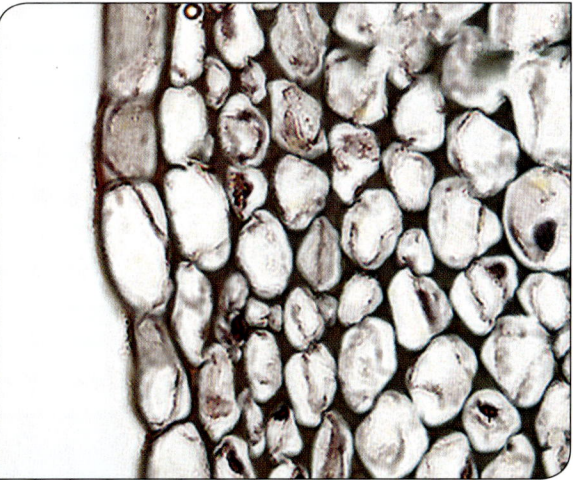

Collenchyma cells

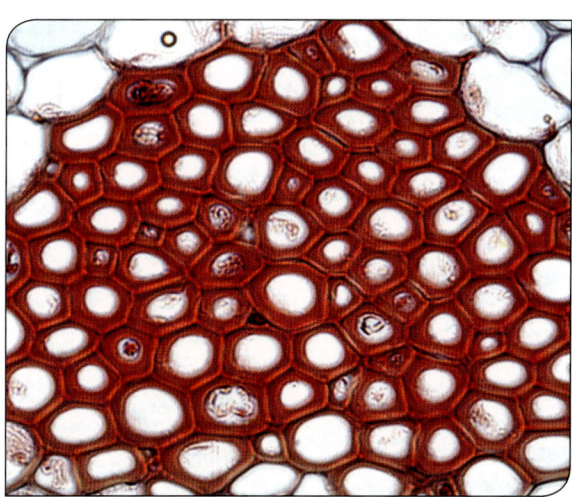

Sclerenchyma cells

PLANT ANATOMY

Vascular plants have specialized parts that control different functions such as photosynthesis, transport, reproduction and nutrient absorption. Some of the main parts of a plant include roots, stem, leaves, flowers, fruits and seeds. Any damage to one or more of the parts can have an effect on the survival of the plant.

Roots

A plant's roots firmly establish the plant in the soil and keep it stable. Roots develop tiny thread-like root hairs that delve deep into the soil to absorb water and nutrients. Roots absorb water and nutrients through a process called osmosis. Water molecules move from an area of high concentration to a region of lower concentration through the semi-permeable root membrane.

The root tip is the actively-growing region and consists of three zones: zone of cell division, zone of cell elongation and zone of maturation.

The roots are also responsible for storing nutrients such as starch or water. Some of the well-known storage roots are potatoes, carrots, beets, sweet potatoes and turnips.

The type of root system found in plants differs based on whether it is a monocot or a dicot. Monocot plants have one cotyledon (seed leaf) while dicot plants have two. Monocots such as grass and rice generally have thin, branching fibrous root systems. Dicots such as sunflower and rose have a tap root system with a single main root growing downwards.

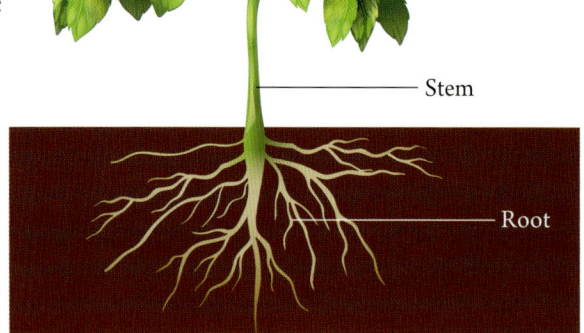

Roots, stem, leaves, flowers, fruits and seeds are the main parts of a plant

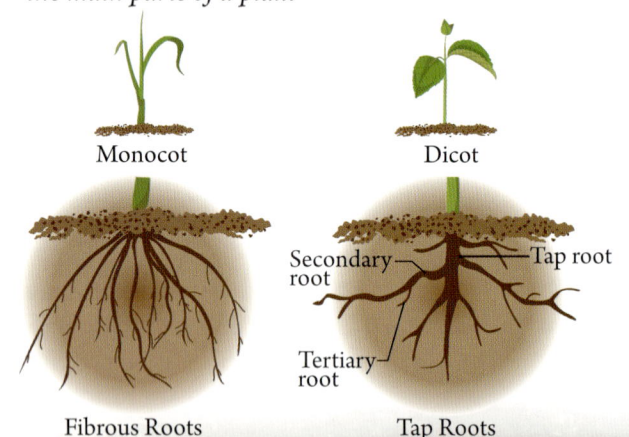

The type of root varies among different plants

Stem

The stem grows after a seed germinates and puts out shoots. A stem grows towards sunlight and bears leaves on smaller stems. Water and nutrients from the soil flow to the leaves through the stem.

Leaves

Leaves come in different shapes and are attached to the stem with the help of the leaf stalk, called a petiole. Leaves have specialized cells to perform photosynthesis and transpiration. Photosynthesis is the production of sugars with the help of sunlight. Transpiration is the process by which water is expelled out of the leaves. Leaves are usually green in color due to the presence of chlorophyll pigment. In dry places, where water is scarce, leaves have a waxy coating that reduces transpiration.

Fact File

The growing tip of the root is protected by a 'root cap'. If it is removed, the roots will grow in a haphazard manner.

Leaves exhibit diversity in size and shape

Fruits carry the reproductive part of the plant - seed

Fruits

The seed-bearing structures of plants are referred to as fruits. Like flowers, there is sheer variety in the morphology of fruits. Many fruits are edible, and the outer edible portion is called 'pericarp'. Fruits can be classified as simple, aggregate, multiple or accessory depending on their development from the ovary.

Flowers

Flowers come in different colors, fragrances and sizes. Flowers that are brightly colored or fragrant have evolved that way to attract insects and other agents that assist in pollination. Pollination is essential for transferring pollen to other flowers for fertilization. Flowers can be imperfect with either male or female parts or perfect with both female and male parts, ovary and stamen respectively.

Flowers that are pollinated by external agents are attractive

LEAF STRUCTURE

Leaves have a distinct green color that is due to the presence of the pigment chlorophyll. They play a major role in photosynthesis by absorbing sunlight across a large surface area. The structure of leaves varies and is usually modified for specific habitats and climatic conditions.

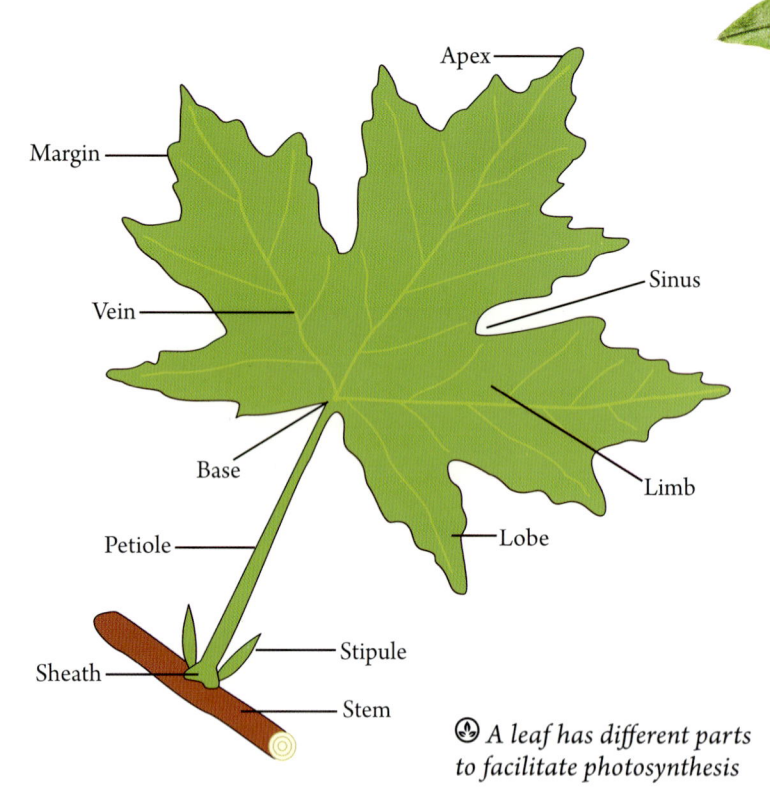

A leaf has different parts to facilitate photosynthesis

Leaf Anatomy

Despite variations in shape, size and texture, most leaves have certain common features. These are midrib, vein and blade. The midrib runs all the way from the stem where it is attached to the tip of the leaf. It branches out into tiny veins through which water is transported throughout. The blade, also called lamina, is the broad, flat portion of the leaf. It is in the lamina that photosynthesis occurs.

Cell Layers

A typical leaf is made up of two layers: the upper epidermis and the inner mesophyll.

Epidermis: It is the outermost layer that makes up the upper and lower outer layers of leaves. It acts as a physical barrier for the inner cells. The epidermis consists of tiny pores called stomata that are responsible for exchange of gases and water.

Mesophyll: The mesophyll layer is sandwiched between the two layers of epidermis. It is here that photosynthesis occurs. Mesophyll is, in turn, made up of two layers: an upper palisade layer and an inner spongy layer. Chloroplasts are found occurring in the palisade layer. The cells here are packed in tight layers and can effectively absorb carbon dioxide. The spongy layer consists of loosely-packed cells with very few chloroplasts.

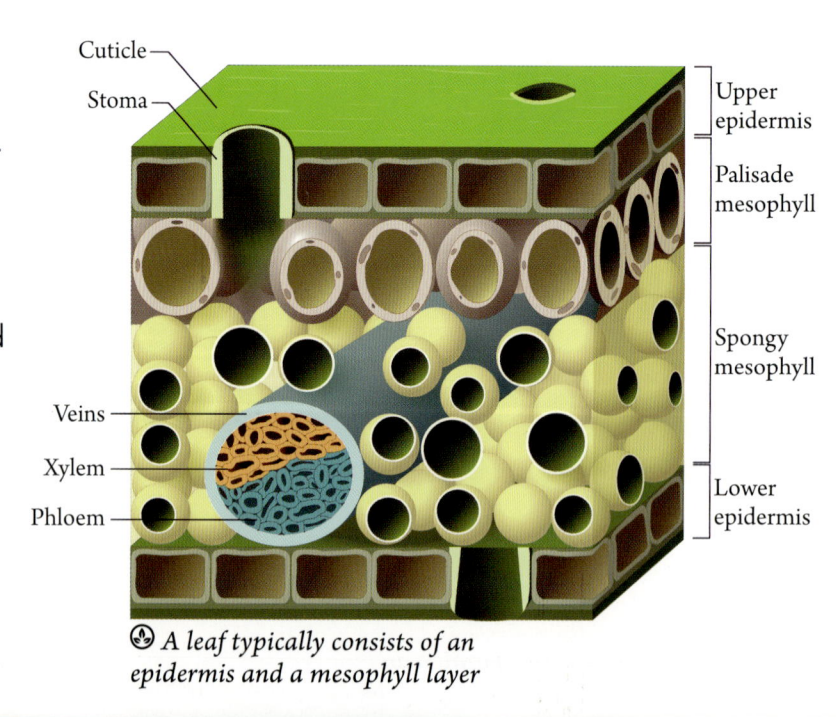

A leaf typically consists of an epidermis and a mesophyll layer

Functions of Leaves

Leaves generally have a large surface area to capture more sunlight. They are also mostly thin, so that carbon dioxide in the atmosphere can diffuse into the leaf through stomata more easily. The chlorophyll pigment present in the leaf absorbs sunlight and transfers the energy to other chemical components.

The network of veins not only transport water and nutrients, but also acts as a structural framework. The stomata present on the underside of leaves help in gas exchange and transpiration.

Leaf cells have chloroplasts that contain chlorophyll pigment

Fact File
Some leaves are covered with tiny hairs that are called 'trichomes'. In carnivorous plants, trichomes secrete digestive enzymes.

Leaf Adaptations

Leaves adapt to the habitat they grow in and the climatic conditions. Some leaves have a thin epidermis that is almost transparent to enable more light to reach the palisade cells located underneath. It is here that photosynthesis is carried out. A few leaves have a waxy coating that protects them from damage caused by heavy winds.

Some leaves have palisade cells as the top layer to enhance photosynthesis. A few leaves are thick and spongy to allow carbon dioxide to diffuse easily through the leaf and also to increase the surface area. Coniferous trees are found in dry and cold regions and possess needle-like leaves to avoid dehydration. Cacti living in hot deserts have small leaves that fall off during spring.

Cacti have small leaves that fall off during spring

Waxy leaves reduce transpiration and prevent damage

PHOTOSYNTHESIS

Plants are referred to as 'autotrophs'. This means that they can make their own food in the form of sugars using sunlight, water and carbon dioxide. This process is called photosynthesis and is of enormous significance to us and other living organisms that depend on plants for food and oxygen.

What Is Photosynthesis?

Photosynthesis is a series of chemical reactions that use sunlight, carbon dioxide and water to produce glucose and oxygen. It occurs in plants, algae and certain types of microorganisms. This process is vital to all other organisms not only for the food but also for the oxygen that sustains life on the planet.

Plants use the sugars produced during photosynthesis for respiration. During respiration, the sugars are broken down to release energy for growth and reproduction. The excess sugars are also converted into starch, proteins or fats and stored for future use.

✿ *Sunlight, water and air are essential for plants to survive and make their food*

✿ *Green leaves have chloroplasts that perform photosynthesis*

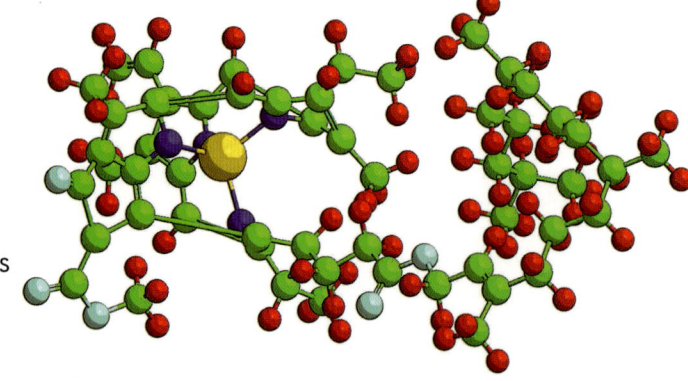

Chlorophyll

Chlorophyll is an essential pigment that takes part in photosynthesis. A pigment is a substance that is capable of absorbing light. The pigment's color is derived from the wavelength of light it absorbs from the visible spectrum. Chlorophyll is a green pigment that absorbs all wavelengths of light except green. Chlorophyll is a complex molecule that exists in different variations in different photosynthetic organisms. 'Chlorophyll A' is the most common type of pigment found in most plants and blue-green algae.

✿ *Chlorophyll A is one of the main pigments used in photosynthesis*

Light and Dark Reactions

Photosynthesis is divided into two parts: the light-dependent (light) reaction and the light-independent (dark) reaction. The dark reaction uses the output products of the light reaction and will stop if light is deprived for a long time.

Light Reaction: The light reaction occurs in the thylakoid membrane of the chloroplast. In the light reaction, sunlight is the main source of light, though artificial light can also be used in controlled environments to stimulate photosynthesis. Light energy that is absorbed breaks down water into hydrogen (H+) and hydroxyl ions (OH-), oxygen and energy in the form of adenosine triphosphate. NADP, a special molecule present in the chloroplast, is reduced to $NADPH_2$.

$$H_2O + \text{Light Energy} \rightarrow NADPH_2 + ATP + O_2$$

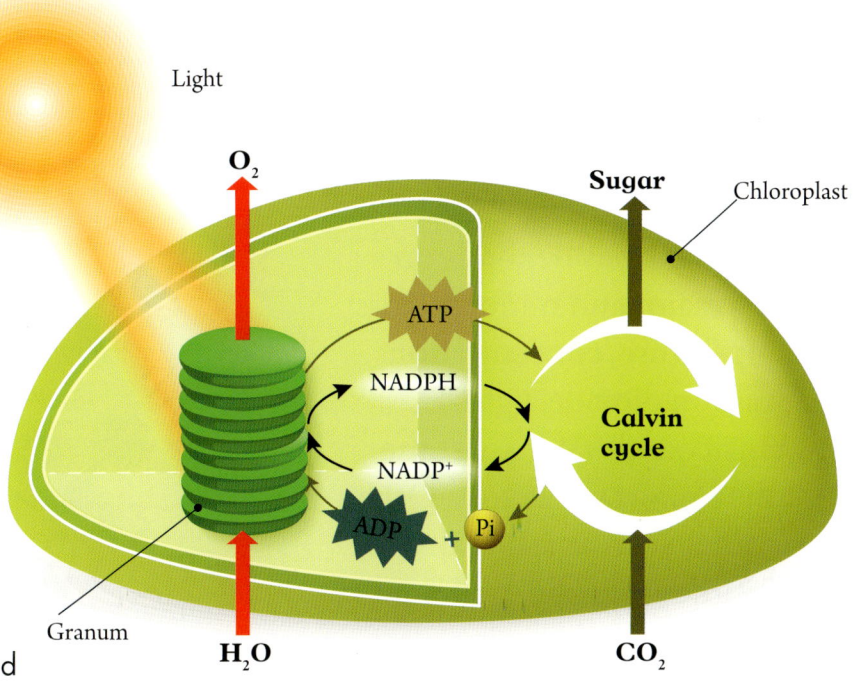

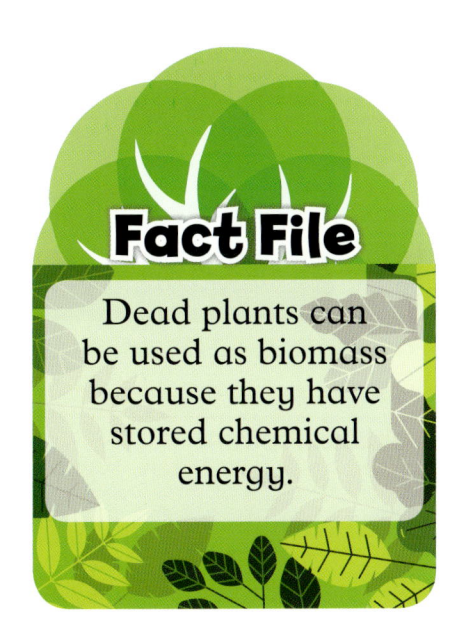

The light reaction occurs through a series of steps

Dark Reaction: The dark reaction, also called the Calvin Cycle, occurs in the stroma of chloroplasts. This reaction depends on the products of the light reaction to occur. The dark reaction can occur in the presence and absence of light, but it is called so because of its dependence on the products of light reaction. Using ATP, hydrogen ions and carbon dioxide, it produces sugars.

$$6\ CO_2 + 12\ NADPH + 12\ H^+ + 18\ ATP \rightarrow C_6H_{12}O_6\ \text{(glucose)} + 6\ H_2O + 12\ NADP^+ + 18\ ADP + 18\ Pi$$

The dark reaction is mostly an enzymatic reaction and occurs more slowly than the light reaction.

Fact File
Dead plants can be used as biomass because they have stored chemical energy.

Coal is formed from dead remains of plants that died millions of years ago

Importance of Photosynthesis

Photosynthesis sustains life on Earth. Plants use the glucose created for growth and energy. Animals then consume plants for energy needs and survival. The animals that feed on plants are known as primary consumers or herbivores. Photosynthesis facilitates respiration for animals because the oxygen produced by the plants is used for respiration. Photosynthesis is therefore directly related to the life and survival of all living creatures on earth.

Coal and natural gas are products of dead and buried plant material from millions of years ago. We use these fossil fuels for generating electricity.

Fossil fuels form in the Earth's crust from buried parts of plants and animals

FACTORS AFFECTING PHOTOSYNTHESIS

Photosynthesis depends on many major and minor factors. Temperature, concentration of carbon dioxide, light intensity and water are some of the important factors. Other variables such as mineral constituents in soil, pollutants and duration of reaction also regulate the efficiency of photosynthesis.

Major Factors

Temperature: The rate of photosynthesis increases with a rise in temperature until about 37°C. Above this temperature, the trend reverses with the rate falling rapidly. At 43°C, plant tissues die. At high temperatures, the enzymes responsible for the dark reaction are inactivated.

The optimal temperature range for photosynthesis varies across species. Lichens photosynthesize most efficiently at 20°C while for coniferous trees, the ideal temperature is 35°C. Cacti and hardy desert plants, acclimatized to very hot and dry weather, can carry out photosynthesis at 55°C. Certain species of bacteria and blue-green algae that reside in hot springs can photosynthesize at temperatures as high as 75°C.

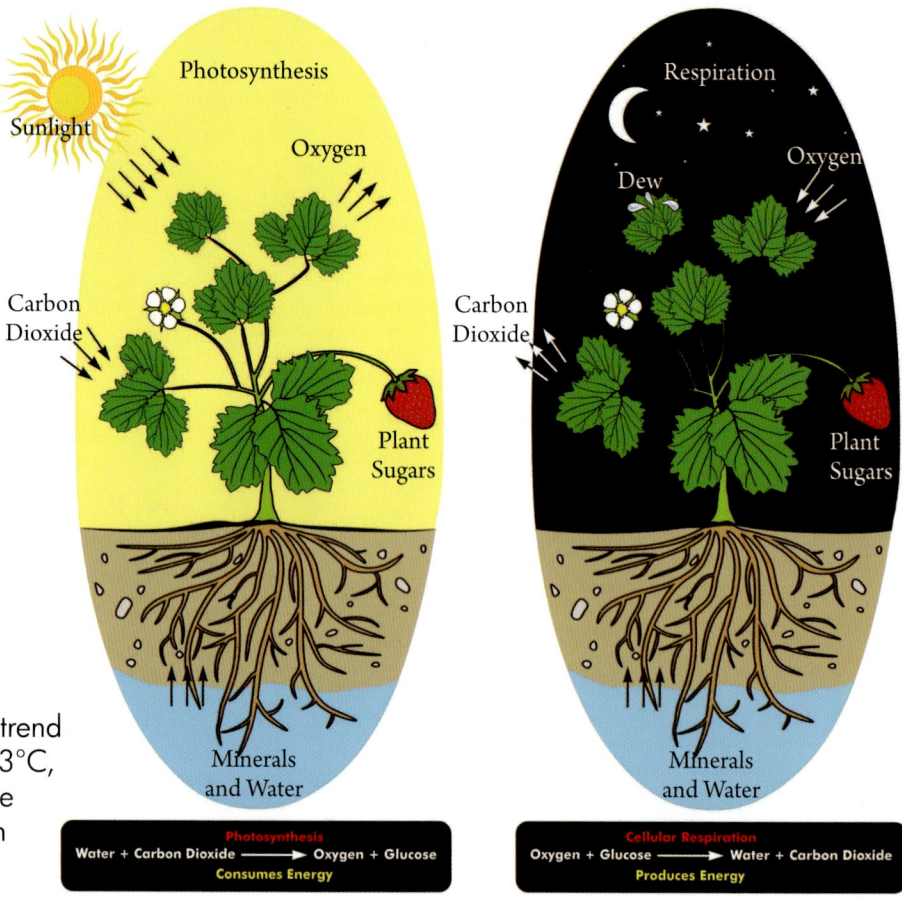

Photosynthesis: Water + Carbon Dioxide ⟶ Oxygen + Glucose — Consumes Energy

Cellular Respiration: Oxygen + Glucose ⟶ Water + Carbon Dioxide — Produces Energy

☘ *Photosynthesis occurs during the day when sunlight is abundant*

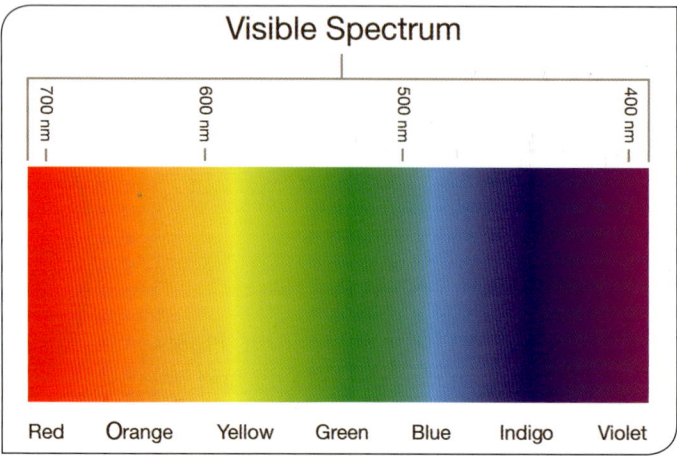

☘ *The green region of the visible spectrum is important for photosynthesis*

Light Intensity: The wavelengths from 400 to 700 nanometers of the visible light region in the light spectrum correspond to the active photosynthesis region.

☘ *Blue-green algae can photosynthesize even at 75°C*

The green light (550 nm) is important for the process. A plant cannot carry out photosynthesis efficiently even if sufficient amounts of water and carbon dioxide are present. When light intensity increases, the rate of photosynthesis also increases up to a saturation point.

Carbon Dioxide Concentration: The atmosphere consists of 0.03% by volume of carbon dioxide. This low concentration of the gas acts as a limiting factor during photosynthesis. A limiting factor is anything that ensures that a population of living organisms, in this case plants, remain controlled in size and reproduction. A rise in carbon dioxide concentration from 0.03 to 0.1% increases the rate of photosynthesis. Above this concentration, the rate remains constant.

Water: Water is an important component in the process, but less than 1% of the absorbed water is used for photosynthesis. Any decrease in soil water results in leaf wilting and decreased photosynthesis. Severe dehydration can even lead to damage of chloroplasts.

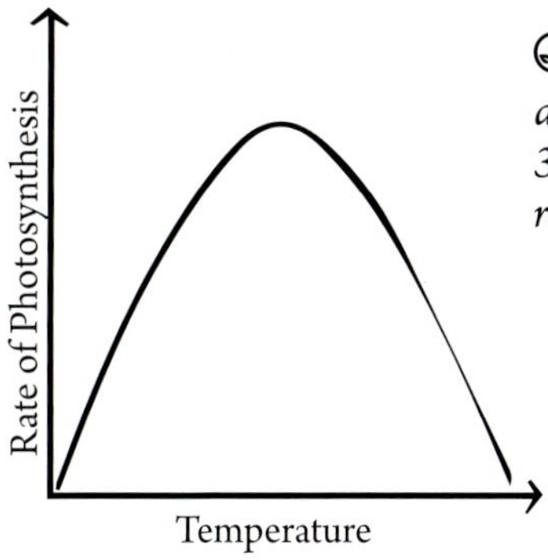

Temperature, light intensity and CO_2 concentration are 3 major factors that control rate of photosynthesis

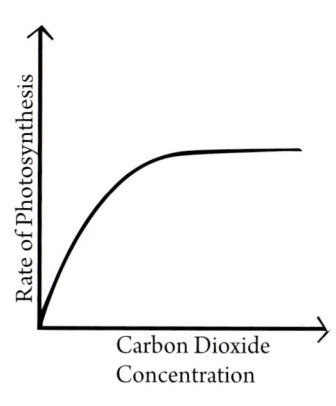

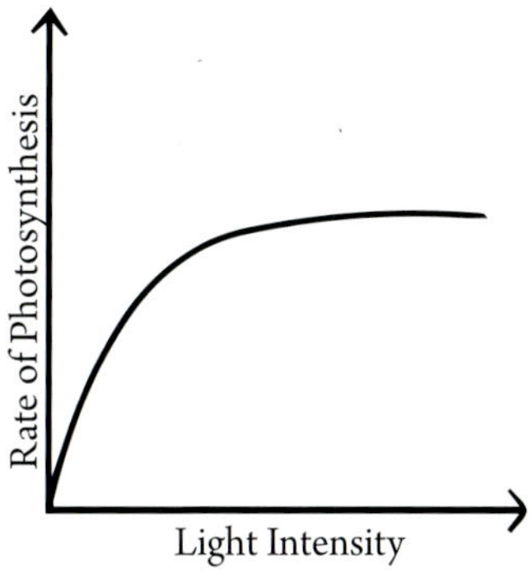

Minor Factors

Minerals: Minerals such as magnesium, iron, copper, chlorine, manganese and potassium are directly involved in regulating photosynthetic enzymes. Any decrease in the concentration of minerals will affect the rate of photosynthesis.

Pollutants: Gaseous pollutants such as ozone and sulphur dioxide decrease photosynthetic activity.

Accumulation of Sugars: Photosynthesis results in the formation of sugars and their accumulation leads to a slowdown of the process and eventually stops it. Sugars are converted into starch which also starts accumulating inside chloroplasts, reducing their efficiency.

Farmers and agriculturists use this knowledge to maximize plant growth. Artificial lights and paraffin lamps in greenhouses are often used to provide extra heat, light and carbon dioxide to boost growth.

Fact File

The concentration of carbon dioxide was as high as 20% in Earth's early atmosphere.

Pollutants in air can decrease rate of photosynthesis

Plants can be grown in greenhouses under controlled conditions

TRANSPIRATION

Transpiration is a process by which excess water in plants is carried to the pores on the underside of leaves to be released into the atmosphere as water vapor. Transpiration is a type of evaporation that occurs from leaves. Water can be lost in liquid form through intact leaves or stems in a process called guttation.

Water evaporates from leaf surface

Water travels though plant

Water absorbed by root hairs

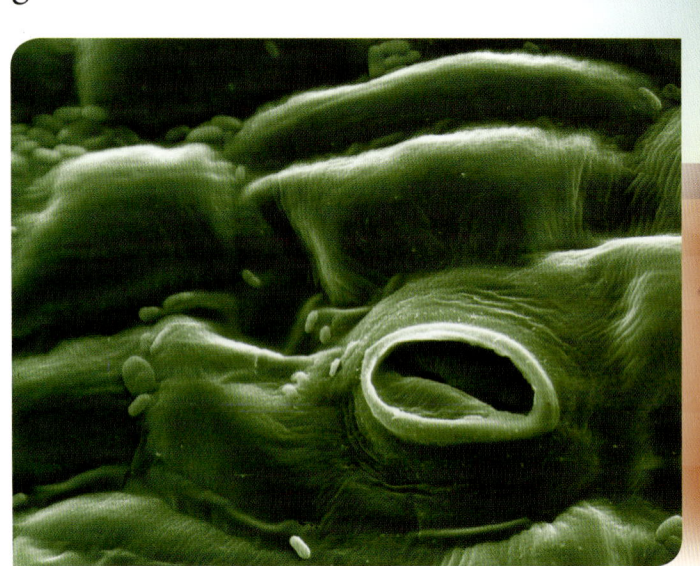

🌱 *Transpiration occurs through openings called 'stomata'*

Stomata

A 'stoma' is a microscopic opening in a leaf through which transpiration and respiration occurs. Stomata are located on the underside of leaves. Plants take in carbon dioxide and expel oxygen through stomata. Water vapor is also expelled through these openings. The opening and closing of each stoma is controlled by two guard cells. The number and distribution of stomata varies across plant species. Stomata are found on the upper side of leaves in aquatic plants such as water lily and lotus.

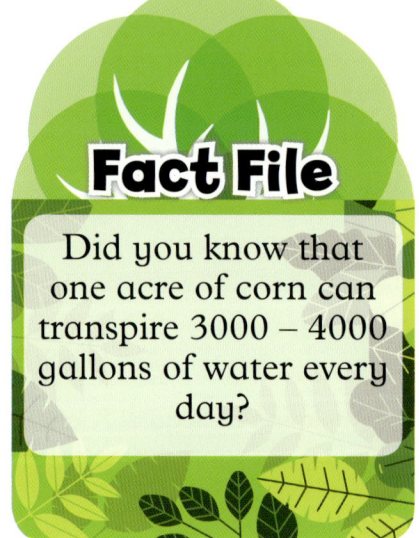

Fact File

Did you know that one acre of corn can transpire 3000 – 4000 gallons of water every day?

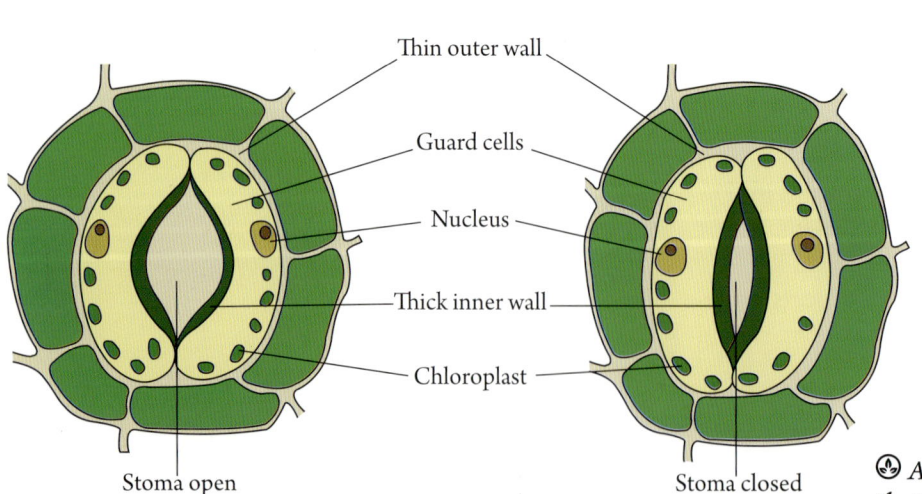

Thin outer wall
Guard cells
Nucleus
Thick inner wall
Chloroplast

Stoma open   Stoma closed

🌱 *A stoma consists of two guard cells that control opening and closing*

Mechanism of Transpiration

Plants use only about 5% of the water they absorb for growth. Transpiration is the process by which plants lose water in the form of water vapor.

Plants absorb water from the soil and transport it to all parts through specialized tubes called xylem. The water transported to leaves is expelled out through small pores. Water moves up against gravity and spreads across the leaf's cells and diffuses out.

Why Do Plants Transpire?

When leaves transpire, the water evaporates and transforms from liquid into gas. This process is useful to plants in different ways. During transpiration, energy is released. The release of water vapor and energy into the atmosphere cools the plant. Transpiration is also useful for enhanced intake of nutrients to different parts as water with the dissolved minerals rises up to the leaves. When plants are transpiring, the stomata are open, allowing gas exchange to occur simultaneously.

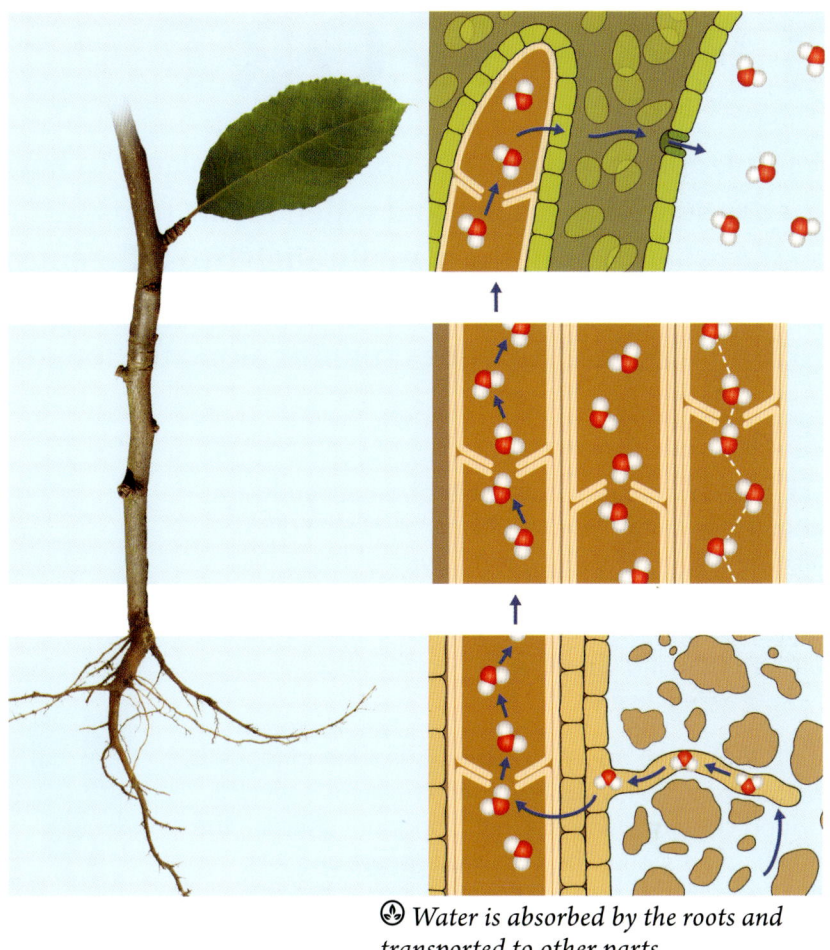

Water is absorbed by the roots and transported to other parts

Factors Affecting Transpiration

Some of the factors that affect the rate of transpiration include:

Light: Transpiration rate is high in bright light as the stomata open wider to allow entry of carbon dioxide and expulsion of water.

Temperature: The higher the temperature the faster the transpiration occurs, up to a certain point.

Wind: It can hasten transpiration by quickly removing water vapor and speeding up diffusion of water.

Humidity: Transpiration falls as the relative humidity rises. Humidity is the amount of moisture present in the atmosphere.

Factors that affect transpiration can also cause an increase in the uptake of water from the soil. When water is scarce or if the plant's roots have been damaged, slowing down the transpiration rate is essential for its survival. Plants can lower the rate of transpiration naturally through wilting until water becomes available.

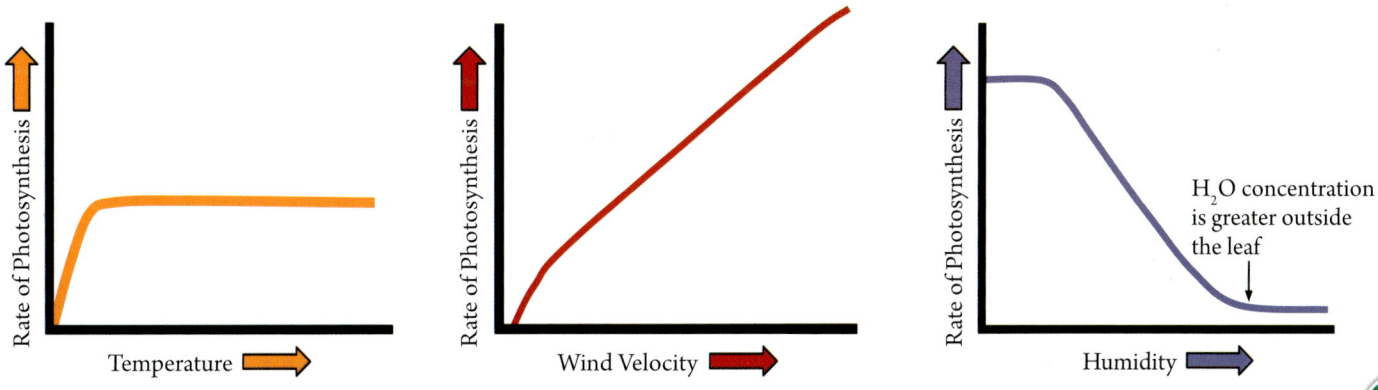

H$_2$O concentration is greater outside the leaf

TRANSPORT

Vascular plants differ from non-vascular plants in having specialized tissues for conducting nutrients and water. Plants transport water and minerals to the other parts of the plant through two different systems – xylem and phloem. Both these transport systems are made up of cells arranged in rows to form tube-like structures running along the length of the plant.

Xylem

The roots absorb water and dissolved minerals from the soil. This, in turn, travels up a network of tubes called 'xylem'. Xylem is a type of tissue that transports water absorbed by the roots to other parts of the plant like leaves and stem. The word 'xylem' is derived from the Greek word 'wood' since wood is a type of xylem tissue.

Cells that make up xylem develop like the other cells, but after the cell walls form, the chemical 'lignin' is added. This addition has two important effects – the lignification makes the cells waterproof and kills the cells. The xylem tissue then becomes long tubular networks made up of sturdy, dead cells ideal for transporting water and minerals across long distances.

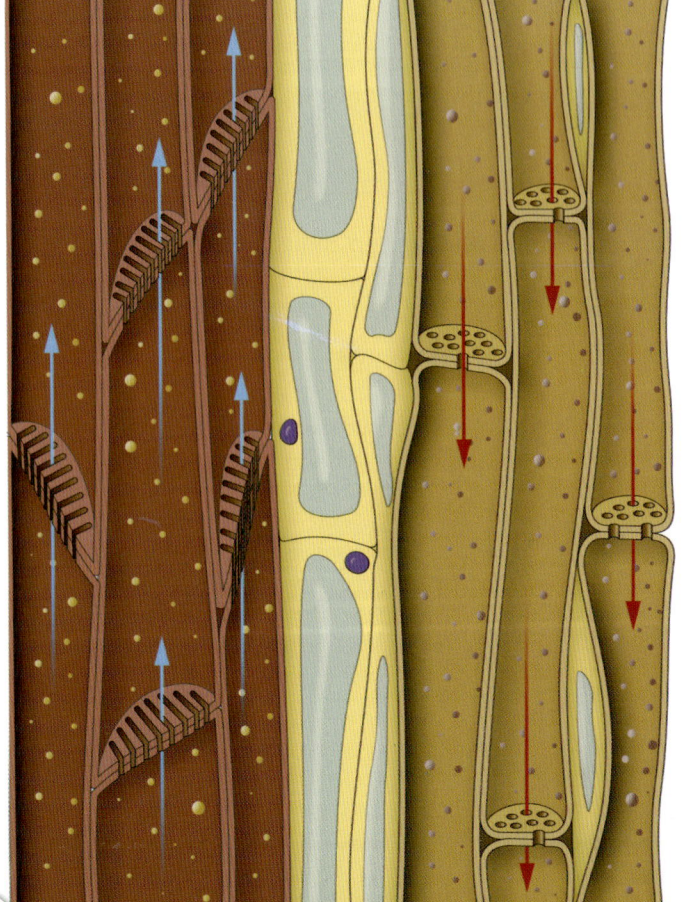

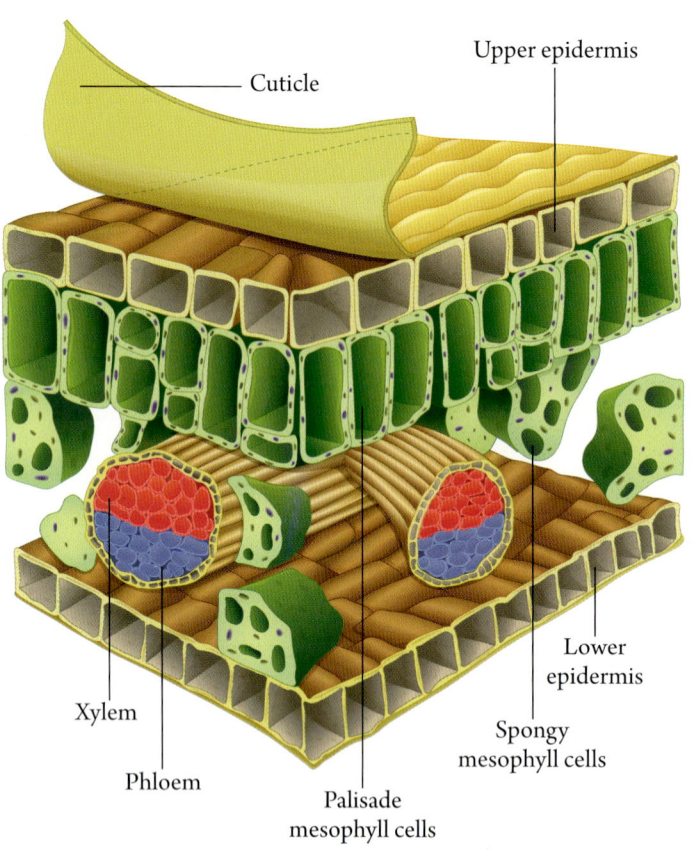

🌱 *Xylem and phloem are the major conducting vessels in plants*

The transport of water through xylem is passive and energy is not spent on this process. Since the upward transport of water becomes challenging with increase in height, it becomes a limiting factor in deciding how tall a tree or plant grows.

The most common types of xylem cells are tracheids and vessel elements. They are distinguished by shape and size. Tracheids are elongated cells with thick, lignified walls that provide structural framework in many woody coniferous trees. Vessel elements are shorter than tracheids and connected together to form long tubules.

🌱 *Xylem transports water from roots while phloem transports nutrients from leaves*

Phloem

Phloem, also known as bast, is the plant tissue responsible for transporting nutrients and minerals prepared in the leaves to other parts of the plant. The word 'phloem' is derived from the Greek word meaning 'bark' since phloem forms the innermost layer of bark. It forms in the apical meristems or growing zones of roots and shoots. The process by which it transports sugars is known as translocation. The main difference between xylem and phloem is that while xylem is mostly made up of dead cells, phloem cells are living.

There are many specialized cells that make up phloem. They are:

Sieve tubes: They are designed for transporting sugars across long distance by acting as channels.

Phloem fibers: They support the conducting cells and offer structural strength to the stem.

Phloem parenchyma: Also called 'transfer cells', they are located near leaf veinlets and fine branches in locations where sieve tubes end. Parenchyma cells, in turn, are of two types: chlorenchyma and aerenchyma.

Companion cells: They assist phloem cells and regulate activity to keep them alive.

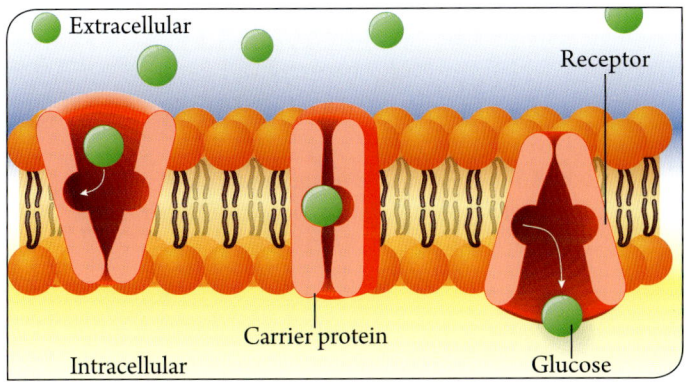

◉ *Facilitated diffusion occurs through certain transport proteins*

Fact File

The sap that we see in certain plants is actually the water and nutrients transported by xylem and phloem.

Transport Mechanisms

Water, minerals and nutrients are transported across the plant through these three means:

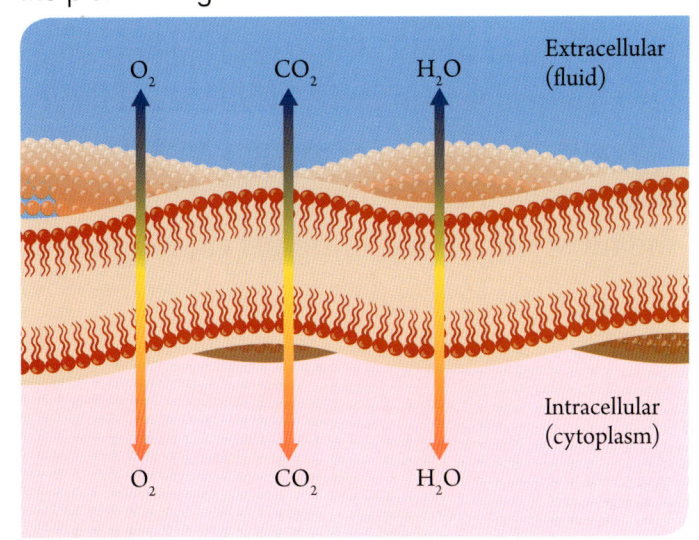

◉ *Simple diffusion of molecules occurs from higher to lower concentrations*

Simple Diffusion: In this type of transport, molecules make their way into the plant cell membrane due to the difference in concentration. Diffusion is the process by which molecules move from a region of higher concentration to a region of lower concentration. It is a slow process but does not use up energy. Water and gases enter cells through diffusion.

Facilitated Diffusion: Certain molecules are taken up selectively based on their ability to pass through membrane transport proteins. The protein facilitates movement of molecules without expending any energy.

Active Transport: This is a process by which molecules are taken into plant cells by spending energy in the form of ATP. Unlike diffusion, which can occur only from high to low concentration, this type of transport can occur even against the gradient. It is of 2 types:

- **Symport:** Two molecules enter through the membrane simultaneously.

- **Antiport:** One molecule enters in while another molecule is expelled out.

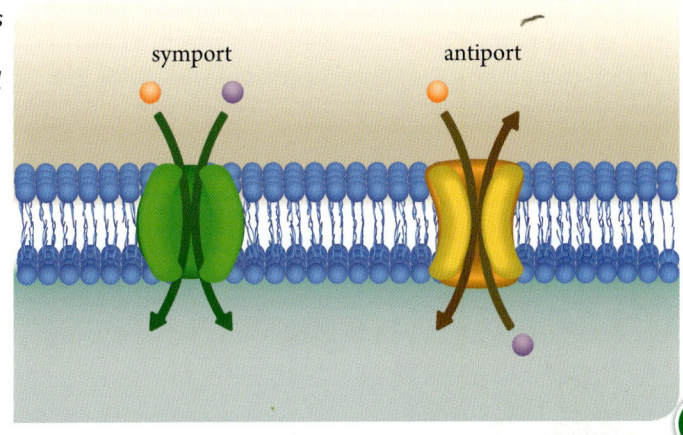

◉ *There are two types of active transport systems - symport and antiport*

PLANT NUTRITION

Apart from sunlight, water and carbon dioxide, plants also need different minerals from the soil for survival. While animals consume food that already contains minerals, plants have to obtain minerals from the soil to produce complex macromolecules. The roots absorb the minerals from the soil for the plant's needs. The most important minerals are magnesium and nitrates.

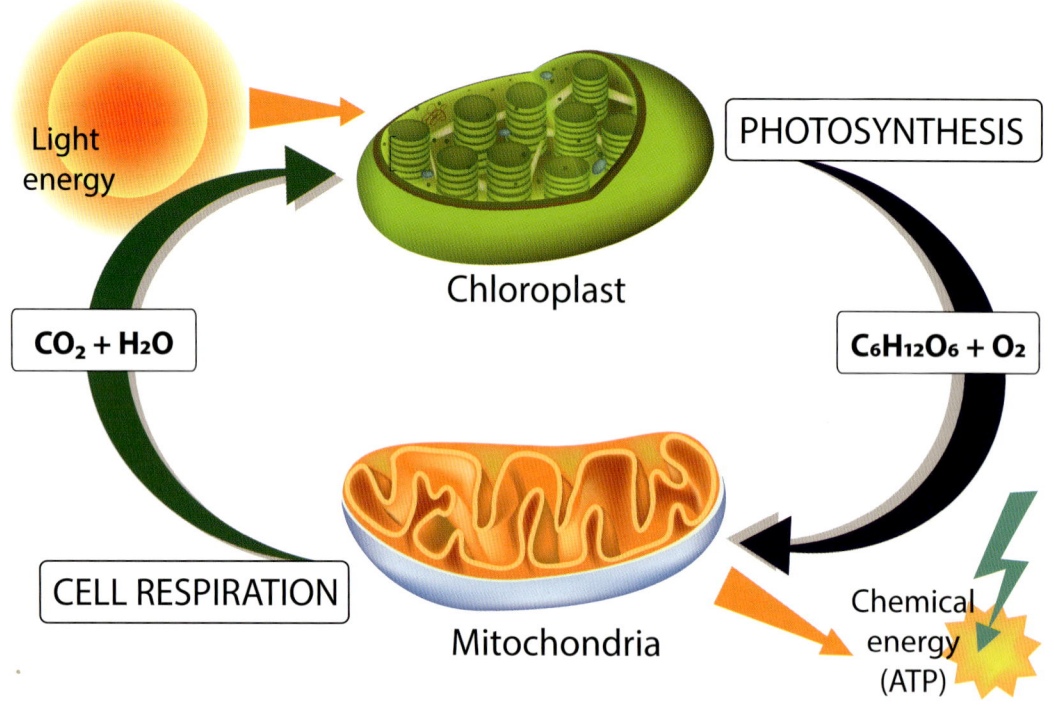

Chloroplasts and mitochondria are vital organelles that perform important functions

Macronutrients and Micronutrients

Plants need seventeen nutrients for normal growth and development. The macronutrients that plants need are: nitrogen, phosphorus, sulfur, potassium, magnesium, calcium, hydrogen, carbon and oxygen. The minerals or micronutrients required include: iron, nickel, zinc, copper, manganese, boron, chlorine and molybdenum.

The gases such as hydrogen, carbon, oxygen and nitrogen are available through water and the gases found in the atmosphere. The macronutrients are required in large quantities and roughly make up 95% of the plant's biomass. Minerals are required in trace quantities and make up about 0.02% of the plant's dry weight.

Absorption of Minerals

Minerals are present only in tiny quantities in the soil. In the presence of water, the minerals are dissolved and available in the form of a solution. The cells in root hairs are specialized in absorbing the water from the soil through osmosis or simple diffusion.

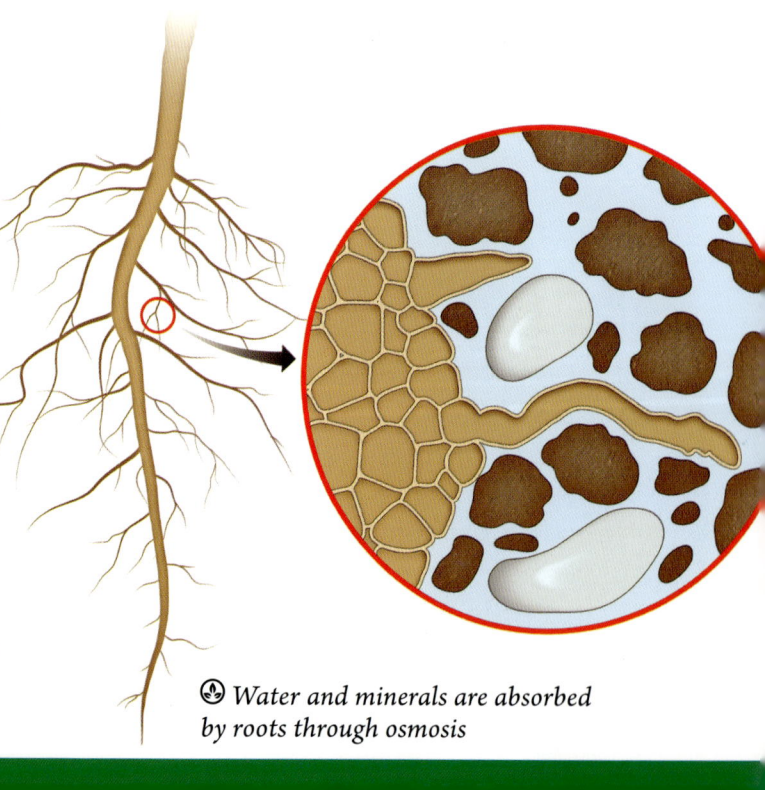

Water and minerals are absorbed by roots through osmosis

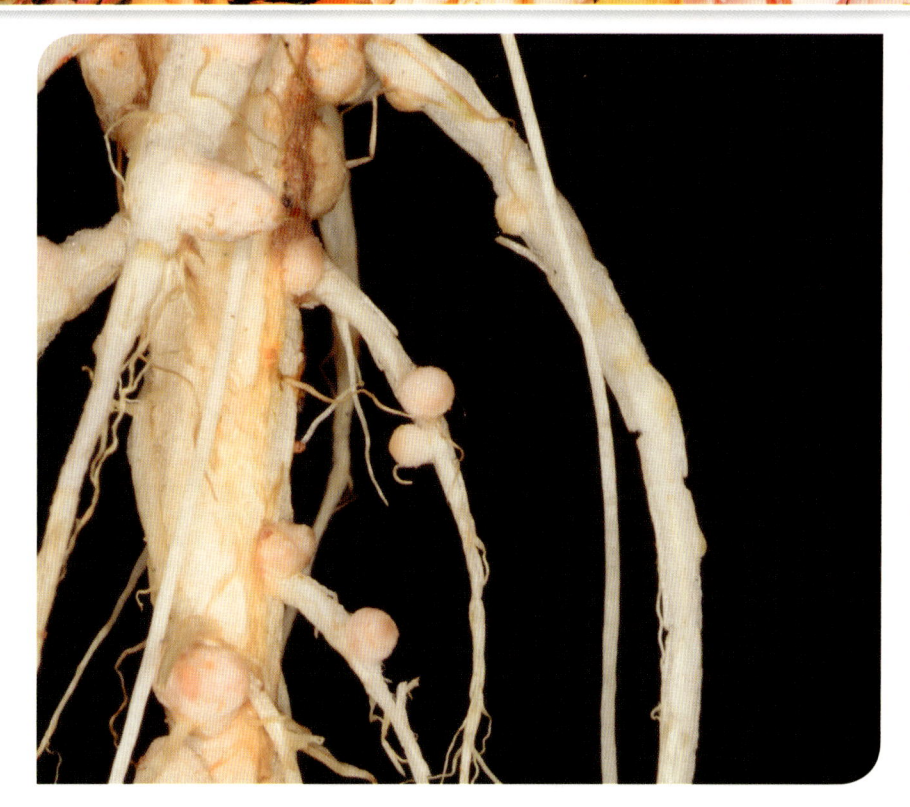

Minerals are also taken in through active transport against a concentration gradient by spending energy. To achieve this, root hair cells have special carrier molecules on the surface that can selectively pick up minerals needed by the plants.

Certain legume plants such as pea and groundnut have root nodules containing bacteria that help fix nitrogen for plants to use in exchange for nutrients.

Root nodules in legumes contain bacteria that help fix nitrogen

Fact File
In the United States, the three crops that require the most fertilizers are corn, soybean and wheat.

Fertilizers for Plant Growth

Plants adapt to the habitat they grow in and most soil types across the world are suited for providing sufficient nutrition for the complete life cycle of a plant. A plant that exhibits stunted growth or yellowing leaves may be deficient in one or more micronutrients.

In agriculture, to facilitate the mass production of crops for large-scale consumption, the soil nutrients alone are not sufficient, especially for repeated cultivations. So nutrients are provided in the form of fertilizers. The use of fertilizers has improved growth, increased yield and compensated for soil deficiency. The commonly used fertilizer is called NPK (N – Nitrogen, P – Phosphorus, K – Potassium) fertilizer.

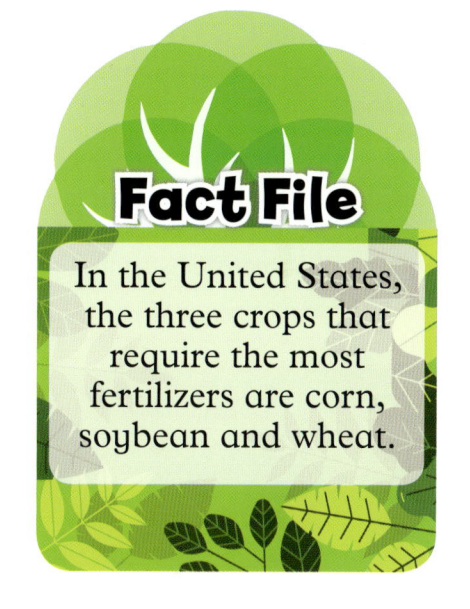

Mineral	Use	Deficiency
Nitrates	Building blocks of amino acids	Poor growth; yellowing leaves
Phosphates	Required for DNA synthesis and respiration	Discolored leaves; poor root growth
Potassium	Needed for photosynthesis and respiration	Poor development of flower and fruit
Magnesium	Essential in chlorophyll for photosynthesis	Yellowing leaves

Overuse of Fertilizers

While fertilizers are essential for large-scale plant cultivation, overuse can cause problems. A common problem that occurs either from the overuse of fertilizer or from the use of poor quality fertilizer is 'fertilizer burn'. This causes the wilting of roots or leaves.

Other issues resulting from the indiscriminate use of fertilizers include soil pollution, reduced plant health and making plants more attractive to pests.

Fertilizer burn observed on a patch of grass

PLANT GROWTH

Most plant species grow throughout their lives. Like other multicellular organisms, plants grow through a combination of cell growth and cell division. Cell differentiation results in the production of specialized types of cells.

Meristem

The area where growth occurs in plants is called 'meristem'. It is found in roots and shoots. Meristem is a type of plant tissue with undifferentiated cells that are capable of continuous growth and differentiation. Apical meristem is found at the apex or tip of roots and buds. It allows roots and stems to grow and enables flowers to differentiate.

It is common to find one branch of a plant becoming the dominant 'apical meristem'. The 'dominant meristem' will supress the growth of other meristems so that only a single trunk develops.

The dominant meristem ensures development of a single trunk

Primary Meristem

Primary apical meristem differentiates into three types. These three meristems are responsible for primary growth such as increase in length and height.

Protoderm: It produces new epidermis or the outermost layer of cells

Procambium: It produces new xylem and phloem

Ground meristem: It gives rise to new ground tissue

Apical meristem is present at the growing tips of plants

Fact File

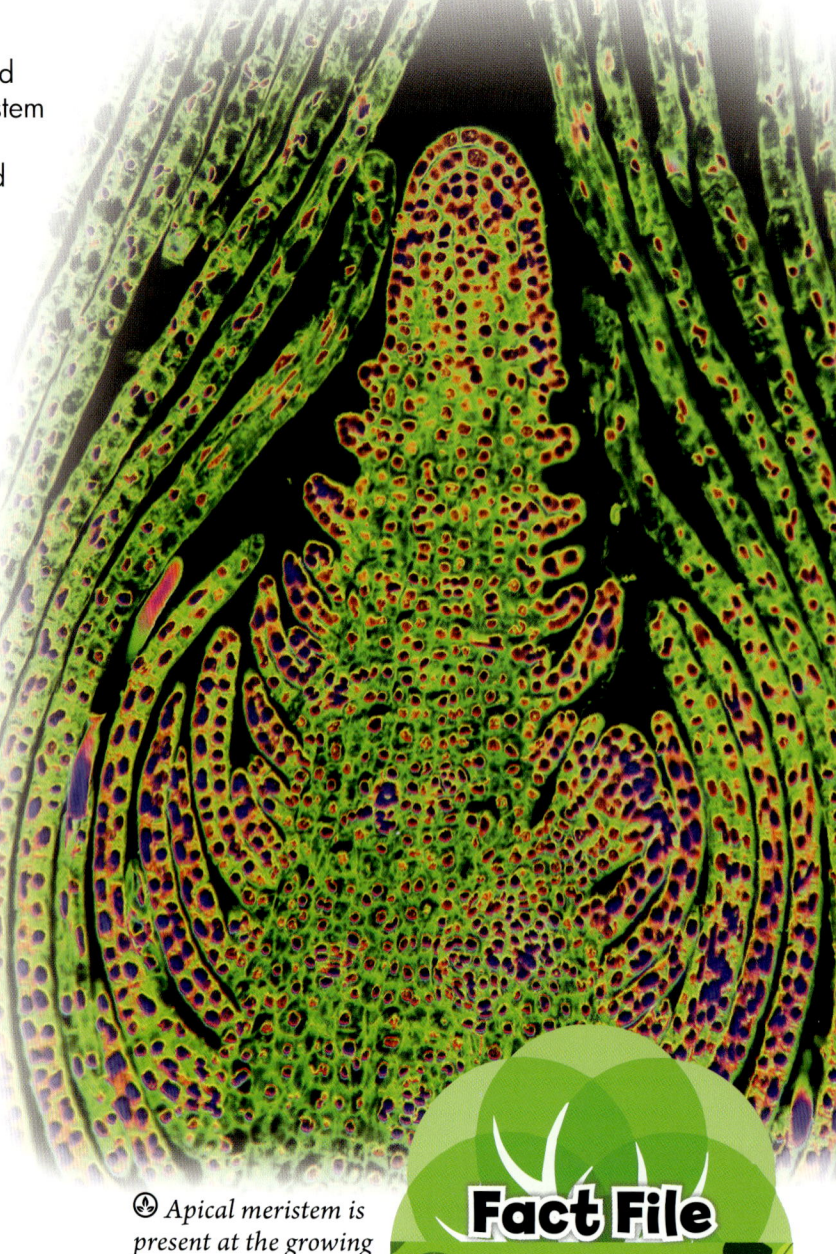

Grasses have apical meristems at the base of leaf blades – that's why they regrow easily after being mowed or grazed.

Secondary Meristem

Secondary meristem is essential for enabling increase in radius or secondary growth in woody plants. Secondary growth is not observed in herbs and shrubs. The two types of secondary meristem are:

Vascular cambium: It produces secondary xylem and phloem and adds diameter to the trunk.

Cork cambium: It lies between the epidermis layer and phloem and is responsible for replacing root and stem epidermis with bark, the tough outer covering found on trees.

🌱 *Vascular cambium forms the rings in tree trunks*

🌱 *Cork cambium makes up the outer bark of trees*

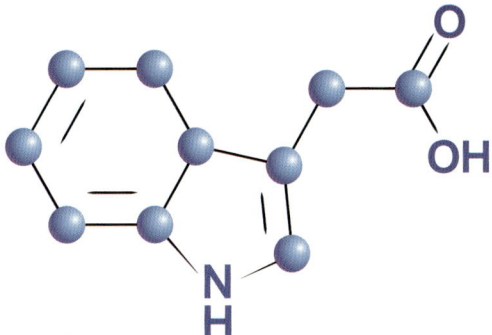

🌱 *Auxins are a class of plant hormones that assist in cell growth*

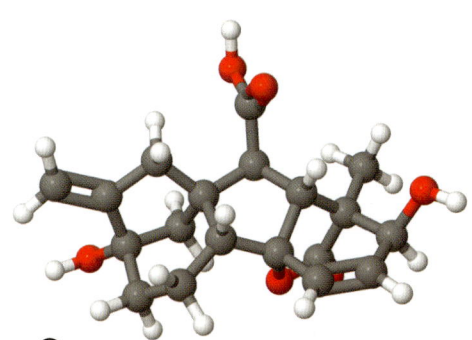

🌱 *PGibberellin is a plant hormone responsible for cell elongation*

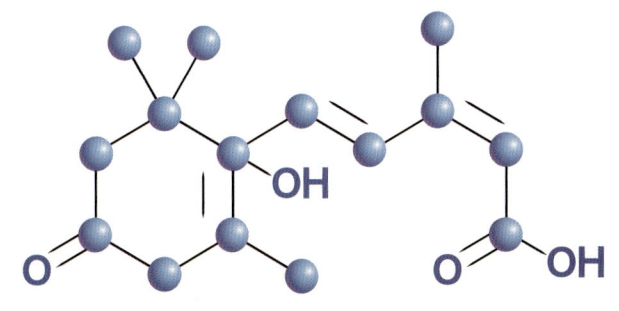

🌱 *Abscisic acid is produced in response to water stress*

Growth Hormones

Plants synthesize five major hormones that influence growth, development and ageing. They are: auxins, gibberellins, cytokinins, abscisic acid and ethylene.

Auxins: Auxins are responsible for inducing cell growth and expansion. The highest concentration of auxins is found in the growing tip of the plant. Auxins are vital for maintaining the shape of plants.

Gibberellins: Gibberellins function in a similar way to auxins and promote elongation of stems between nodes. A node is the place where a leaf is attached to the stem. Gibberellin was named after a fungal species that caused rice plants to grow very tall. Farmers sometimes use gibberellins to elongate sugarcanes for higher sugar yield.

Cytokinins: Cytokinins are responsible for stimulating cell division in roots and shoots. They are produced in the apical meristems or the growing tips. These hormones are responsible for delaying ageing in plants.

Ethylene: Ethylene is responsible for the ripening of fruits. It is the only plant hormone that exists in gaseous form. Since ethylene can only form in the presence of oxygen, fruits and vegetables are transported in trucks with low oxygen and high carbon dioxide to delay ripening.

Abscisic acid: This is a hormone produced by the plant in response to water stress. It in turn signals the stomata to close to reduce transpiration or loss of water.

GERMINATION

The process by which a seed develops into a whole plant is known as seed germination. The fruits produced by a plant are actually ripened ovaries with seeds inside. The seeds are spread across the environment to develop into new plants. The success of seed germination depends on a lot of factors.

Germination of seeds occurs in stages

Formation of Seed

Male plants release the pollen grains that fertilize the ovaries. The fertilized ovaries develop into seeds. The fertilized ovaries develop and accumulate plenty of carbohydrates and proteins inside the seed. This provides nutrition for the developing seed and helps it give forth roots and shoot.

The seeds are carried away from the plant by different pollinating agents; this is known as dispersal. When the seeds fall onto suitable soil, under the right conditions, they develop into new plants.

The ideal conditions of seed germination vary across species

🌱 *A seed germinates after it breaks open from its seed coat*

Germinating Conditions

Seeds start growing by absorbing moisture from the surroundings through their seed coat. The water essentially brings the seed back to life. The seed coat cracks open and the roots start growing.

The stem also develops above the ground. When it first pushes out through the soil, the shoot is usually curved. This is a process to protect the developing plantlet from physical damage. As the shoot is exposed to sunlight, it slowly grows towards the light and begins photosynthesis.

🌱 *A germinated seed has a root and a shoot*

Germination – Optimal Conditions

The right environmental conditions are vital for the germination process. The germination of a seed depends on how deeply in the soil it is embedded and the availability of water and warmth. If plentiful water is available in the soil, the seed takes up as much water as it can hold in a process known as 'imbibition'.

Water: The water activates enzymes in the seed that triggers the process of seed growth. The seed first grows roots to access the water and nutrients underground. Then it puts out shoots and leaves that grow towards the sun. The affinity for shoots to grow towards sunlight and away from the ground is called photomorphogenesis.

Oxygen: It is essential for metabolism and is the main source of energy for the developing seed until it produces leaves. A seed that is packed too deep inside the soil or waterlogged will not get sufficient oxygen.

Temperature: The amount of sunlight and temperature needed by seeds to germinate varies among species. Sometimes, even seeds from the same plant can germinate at different temperatures. The optimal temperature for most seeds to germinate is 16 – 24 C. There are seeds that germinate at temperatures just above freezing point. There are some seeds that need to be exposed to cold temperatures to begin germination. This process is known as 'vernalization'. At the other extreme, certain types of seeds require temperatures as hot as forest fires to crack open their seed coats.

🌱 *Germination, in most cases, is initiated by absorption of water*

Fact File

It takes a coconut 3 to 6 months to germinate after landing in an ideal spot.

POLLINATION

The process by which pollen grains from the stamens are transferred to the ovules is called pollination. Many plants are capable of self-fertilization. However, there are plants that depend on wind, water, insects and animals for pollination. Pollination is an important process and any change in the pollinator population can be a major threat to plants.

Process of Pollination

In gymnosperms, pollination is relatively simple. The ovules are exposed and the pollen is received in a drop of sticky fluid secreted by the ovule. In angiosperms, the process is more complicated. The ovules are embedded in a hollow organ in the flower called 'pistil'. The pollen grains are deposited on the stigma. The pollen germinates and develops into a pollen tube all the way to the ovule.

Out of the two sperm cells in the pollen tube, one fuses with the egg cell in the ovule and gives rise to the embryo. The other sperm cell fuses with two sexual nuclei of the ovule to form the reserve food tissue or endosperm. This process is known as 'double fertilization'. As the ovule develops, it becomes the seed.

❀ *The shape and size of pollen grains vary*

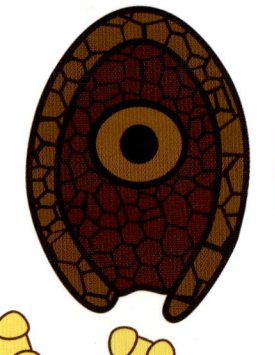

❀ *Fertilization occurs in a series of stages following successful pollination*

Abiotic Pollination

This is a type of pollination that involves non-living methods for transferring pollen from a plant. Plants that use this type of pollination spend energy on distributing pollen rather than attracting pollinators or secreting nectar.

Some of the common abiotic pollinating agents are:

Wind: This is the most common pollinating agent, making up 98% of all abiotic pollinations. The transfer of pollen is achieved effectively through the wind which can disperse pollen and seeds across a large area and increase the success rates of germination. Plants that depend on wind for pollination have specially-designed seeds capable of floating. Dandelion is an example of a plant that disperses its seeds through wind.

Rain: While rain can destroy delicate flowers and discourage insect pollinators, it can help disperse pollen of certain flowers. Orchids allow rain to remove the anther caps thus exposing pollen. The pollen shoots upwards and falls into the stigma of another flower. This method is useful in places where biological pollinators are rare.

Dandelion seeds get dispersed across a wide area through wind

Rain is an abiotic pollinating agent of orchids

Fact File
Honey bees are so vital for pollination that agriculture, and, in turn, food supply for us would be affected if their population dwindled.

Water: Water can transport pollen across its surface and deposit it far from the source. This method is useful for aquatic plants. Waterweeds and pondweeds rely on this effective method of transmitting pollen.

Pollinators

A pollinator is an animal, bird or insect that helps move pollen from the anther to the stigma of a flower. Only after this does fertilization of ovules occur in the flower.

The common insect pollinators are honey bees, bumble bees, butterflies, moths and beetles. Bats and birds are also important pollinators. Monkeys, possums, rodents, lizards and lemurs also assist in pollination.

Animals such as rodents and possums also assist in pollination

REPRODUCTION

Plants reproduce sexually or asexually to produce offspring. Asexual reproduction occurs without the fusion of gametes and the offspring are identical to the parents. Sexual reproduction occurs through the fusion of gametes. The offspring from this type of reproduction are different from the parent plants.

Asexual Reproduction

Asexual reproduction is common among plants. In lab conditions, it is possible to regenerate an entire plant from plant tissue by providing the appropriate stimuli and conditions. The undifferentiated parenchyma cells give rise to new plants.

Plants that adopt asexual reproduction invest less energy in flowers and pollination. Another advantage of asexual reproduction is that plantlets produced by this method will reach maturity faster.

Asexual reproduction commonly occurs through the following ways:

- Budding
- Fragmentation
- Fission
- Spore formation
- Vegetative propagation

Plantlets can grow from certain parts of the plants like leaves

Asexual reproduction can also be artificially induced by farmers and agriculturists. Grafting, cutting, layering and micro propagation are a few methods used. Grafting involves uniting two plant sections using tape or string. In cutting, a small piece of a plant is grown in soil. Layering is a technique in which a low-lying stem is pinned to the ground and covered in soil to encourage growth of a new plant. These artificial methods are useful for producing novel varieties of roses, citrus plants and a few other species.

Vegetative Propagation

Plants such as ginger, onion and dahlia grow from buds present on the surface of the stem. In other plants such as the sweet potato, roots called 'stolons' can produce new plants. Vegetative propagation also occurs naturally in aquatic plants. Fragments of the plant break off, disperse in the water and develop into whole plants. Eelgrass and surf grass are examples of aquatic plants that reproduce through vegetative propagation.

Many aquatic plants reproduce through vegetative propagation

Grafting is an artificial method of inducing asexual reproduction in plants

Parthenocarpy

Flowering plants produce seeds without fusion of male and female gametes. During meiotic cell division, a diploid egg cell develops in the ovule which functions as a zygote. Citrus plants, dandelion, buttercup, blackberry and raspberry plants reproduce in this manner.

Raspberry reproduces through parthenocarpy

Sexual Reproduction

The majority of flowering plants reproduce sexually. The flower is the reproductive part of a plant and has distinct male and female reproductive organs. The pistil or carpel is the female reproductive organ while the stamen is the male reproductive organ. The pistil consists of style, stigma and ovary. The stamen consists of the anther and supporting filaments. The anther produces the male reproductive cells: pollen grains.

Fact File

The plant 'Bryophyllum' reproduces through buds that form on its leaves and develop into complete plantlets.

Flowers may have both pistil and stamen or only one. Bisexual flowers have both female and male reproductive parts. Rose is an example of a plant with bisexual flowers. Papaya and cucumber produce only unisexual flowers.

Plants that depend on pollinating agents use different methods to attract pollinators such as nectar, scent, and bright colors.

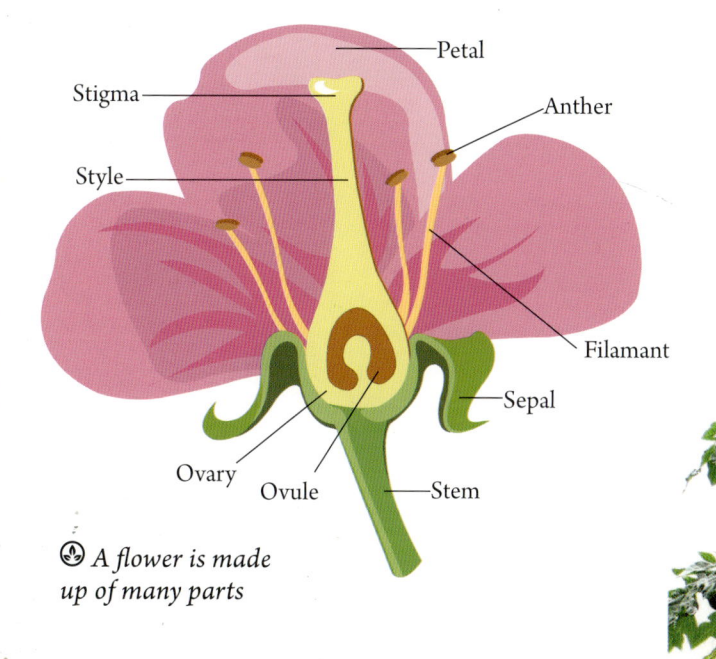

A flower is made up of many parts

Papaya produces male and female flowers in separate trees

PLANT DEFENSE

Plants, unable to move, are vulnerable to attacks by different herbivores. To effectively defend themselves and minimize mechanical wounding, plants have developed different types of barriers, adaptations and chemical defenses. Plant defense mechanisms range from chemical reactions to physical adaptations that reduce digestibility or act as repellents or toxins.

Defense against Herbivores

Mechanical barriers

The primary defense against plant eaters is a mechanical barrier. Most trees have thick bark and stout trunks that cannot be harmed by animals. Smaller herbs and shrubs have a wide range of barriers, ranging from thorns to waxy layers and bitter tasting fruits that are unappetizing. Unripe persimmon fruits have high tannin content that gives them a bitter taste so herbivores avoid them.

Thorns are one of the most common and effective physical barriers

Stinging nettle produces physical reactions simply upon contact

Chemical defenses

Herbivores can still easily breach the mechanical barriers. Some plants have evolved a secondary mechanism in which toxic compounds are released. Herbivores that feed on the compounds experience a wide range of physical reactions ranging from bitter taste, rashes, allergic reactions to dangerous convulsions. However, through learned behavior herbivores learn to avoid these plants. Nettle is an example of a plant that is avoided because of the stinging sensation it can evoke upon touch.

Another mechanism is triggered when a plant is mechanically wounded. The plant produces a set of volatile compounds that attract parasites that can attack the predators.

Some plants host insects that defend against predators

Damage response

When a plant experiences mechanical damage, it makes way for pathogens to enter inside. Like the immune system in animals, plants trigger toxins and enzymes to fight against the pathogens. These chemical compounds are not derived from photosynthesis or essential for the plant's growth.

Foxglove is an example of a plant that is capable of releasing many deadly chemicals, the ingestion of which can cause a wide range of symptoms such as nausea, vomiting, hallucinations, convulsions and even death.

Response to Pathogens

Plants have a variety of other defenses that are induced when they are attacked by specific pathogens. The plants can produce antimicrobial chemicals, proteins or enzymes to fight the pathogens. Sometimes, chemical signals trigger the stomata to close down to prevent pathogen entry. Plants can even elicit a hypersensitive response which causes them to undergo rapid cell death to fight off an infection. Some plants have a mechanism of inducing their roots to produce chemicals to attract beneficial soil bacteria to fight against the pathogens.

Foxglove plants produce chemicals that cause serious symptoms when ingested

The touch-me-not plant responds to touch by closing

Thigmonasty

The movement of plant parts in response to touch stimulus is called thigmonasty. The most well-known example of this mechanism is the touch-me-not plant. The leaves of the plant can close up in response to touch, vibrations or heat. The closed leaves give a wilted appearance that makes them unappealing to herbivores. The physical movement can also dislodge small insects.

Mimicry and Camouflage

Plants can have leaves with patterns that resemble insect eggs to dissuade insects from laying eggs. Female butterflies will choose not to lay eggs on leaves that already seem to have other butterfly eggs on them.

Fact File

Certain Acacia tree species offer homes to ant colonies in return for the ants defending them against predators.

PLANT DISEASES

Like other organisms, plants also develop diseases that affect their normal appearance and functions. Irrespective of whether a plant is cultivated or grows in the wild, it is susceptible to disease. The nature and severity of diseases varies across species and depends on many environmental factors.

History of Plant Diseases

Plant diseases have existed for millions of years. Fossil evidence has shown that plant diseases were common even 250 million years ago. Diseases such as mildews, blight and rusts have been documented. These diseases are significant because they have resulted in massive famines and economic changes.

Mildew is a disease that affects different plant species

Fact File

The late blight disease that affected potato plants on a large scale in 1845 led to the Great Famine and mass migration in Ireland.

Plant Pathology

A plant is said to be diseased when its normal growth and development is hindered by disease agents. The disease agents affect one or more essential physiological process or biochemical pathway.

Plant diseases are caused by pathogenic organisms such as fungi, bacteria, viruses, nematode worms, insects or other parasites. Plants can also develop non-infectious diseases due to extreme temperatures, toxins in the soil, water or air, and mineral deficiency.

The study of plant diseases and prevention is of vital importance because we are directly dependent on many crop plants for food. Since diseases spread quickly, large fields with crops are susceptible. Farmers are affected when an entire field is affected by a disease.

Citrus canker is a bacterial disease that affects citrus species such as lemon and lime

Cause and Prevention

Growing in a natural environment, plants are often subjected to more than one unfavourable condition and a wide range of pathogens. When a plant is affected by nutrient deficiency or soil imbalance, it also becomes easily susceptible to pathogen infection.

Any plant that has succumbed to infection by one pathogen is also prone to infection by secondary pathogens. The plant will exhibit different physical deformities and characteristics as a result of its infections. Knowledge of normal plant morphology and development is essential for identifying the diseases.

Late Blight is a disease that affects potatoes

Plant diseases that have global implications for whole populations include:

- Late blight in potato
- Powdery mildew in grapes
- Coffee rust
- Fusarium wilt in cotton
- Bacterial wilt in tobacco
- Panama disease in banana
- Corn leaf blight

Genetically modified banana plants are resistant to disease

Corn leaf blight disease can destroy an entire field of corn

Plant diseases can be prevented or controlled by addressing the following factors:

- Use of healthy seeds
- Crop rotation practice
- Control of moisture in the fields
- Use of pesticides
- Use of genetically modified seeds resistant to diseases

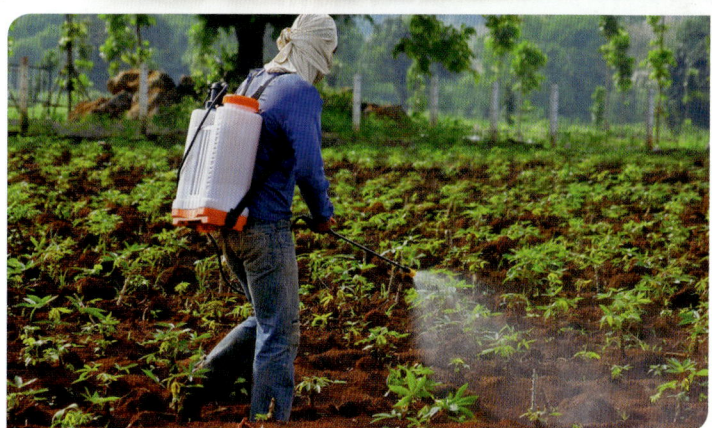

Pesticides are the most common form of protection against insects

CLASSIFICATION OF PLANTS

Of the millions of plant species thriving on Earth, flowering plants make up the major percentage. Plants are classified into two major groups – vascular plants and non-vascular plants. Classification of plants is important for identification and comparison of the different species of plants.

Non-Vascular Plants

These plants are called 'non-vascular' because they lack the tissues needed for transport of water and nutrients. Non-vascular plants are considered to be the earliest living plants that evolved on the planet. Bryophytes are the most common type of non-vascular plants. Mosses, hornworts and liverworts are some of the members of this family.

Considered the simplest, bryophytes lack parts such as leaves, stems or roots. As a result, these plants can survive only in moist habitats where water is plentifully available. Even though they lack essential parts, they are extremely versatile at survival.

Bryophytes also play an important role in nutrient recycling within the environment, regulating temperatures and reducing soil erosion around water. Since they do not produce seeds, they reproduce through spores.

Non-vascular plants are considered to be the earliest plant forms

Club moss is an example of vascular plant

Fact File

Gymnosperms consist of the thickest, tallest and oldest-living tree species among all plants.

Vascular Plants

Vascular plants are characterized by the presence of distinct tissues, xylem and phloem. Xylem transports water and minerals from the roots to other parts of the plant. Phloem transports the products of photosynthesis from the leaves. Club mosses, horsetails, ferns, gymnosperms and angiosperms are categorized under vascular plants.

Pteridophytes

Pteridophytes comprise over 12,000 species of seedless plants that reproduce through spores. These spores are usually located on the underside of the leaves and are called 'sporophylls'. The spores are catapulted across long distances through spring-like structures in the sacs that contain the spores.

Ferns are the most well-known species of pteridophytes. They have leaf-like structures that are diverse in appearance. Ferns have fronds that remain coiled until maturity.

Pteridophytes also have simple stems called 'rhizomes'. They have adapted to different terrestrial and aquatic habitats, though most pteridophytes are found in tropical regions.

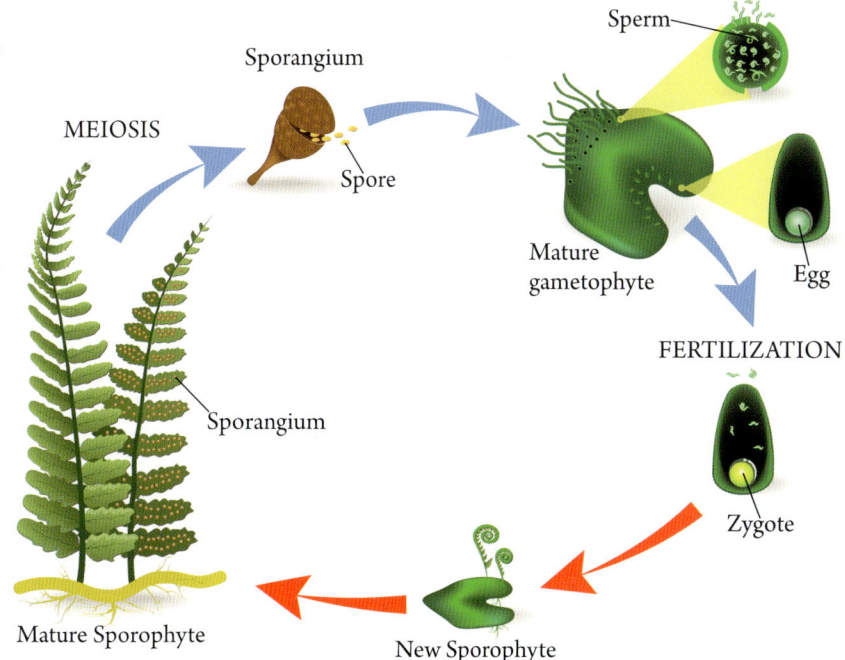

Pteridophytes reproduce through spore formation

Gymnosperms

The word 'gymnosperm' means 'naked seed'. The seeds of Gymnosperms are exposed and are present in the form of cones instead of seeds. Gymnosperms produce two types of cone, female and male.

These plants are distributed across many regions though they are abundant in the Arctic region and temperate forests. Some well-known gymnosperm species include fir, pine, spruce and hemlock. They are a good source of wood.

Gymnosperms reproduce through cones instead of seeds

Angiosperms

They exhibit the highest diversity among plants and include about 240,000 plant species. Angiosperm means 'covered seed'. The seeds are usually enclosed in fruits or protective cases. The oldest known angiosperms are thought to have diversified from gymnosperms in the Triassic Period. Over time, they gradually replaced the coniferous population dominant until then.

Flowering plants, also called angiosperms, are a diverse group

CROP PLANTS

Crops are plants that are grown and harvested on a large scale for providing food, or fodder for livestock. Agriculture is the science of growing crops on a commercial scale and since it directly supplies food to humans, it is a vital industry. While most crops are grown in fields and farmlands, some crops are harvested from the wild.

Agriculture Types

Food crops that include cereals and grains form the major portion of agriculture. Wheat, rice, corn, maize and millets form the basis of many foods consumed across the world. Horticulture deals with the growth of crops other than grains, such as fruit trees. Floriculture is the cultivation of flowers and potted plants. Crops are also grown for clothing fibers, biofuel and medicines.

History of Agriculture

Agriculture is believed to have started in the Fertile Crescent along the Nile Valley, Mesopotamia and the Levant. Wheat and barley were some of the first crops to be cultivated.

By the 20th century, major reforms in agriculture improved the ability to feed more people. Chemical fertilizers providing nutrients, pesticides and herbicides to kill pests and weeds were used extensively.

Agriculture has been the major backbone of human development

Agriculture Techniques

Crop Rotation
Sometimes, crops are grown one after another, in fixed rotation. This is done to maintain the fertility of the soil. Sometimes, crops are rotated on a yearly basis, while at other times, it may involve a few years.

Crop rotation is useful for maintaining soil fertility

Chemical fertilizers are used in intensive farming

Intensive Farming
In areas where irrigation is difficult, farmers depend heavily on fertilizers and pesticides to improve crop growth. Farmers also use high-yielding seed varieties and machinery for different processes. The yield is considerably high per unit area. While it has increased production, intensive farming also results in environmental pollution and soil erosion.

Plantations require high capital and maintenance

Fact File

The rice terraces of the Philippine Cordilleras date back thousands of years and are a World Heritage Site.

Plantation
In this type of farming, a large area is dedicated for the growth of a single type of crop such as tea, coffee, spices, cocoa, coconut or fruits. It is capital and labor-intensive and involves management and use of sophisticated machinery, fertilizers, irrigation and transportation. Plantations require large areas of land and are typically successful in regions with high annual rainfall.

Shifting Cultivation
Forest land is cleared by felling and burning trees. The cleared land is then used for growing certain crops for two or three years. The land is then abandoned as the soil loses its fertility over time. The farmers move to different areas and repeat the process. Maize, millet, rice and vegetables are grown in this type of farming.

Terrace Farming
In naturally hilly areas with slopes, terrace cultivation is practised. The hills and mountain slopes are cut into terraces and the land is used for agriculture. The terrace formation is useful in reducing soil erosion. When it rains, instead of the top nutrient layer of the soil getting washed away, it is carried to the next layer below.

Terrace farming is practiced in hilly areas

RESOURCES FROM PLANTS

Plants are grown for different purposes, and especially for their resources. Some trees and plants are very useful and virtually every part of them is of commercial value. There are four major types of plant resources – food crops, raw textile materials, wood and medicines.

Food crops

Some of the major food crops that are cultivated for consumption include: cereal grains, vegetables, fruits, nuts, seeds, oil and tubers. Cereal grains are essential for the major food products that make up everyday meals across the world. They provide carbohydrates and proteins.

Vegetables, fruits and nuts are supplements that are eaten to provide vitamins, minerals and other nutrients. Oils are extracted from the seeds of different plants such as groundnut, cotton, sunflower, palm and coconut. The oil provides the fats needed for the body. Tubers such as potato, sweet potato and yams are a rich source of starch.

Textiles

Most knitted and woven garments and products are made from yarn derived from processed plant fibers. Plants such as jute, hemp, straw, flax, bamboo, coconut leaves and cotton are used for producing fibers that can be made into ropes, clothing, baskets and mats.

Cereal grains form an important part of the diet across the world

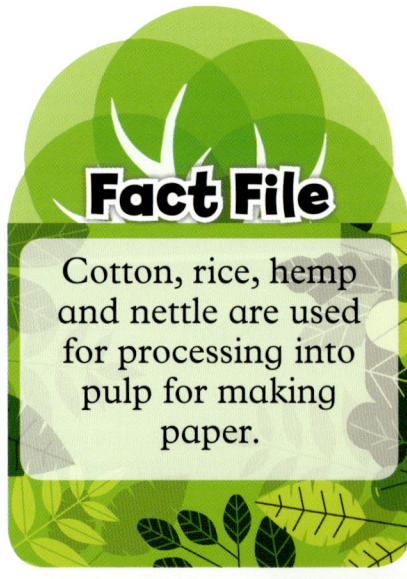

Plant fibers have been used for making different products

Fact File

Cotton, rice, hemp and nettle are used for processing into pulp for making paper.

Wood and Timber

Both hard and soft wood are employed for different purposes. Hard wood is used for building and construction as well as for making furniture. Ebony, teak and mahogany are examples of hard wood.

Soft wood is more suitable for preparing wood pulp which in turn is used for making paper. Soft wood is also used as firewood for making fires. Cedar, pine and redwood are examples of softwood.

Large scale deforestation for timber and wood pulp can have a devastating effect on forests and the environment. Timber industries and paper manufacturers plant trees in place of the cut ones for conservation and sustainability.

Wood and timber are used extensively in construction and furniture industries

Medicines and Drugs

Since ancient times, people have depended on various plants for preparing medicines for various ailments. As many as 800 medicinal herbs have been listed in papyrus scrolls from ancient Egypt. Several important medicines and drugs are manufactured from plant compounds extracted from bark, roots, stems, flowers and leaves. About 17,810 plant species have been listed to have proven medicinal use as estimated by the Royal Botanic Gardens, Kew in 2016.

Many drugs and medicines are plant products

Cash Crops

Certain crops are grown for the sole purpose of exporting to other countries. Some examples of cash crops include oil palm, cotton, groundnut, mahogany, rubber, coffee, tea, coconut, cocoa, sugarcane and tobacco. The type of cash crops that can be cultivated depends on the climatic conditions. Cereals, vegetables and oil-yielding crops grow in moderate climates. Coffee, oil palm, cocoa, bananas, sugar cane and cotton are grown in tropical and sub-tropical regions. The Arctic and Antarctic regions are unsuitable for crop cultivation.

Oil is an important product extracted from different seeds and plant parts

PLANT TISSUE CULTURE

Plant tissue culture is a valuable tool for scientists to grow plants under controlled environments for observation and monitoring. Using small pieces of plant tissue, such as a bit of leaf or section of root, a whole plant can be generated. Tissue culture is useful for research and commercial production of plants.

Totipotency

The ability of plant tissue to develop into a whole plant is known as totipotency. The plant scientist, Gottlieb Haberlandt, was the first to initiate plant tissue culture in 1902. Since then, much advancement in the technique has helped scientists grow a wide range of species more efficiently.

Totipotency is the ability of plant tissue to develop into whole plant

Gottlieb Haberlandt was a pioneer of plant tissue culture studies

Maintaining sterile conditions is necessary for preventing microbial infections

Tissue Culture Method

Plants need appropriate growth medium to grow and develop. The growth medium will act as the soil and provide all the nutrients that the plants need. The growing conditions such as temperature, light and water can also be easily taken care of in the laboratory.

In appropriate conditions, the roots and shoot begins to develop in about 3 – 6 weeks. At this stage, the plant is still in test-tubes. The laboratory is maintained in a strictly sterile environment and all equipment carefully sterilized. If bacteria or fungal spores come in contact with the growth medium, they will grow and multiply and interfere in the plant growth.

Growth and Development

The exact conditions needed to stimulate growth vary across species. For growing plants in the laboratory, scientists use specially-designed medium. It is prepared by adding a number of separate ingredients in sterile water and a gelling agent for providing a firm soil-like material for growth.

Murashige and Skoog (MS) growth medium is the most well-known and versatile medium used for growing plant tissues of different species. It consists of organic and inorganic compounds, minerals and growth hormones needed for development.

Laboratories are equipped with artificial lights and maintained at optimal temperatures to encourage growth. Plantlets that develop in test tubes or jars are transferred to pots and tended inside greenhouses to develop into plants.

Murashige and Skoog medium is commonly used for plant tissue culture

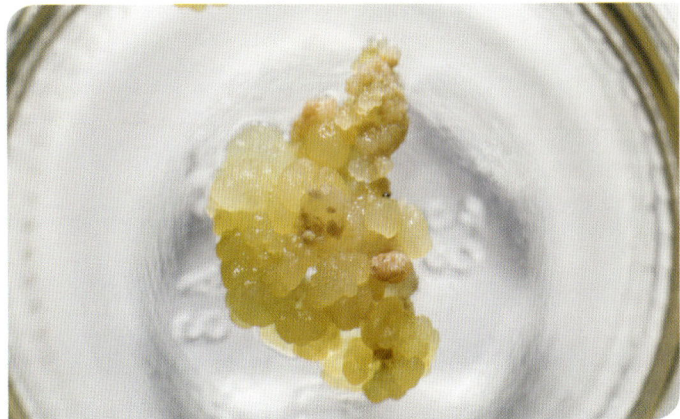

Nature of Cultured Cells

Plant cells grown through tissue culture are distinct from regular plant cells. They have smaller vacuoles, lack chloroplasts and the ability to photosynthesize and lack variety in structure and properties. They are a mass of undifferentiated cells similar to those found in meristems. These clumps of cells, called 'callus', can be artificially induced to develop into different cell types.

Callus refers to the undifferentiated mass of plant tissue

Advantages of Plant Tissue Culture

The advantage of plant tissue culture is that a plant can be grown from any part of the plant. Plants with desired features can be chosen to artificially propagate more plantlets with those features. The parent plant should be healthy and free of disease or decay. The plant must be actively growing and not in a state of dormancy. The plant part used for tissue culture is termed 'explant'. Generally, younger plant tissue is chosen because it has a higher proportion of actively dividing cells, which can be artificially induced to develop into different cell types.

Plantlets developed in labs can be grown in greenhouses later

Fact File

Tissue culture is useful for growing plants such as orchids or Nepenthes that are difficult to cultivate under normal conditions.

GENETICALLY MODIFIED CROPS

Genetic engineering is playing a vital role in producing plants with unique qualities not naturally found. The technique involves inserting foreign DNA (genetic material) into the plant's genome to confer unique properties. Many genetically modified crops have been designed, but there is growing opposition to them.

Need for GM Crops

As the world population increases, so too do the demands of agriculture. Genetically modified (GM) crops are produced with the aim of improving productivity by artificially providing the plants resistance to pests and herbicides. In other cases, useful traits are introduced to make the crops more nutritious or with better shelf life for easy transportation. As GM crop production rises, it faces increasing opposition and controversy owing to safety concerns.

Introducing Foreign Genes

The physical and chemical characteristics of living organisms are determined by their genetic makeup. The genome of a plant consists of all the genes that code for different proteins and enzymes needed for growth and reproduction. Genetic engineering can confer different characteristics to the genes. To make this possible, the genes have to integrate with the genome. Upon successful integration, when the plant reproduces, the genes and consequently the traits are transferred to the progeny.

Fact File
About 90% of soy, corn, cotton and beets sold in the US are genetically modified.

Transferring DNA to Plant Genome

The first stage in growing a genetically modified plant is to transfer the DNA into the cells. Plant cells have thick cell walls which make it more challenging to transfer DNA than in animal cells. A special method called 'gene bombardment' is used for transferring DNA. Microscopic metal particles coated with DNA are bombarded onto developing plant tissue using a gene gun.

Another method of transferring DNA to plant cells is through bacterial or viral infection. The bacteria or viruses will be tailored to have the genes to be transferred. Agrobacterium tumefaciens is a bacterium that is commonly used as a vector for transferring genes. This bacterium naturally occurs in soil and causes crown gall disease.

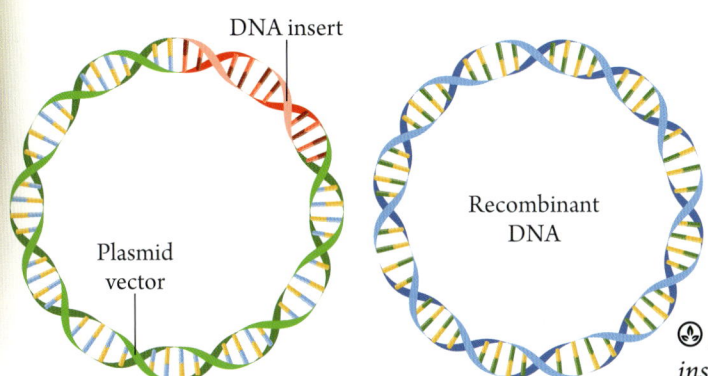

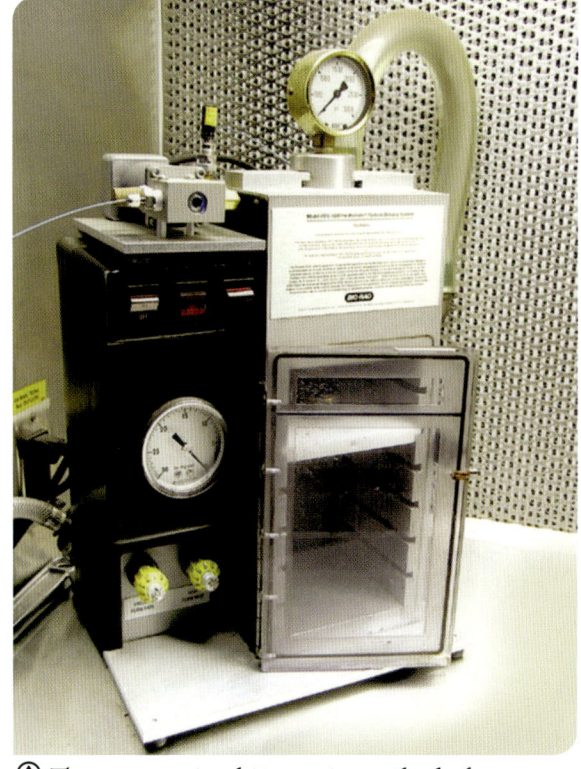

The gene gun is a hit-or-miss method of transferring genes

Recombinant DNA technology attempts to insert foreign genes into the genome

Genetic engineers modify the genome of the bacteria by disarming the genes that cause the disease and insert the required genes into the genome. Through this method, genes are incorporated at a better success rate than the 'hit or miss' gene gun approach of gene transfer. Sometimes, the gene of interest is inserted into the bacteria's extra-chromosomal DNA called 'plasmid' to form the 'recombinant DNA'.

Plants that have successfully taken up the genes develop into plants exhibiting the required traits. Genetic engineers evaluate the plant's growth and produce at many stages to identify desirable traits and evaluate for negative effects. Even when the plants are transferred to the field, they are isolated from other plants to avoid cross-pollination and contamination.

GMO Crops

Crops are genetically modified to maintain resistance to pests, insects or herbicides. Alternatively, they produce vitamins or other useful compounds. GM crops are also designed to ripen more slowly than normal varieties thus improving their shelf life.

Some well-known genetically modified plants include:

- Flavr Savr Tomato with longer shelf life
- Bt Cotton with resistance to bollworm infection
- Golden Rice enhanced with Vitamin A

Tomatoes have been genetically modified for longer shelf life